NEANDERTHAL

NEANDERTHAL

NEANDERTHAL MAN
AND THE STORY OF
HUMAN ORIGINS

PAUL JORDAN

SUTTON PUBLISHING

First published in the United Kingdom in 1999 by
Sutton Publishing Limited · Phoenix Mill
Thrupp · Stroud · Gloucestershire · GL5 2BU

Paperback edition first published by Sutton Publishing Limited in 2001

Reprinted in 2001

British Library Cataloguing in Publication Data
A catalogue record for this book is available from the British Library.

ISBN 0 7509 2676 7

Cover illustration: A Neanderthal skull from La Ferrassie, France (E.T. Archive)

Typeset in 11.5/15 pt Garamond.
Typesetting and origination by
Sutton Publishing Limited.
Printed in Great Britain by
J.H. Haynes & Co. Ltd, Sparkford.

Contents

Acknowledgements

The author would like to thank Dr Robert Foley of the Department of Biological Anthropology, Cambridge University, for his generous permission to photograph the casts in the department's collection, and his assistant Maggie Bellatti for her help with the photography. All photographs were taken by the author unless otherwise stated – particular thanks go to the Neanderthal Museum, Mettmann, Germany, for their colour pictures. Thanks are also due to Dr John Wymer for the use of his drawing of the Molodova finds and to Chicago University Press for permission to reproduce the jaw picture from *The Middle Stone Age at Klasies River Mouth* by Ronald Singer and John Wymer. Special thanks go to Professor Paul Mellars of Cambridge University for many helpful conversations in the course of writing this book.

List of Illustrations

Colour plates

(between pp. 112 and 113)

Dardé's imaginative statue of Neanderthal Man at the museum of les Eyzies.

A modern reconstruction of a Neanderthaler in the new Neanderthal Museum at Mettman in Germany.

Neanderthal home-life as portrayed at the new Neanderthal Museum at Mettman in Germany.

The bellowing, drinking mammoth of le Thot near Lascaux in the Dordogne.

The woolly rhino at Préhisto-Parc near les Eyzies in the Dordogne.

Reindeer and wolves at Préhisto-Parc.

European bison at le Thot.

Przewalski's horse – the ice age type with distinctive mane – at le Thot.

Préhisto-Parc's fearsome cave-bear.

A cave lion menaces a Neanderthaler at Préhisto-Parc.

Neanderthal Man looks out at dusk from the museum terrace of les Eyzies in France.

The Vezère river near le Moustier, with limestone cliffs and caves.

Caves at Mount Carmel in Israel.

Neanderthalers in at the kill at Préhisto-Parc.

Coming home from the hunt through the woods of Préhisto-Parc.

Neanderthalers at home in Préhisto-Parc.

A Neanderthal hunting band traps a mammoth at Préhisto-Parc.

Neanderthalers take on a giant elk in a glade of Préhisto-Parc.

The site of the burials at Regourdou.

Brown bears are still in residence at Regourdou.

A Neanderthal family faces up to a cave-bear in a reconstruction at Roque Saint-Christophe in the Dordogne.

Horses were frequently painted and carved in the Upper Palaeolithic art.

Neanderthal Man gazes from the terrace of the les Eyzies museum at gathering autumn mists across the Vezère valley.

Introduction
The Man from Newmandale

The very name 'Neanderthal' makes an impact all by itself – and so, if you prefer it, does 'Neandertal', without the 'h'. The branch of fate that determines the names (and thereby the flavours) assigned to our various remote ancestors and the productions they left behind them – Crô-Magnon, Magdalenian, Oldowan, Heidelberg and all the rest – has endowed Neanderthal Man with the most flavourful name of them all. Germanic but with more than a hint of the classical, the name looks strong on the page and, however pronounced, sounds as strong to the ear. Especially when mispronounced by English-speakers, it carries a powerful charge of primitive and cloddish associations: 'knee-and-earthal', a fitting name for the bent and shuffling cave-man, hardly risen up out of the mud, that popular imagination still too often imagines Neanderthal Man to have been. 'Nayandertaal' sounds cleaner altogether. Because the name starts with 'N' and contains (at least in its older spelling) the 'th' combination, a surprisingly large number of people go on to confuse Neanderthal Man with the Neolithic period, to the detriment of the latter, imagining that innovative time of the first farmers to have been the heyday of the shuffling cave-men. In fact, the last of the Neanderthal people missed the Neolithic by more than twenty thousand years.

The German spelling reforms at the start of the twentieth century removed the 'h' from Thal and so from the name of the dale in North Rhine–Westphalia after which Neanderthal Man was called. By then, the scientific world was committed to the classification *Homo neanderthalensis* with the 'h' in place, but we are at liberty to write either Neanderthal or Neandertal in common usage concerning this fossil man. With its nineteenth-century echoes of the beginnings of scientific anthropology, 'Neanderthal' appeals, but there's no doubt that 'Neandertal' would help English speakers to pronounce the name more accurately: most American and Continental writers prefer it, but the British often stick with Neanderthal.

The Neander Dale was an appropriate place in which to find the first correctly identified remains of an earlier form of Man, distinct from the modern worldwide species *Homo sapiens sapiens*. The old bones from the Neandertal were evidence of a form of Man new to science in the middle of the nineteenth century: a New Man indeed for the contemplation of both the scientific and the wider world of the time. A nice turn of fate, then, that this New Man should have been discovered in a valley named, circuitously, after a 'new man' of the seventeenth century, who came from a family with the unremarkable name of Neumann (Newman in English). He was the vicar of St Martin's, Düsseldorf, where he was also the organist, and a composer of hymns. As we could expect of a clergyman of his time, he was a classical scholar, too, and headmaster of the town's Latin College. He chose to use a Graecized form of his name for his hymn-writing, and you can come across Neander in hymn books to this day. In his late twenties, he often liked to pass his time, composing no doubt, in a particular little valley close to his home and the locals soon called the place after him, Neanderthal = Newmandale. And when the bones discovered in a quarry in the valley in 1856 came to be assigned to 'Neanderthal Man', a New Man in the human story was recognized for the first time.

Nearly 150 years after his first discovery, the New Man from the Neanderthal may sometimes seem a bit old hat now, overshadowed by the more recent discoveries of much older and much more primitive types like *Homo erectus* (first encountered in Java and China) and the early men and pre-men of East and Southern Africa. A lot more New Men and Near Men and Ape Men have come on the scene since Neanderthal Man put in his first appearance. These more recent arrivals have rightly had their due since they belong to the very early and crucial epochs of human evolution, when the first decisive steps towards 'hominization' or 'anthropogenesis' were taken, without which we would not be here to be interested in our origins. But interest, including scientific interest, in those earliest phases of the human story has perhaps reached the point where the newcomers – who continue to back into the limelight, especially on the very old sites of East Africa – have too far upstaged the old hands like Neanderthal Man, who still has a lot to tell us about the mysteries of the origin and nature of fully modern man: precisely because he is closer to us by far than the ape-men and early men of Africa and elsewhere – closer, but not the same. For Neanderthal Man is the real alien with whom the human race was once in contact, in circumstances over which there has been a great deal of scholarly debate. Our popular culture is obsessed with the idea of aliens from outer space, endowed with intelligence and purpose (often hostile) but skewed away from us in some essential way, different in outlook and desire. It is highly unlikely, to say the least, that any aliens from outer space have ever come anywhere near our Earth, but it is certain that human beings of the modern sort (that is to say representatives of the species *Homo sapiens sapiens*, to which every member of the human race today belongs) have in the not so remote past shared parts of the world with forms of human being significantly different from themselves, both physically and, it must be, psychologically too. The Neanderthalers of Europe and Western Asia are the type par excellence of this sort of alien neighbour. How different they were has recently been a matter of fierce debate among anthropologists and up to a point may always be so, but for the moment a trend in thinking fuelled by new evidence from the field of genetics is unmistakably pointing in a particular direction. So on the grounds both of the new scientific evidence and of this particular fossil man's perennial capacity to throw light on our own nature and origin, a fresh account of the life and times of Neanderthal Man may be timely.

Overview accounts of human evolution, even those written by the anthropologists and archaeologists themselves, often reach Neanderthal Man with a slight but discernible weariness of spirits after the initial excitements of the African ape-men, followed by the expansive exploits of *Homo erectus*. Particularly, perhaps, for those writers already convinced that Neanderthal Man was a byway of human evolution, a dull dead-ender, the Neanderthal epoch looms with a certain boredom, before things look up again with the triumph of modern man in the shape of the cave artists of the last ice age. This book sets out to put Neanderthal Man centre stage, with of course enough of the background story of human evolution to make sense of him — especially in relationship with the emergence of modern man. It isn't the first book to focus on Neanderthal Man and several excellent works are cited in the bibliography, but it does try to be up to date with the crucial genetic evidence and with the vital studies of human mental evolution that, despite their interest and importance for us all, are only now being undertaken — with all their inevitable difficulties and uncertainties.

This book does not aspire to any startling originality: there are no facts and scarcely any interpretations of fact related in it that do not derive from the works of a host of scholars and specialists. Some justice to their labours and insights the writer hopes is done in the bibliographical listings at the back of the book; the authors' names found there record some of the discoverers of the facts and originators of the interpretations discussed here. If those discoverers and originators are not credited with their work line by line, it is certainly not so as to deny them their due but rather so as to be able to present an unbroken and impersonalized account of the material under discussion. Some highly personalized treatments of the scientific inquiry into human evolution have been published, to deserved success: it is often valuable to know what sort of people are engaged in the study and how they go about it, and the story of the ups and downs of controversy makes for colourful reading; the personalized approach also takes care of the aforementioned problem of scholarly acknowledgements and does away with the need for any apparatus of notes. But this book sets out to highlight above all the ideas involved in the study of human evolution, particularly in that latter part of it when the first modern sort of human being and his striking contemporary, Neanderthal Man, were coming on the scene. To present those ideas as vividly as possibly, personalities (and text notes) have been eschewed. This is an account for the interested layperson of the issues involved in the latest and, to us, most important phase of human evolution.

Neanderthal Man is long since dead and gone. His fate, as far as we are concerned, is to illuminate the processes of our own origin and nature. What has come after him, in the form of ourselves, can give point and poignancy to his career. And, after all, he didn't do so badly, his memorial could boast:

R.I.P.

Neanderthal Man

130,000–30,000 BP

CHAPTER 1

The Discovery of Neanderthal Man

When Joachim Neander died in Bremen in 1680, after a short life of only thirty years that aptly matches the life expectancy of the prehistoric people named after him, the little valley in which he had liked to wander was still a charming glen, largely composed of limestone (with many caves), cut by the Düsselbach stream on its way to join the Rhine. Around 175 years later, it was charming no more (and nowadays it is vanished altogether) for industrial quarrying had already removed about half of it, with a narrow gauge railway running along one side. In 1856 quarrying had left only two caves untouched, 20 m up the gorge's face from the valley bottom, called the Feldhof caves. Evidently they were quite hard to enter, with a low entrance that had to be negotiated all that way up the cliffside. But workmen did enter them, from above, using a charge to open the narrow entrance, and in the smaller of them they found, in 1.5 m of mud on the cave floor, a collection of bones (the skull first, nearest to the entrance, and then more bones, all at the same level) that were taken for the bones of a bear. What they had found was in all probability the remains of a deliberate burial of a Neanderthal individual, but the misidentification of the bones as belonging to a bear was not so extraordinary, for bear bones (of both prehistoric and later origins) are to be found in European cave deposits and bear bones do

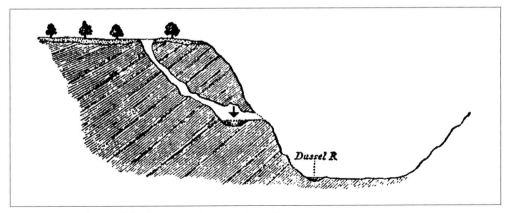

Lyell's sketch of the Feldhof caves in the Neanderthal.

superficially resemble those of human beings, especially ones as rugged as the Neanderthal long bones. (Indeed, the general living resemblance of bears, especially rearing up on their hind legs, to human beings apparently was not lost on the Neanderthal people themselves, as we shall see.) It is not surprising that, in the middle of the nineteenth century when the science of archaeology was in its infancy and the science of anthropology was scarcely conceived, no records were kept of how the bones were found, no sketch was made of the layering of the deposit, no search was made for associated material like stone tools or the bones of other animals associated with the 'bear bones'. Such records and associated materials would be a great help now towards the dating of these original Neanderthal remains, though they can, of course, be generally dated within the last ice age by analogy with the many further remains of Neanderthal humanity that have since come to light in better investigated contexts. At least these original Neanderthal bones from the Feldhof cave have turned out, nearly 150 years after their discovery, to preserve within them vital genetic evidence that it may not be possible to extract so easily if at all from many of the remains of other prehistoric men; and it may be that the varnishing of them soon after their discovery, in a way that would not be done today, has helped to lock in their genetic secrets for us to unpick in good time. The genetic evidence furnished by the bones from Neanderthal is already having a profound impact on our assessment of the status of the Neanderthalers in human evolution, as we shall see in later chapters, and it is wonderfully appropriate that the first genetic tests on Neanderthal remains should have been made on the bones from the place that gave the Neanderthal race its very name.

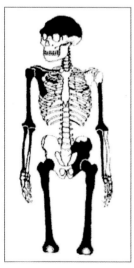

In black, the bones found in the Neanderthal cave.

A part owner in the quarrying named Beckershoff encouraged the workmen to look for more of the 'bear bones' but it seems no more were found by them. The freshly broken condition of the skullcap indicated already that the workmen's methods were none too delicate; in all there were recovered parts of the shoulders, arms, thighs, pelvis, ribs and skull of the individual buried in the cave. Despite its heavy brow arches, so unlike those of any human being Beckershoff had ever seen, it is difficult to believe that he can have gone on thinking he was in possession of bear bones after he examined the skullcap from the cave. He seems to have kept the remains for a few weeks before passing them on to someone who might have a better idea of what they were: Johann Carl Fuhlrott, a grammar school teacher and president of the Elberfeld naturalists' society. Fuhlrott, we may conclude, saw at once that the

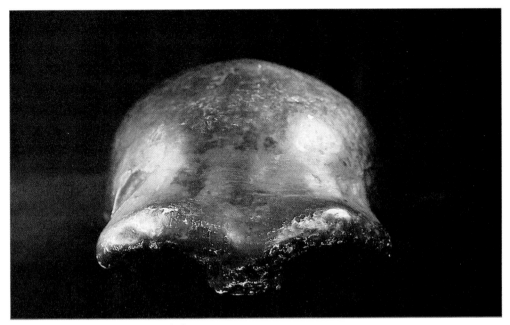

The skullcap from the Neanderthal.

Neanderthal bones were not those of a bear: indeed, he is credited with describing them as belonging to 'a typical very ancient individual of the human race'. Evidently, he thought they were remains from what people were then in the habit of calling 'antediluvian' times – times before the biblical Flood. The geological remains of the last ice age to be found in northern and Alpine Europe were at that time often interpreted as the traces of the Flood. It was easy to imagine the waters of the universal deluge washing remains like the Neanderthal bones into high caves such as the Feldhofer. Fuhlrott evidently believed, noting the freshly broken condition of the skullcap, that a complete skeleton might be there for the finding and went back to the site to search for more human bones and the bones of animals that might have been brought into the cave along with the human ones, but quarrying was far advanced at the Neanderthal and he found no more.

The discovery in the Neanderthal was made in August 1856, three years before the publication of Darwin's and Wallace's theory (they had hit upon the same idea independently) of biological evolution by natural selection. Darwin's *On the Origin of Species*, published in 1859, made at the end only the slightest suggestion of the application of his ideas to the question of human descent and, interestingly, even this passing mention of the theme was left out of the first German translation of the *Origin*. Fuhlrott in 1856 and the whole world of science at the time had, then, no accepted theory of evolution to go by and certainly none that openly embraced the idea of human evolution out of the animal world. But notions of other, previous worlds were being entertained in the middle of the nineteenth century, of worlds different from the present state of affairs, worlds inhabited by creatures now extinct and known only from the fossil record of the rocks and caves. Even of worlds in which human beings might just possibly have coexisted with the vanished animals, though – in the absence of any earlier finds of fossil men with distinctively different features like the brow arches of the Neanderthal skullcap – no one yet envisaged that any men who might have been around in the company of the extinct animals were likely to have looked any different physically from ourselves. Only a few stray thinkers had ever imagined that human beings might have developed out of lower animals. It was comfortable to believe that the extinct creatures of the fossil record were simply monsters destroyed by the Flood, or by some previous catastrophe even before the Flood; in that spirit, even human bones in 'antediluvian' contexts could just about be accepted and, given an estimated date of about 3500 BC for the Bible's Flood, then any human remains found in antediluvian contexts need not be so very old, nor be expected to look so very different from ourselves.

For many if not most people in the middle of the nineteenth century, scientists as well as laymen, the basis of all chronological thinking about the world was still the Bible, with its ragged Old Testament narratives and its New Testament genealogies of Jesus out of which a more or less coherent chronology could be forced with difficulty. It was on this basis that the Flood could be put at about 3500 BC and the Creation (at least of the present world order) at about 4000 BC. (Notoriously, some biblical scholars achieved an astounding precision with their computations, arriving at 4004 BC as the year of Creation, October as the month, the 22nd as the day in question and the time – 9 o'clock in the morning!)

Since the middle of the eighteenth century the idea, foreshadowed by some Greek and Roman writers, of a technological progress from crude stone tools and weapons to better-made ones of stone and then to ones of metal, first bronze and then iron, had been gaining ground. But no one could put any firm dates on these phases of technical advancement and it was easy to imagine it all as happening after the Garden of Eden or even the Flood. Another line of thought about the early state of human affairs drew on what the Greek and Roman authors had to say about the barbarian inhabitants of the fringes of the classical world, with additional information culled from the observations of explorers and colonists, particularly among the American Indians, whose life continued to be lived in a sort of Stone Age. Geology was meanwhile starting to reveal the many stratigraphies of the Earth's fabric, with their startling fossil evidence of other worlds of creation, which some scholars were beginning to think highly indicative of remote antiquity and immense epochs of time, although there was as yet no means of assigning any absolute dates to the record of the rocks. If one accepted the biblical Flood as the last and, for human beings, the most important of a long line of catastrophes (almost certainly divinely contrived), then it was not difficult to see in the fossil record of the Earth's stratigraphy simply a series of previous Creations of purely scientific interest and with no bearing on the Creation of Man, of which the Bible remained a wholly reliable account. (It was a bit uncomfortable, however, to be invited to conclude that human beings, as evidenced by their stone tools or even their own bones, might have existed in any of these previous creations.) Lastly, comparative anatomy of the living creatures of the present world encouraged their arrangement in a hierarchy of forms, from Worm to Man if you like, which suggested to just a handful of thinkers that there might have been an evolution through time from lower to higher forms. Darwin's forerunners Buffon and Lamarck (among others) proposed such an idea in the late eighteenth and early nineteenth centuries, but they were unable to put forward any convincing mechanism by which evolution could proceed and the whole idea was in eclipse by the time of the Neanderthal discovery.

Twenty years before the young Joachim Neander was enjoying the solitude of his little Rhineland valley, a French writer named Isaac de la Peyrère published in liberal Amsterdam *A Theological System upon the Pre-supposition that Men were before Adam* in which he asserted that finds quite commonly made of stone implements or weapons, popularly and erroneously written off as 'thunderbolts', were in fact the artefacts of primitive men who lived before the Adam and Eve of the Bible. His theological views were in general unwelcome to the Roman Church and his assertion of humanity before Adam was quite unacceptable; he was seized and forced to recant and his book was publicly burnt in Paris. But he had placed on record, as early as 1655, the idea that the biblical account of the Creation of Man was, to say the least, incomplete and that men more primitive than ourselves had walked the Earth before the present state of the world was inaugurated.

Through the eighteenth century there were from time to time occasions on which people found, or thought they had found, evidences of human presence in worlds previous to our own. They were usually content to push their finds back before the Flood, avoiding the sort of pre-Adamite views that had got de la Peyrère into trouble. On the very eve of the century, for example, a flint axe was found near Gray's Inn Lane in London in association with the skeleton of an 'elephant', as reports of the time have it, which was probably a mammoth, but on this occasion it was easy enough to dismiss the exotic beast as a Roman import. In 1726 near Oeningen on Lake Constance there was found 'the bony skeleton of one of those infamous men whose fathers brought down on the world the dire misfortune of the Flood', but it was actually the fossil of a giant salamander, millions of years old if only its discoverer could have known it, though we may forgive him for being deceived by the superficially humanoid appearance of his find.

In 1771, near Bamberg in Bavaria, a human lower jaw and shoulder blade together with some stone tools were found in apparent association with various fossils of animals which the discoverer recognized as extinct forms. He could not quite bring himself to conclude that the human remains and the extinct animals belonged together, seeming to acknowledge the possibility of antediluvian humanity but not wanting to plump for it. It is entirely possible that he had come upon what we would call Neanderthal or Crô-Magnon remains, together with their appropriate tools and in association with ice age fauna, in which case this would be the earliest recorded find of its sort, but sadly it remains also entirely possible that the human bones were more recent intrusions among the flints and animal bones or even that bear bones, in a reversal of the Neanderthal case, were misidentified as human!

Near the end of the eighteenth century a still impressive assessment of a find of Stone Age implements was made at Hoxne in Suffolk by an East Anglian country gentleman named John Frere, who was clearly influenced by the growing conviction among some geologists that the world must be much older than people thought. He had seen flint axes (which he described as 'weapons of war, fabricated and used by people who had not the use of metals') coming to light at a depth of 12 ft (3.5 m), in the bottom layer of undisturbed strata in association with the bones of extinct animals. In a letter to the Secretary of the Society of Antiquaries in 1797 he wrote: 'The situation in which these weapons were found may tempt us to refer them to a very remote period indeed, even beyond that of the present world.'

Frere's letter was printed in *Archaeologia* in 1800, but not widely noted at the time. He was, after all, announcing the unwelcome thought that men might have existed before the creation of the present world order at no more than 6000 years ago. It was one thing to conjecture that the remains of men who lived before the Flood might from time to time be found, but altogether another to speculate that evidence of human presence in worlds before the present world could be found in Suffolk gravel pits. By this time, at the start of the nineteenth century, the views of the French biologist Cuvier were very influential; he dismissed the tentative notions of evolution that had already been put forward by two of his fellow-countrymen and insisted that 'fossil man does not exist', by which he meant that no genuine human remains could ever be found in the same geological contexts as those that yielded up the bones of extinct animals. For Cuvier, Man was a special part of this current Creation, with no antecedents in former ones. The French naturalist Buffon, who died in 1788, had taken a different view. He was the first author explicitly to oppose the 6000-year Bible-based chronology, concluding initially that the world was at least 75,000 years old and, at the end of his life, thinking it was likely to be much older still. He formed, moreover, a notion of the evolution of living things: 'they develop in accordance with their surroundings and pass on the new characteristics they acquire to their offspring by a process of hereditary memory.' This was in essence the theory of evolution by inheritance of acquired characteristics that we associate with Buffon's pupil Lamarck, who added to the theory some thoughts specifically aimed at the question of human evolution:

> If some race of quadrumanous animals . . . were to lose by force of circumstances the habit of climbing trees . . . and if the individuals of this race were forced for a series of generations to use their feet only for walking and to give up using their hands like feet, there is no doubt . . . that these quadrumanous animals would at length be transformed into bimanous animals.

Bimana, meaning two-handed, is an obsolete naturalists' term for mankind, so there was no doubt about Lamarck's intention in discussing this hypothesis to point the way to a notion of human evolution. He went on to envisage a process of sharpening of the wits for such a bimanous creature which would 'obtain mastery over others through the higher perfection of its faculties'. Many of the current themes of human evolutionary theory are touched on in these remarks of Lamarck, including descent from the trees, bipedalism, the freeing of the hands for new tasks, the development of the mental faculties. But Lamarck, like all the other evolutionary speculators before Darwin, had no plausible mechanism for the gradual transformation of one sort of creature into another. There is indeed a 'hereditary memory' and 'force of circumstances' does have a great impact on the evolution of living things, but there is no 'inheritance of acquired characteristics' and evolution could not proceed along those lines, as early critics of these evolutionary theories were not slow to demonstrate. It was not until Darwin introduced the concept of natural selection as the means by which evolution might take place that the very idea of evolution could be taken seriously, indeed had to be taken seriously.

Natural selection envisaged blind Nature taking on, but on a global scale through immense periods of time, a role akin to that of the selective breeder of dogs and pigeons – watching out, as it were, for random improvements here and there and, by the harsh rule of the survival of the fittest, granting offspring to the improved and death without issue to the unimproved. Giraffes famously did not grow long necks according to Lamarckian principles by stretching them every day of their lives as they fed on high foliage and then passing on their acquired long necks to their offspring, but rather by Darwinian principles when giraffes-in-the-making who happened to have longer necks than average reached more food, lived longer and bred more often, with the repetition of the whole process through countless generations. Darwin himself lived and wrote before the science of genetics was established, and thus had no idea how random mutations (for longer necks, for example) come about and are inherited, but his theory of natural selection showed at once how the cold workings of Nature could have produced the rich range of life on our world, when given to work in the immensely long reaches of time that the geologists of the early nineteenth century were seeing in the record of the rocks. But Darwin, and the naturalist Wallace who was working along the same lines at the same time, had not published in 1857 when the Neanderthal discovery was announced to the world.

The Neanderthal may have given its name (ultimately Joachim Neumann's name) to the prehistoric race now recognized on the basis of the remains of many hundreds of Neanderthal men, women and children, but it was not in fact the site of the first discovery of a Neanderthal individual nor, more widely, of the first discovery of a fossil human being. Pace Cuvier, with his doctrine that 'l'homme fossile n'existe pas', genuine discoveries of fossil human beings were being made in his lifetime (he died in 1832), but not properly recognized for what they were, if at all. Human teeth were found in association with the remains of mammoth, cave-bear and woolly rhino in gypsum quarries in Thuringia in 1820, but their discoverer was cowed by Cuvier's dogma into regarding them as intrusive into an older deposit. In 1823 a human skeleton erroneously identified as female was found in a cave at Paviland in Wales, with marine shells and bone ornaments on the chest, the whole coloured with red ochre and gaining an unfortunate young man of the last ice age the sobriquet 'Red Lady of Paviland'. The associated fauna included extinct forms of elephant, hyena and rhino. The skull was missing and the whole surviving skeleton (including the pelvis which should have settled the matter of sex) was so modern in form – being, as we know, a Crô-Magnon type of the Upper Palaeolithic period – that it was easy at the time to write it off as again a modern intrusion into an older context. A Roman's camp-follower was the preferred dismissal at the time, but here was, if only the finder had known, the first sure discovery of a fossil human being in clear association with extinct fauna. Another even clearer demonstration of the antiquity of Man came only two years later in 1825 at Kent's Cavern, near Torquay in Devon, where human skeletal material was found not only in association with the fossils of extinct animals and flint tools but sealed with them under a layer of stalagmite. The discoverer was deterred from publishing his correct conclusions about his site and news of his work was not reported at the Geological Society in London until 1840, when the geological circumstances were fully expounded, still to no avail.

If a proper recognition of what was found there in 1830 could have been extended to a piece of cranium bone from the cave of Engis on the river Meuse near Liège in Belgium, then Neanderthal Man would today be known as Engis Man instead. Pieces from the skulls of at least three individuals were turned up together with the remains of extinct animals and flint tools. One skull piece, illustrated at the time, afterwards perished and another has since been shown to be indeed an intrusion from about

8000 years ago, but a third cranium fragment we can now recognize as belonging to a Neanderthal child, with the distinctive brow arch development that even small children of the Neanderthal people exhibited. The discoverer of these things was in no doubt as to what he had found: 'whatever conclusions we like to reach about the origins of mankind, I for one am convinced that a skull of this kind belongs to a person of limited intellectual

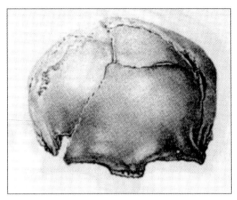

One of the skull pieces from Engis.

faculties, that is a man belonging to a lower level of civilization . . .'. He was talking of the admittedly rugged but intrusive later specimen, but the incipiently heavy-browed Neanderthal child fits his words well.

And if not many of the bones of fossil man were coming to light in the early half of the nineteenth century, then his stone tools were being found and recognized in increasing numbers. John Frere had seen a few axes at Hoxne at the end of the eighteenth century; from 1840 a French customs officer began reporting them in quantity in old gravels of the Somme in northern France. In 1841 he claimed the discovery of such an axe, shaped by flaking, in association with extinct faunal remains and asserted this as proof of the existence of antediluvian man. Sadly, this Boucher de Perthes worked rather shoddily, mistrusted his workmen who foisted the odd fake on him, illustrated his reports badly and neglected geological data. All the same, he rightly persuaded first the Danish and English exponents of the Three Age System (Stone, Bronze, Iron) and then later on some of his own distrustful countrymen that he really was finding proof of human presence in remote epochs. An English geologist of the time declared Boucher to have provided 'just as definite evidence of human activity as the knives of Sheffield'. Importantly, the distinguished geologist Lyell, who had developed the uniformitarian theory of geology, accepted Boucher's 'antediluvian' axes. Uniformitarianism had first been championed by a Scottish geologist of the late eighteenth century named James Hutton who proposed that the main causes of the formation of the geological features of the Earth were not the drastic impacts of some cyclical scheme of divinely imposed catastrophes (as Cuvier thought) but rather the slow workings of familiar processes of sedimentation in oceans, seismic elevation of strata and erosion by the weather. His idea inevitably suggested that long periods of time were involved and he wrote rather poetically of a world with 'no vestige of a beginning, no prospect of an end'. Lyell had taken on Hutton's ideas and was prepared to accept evidence for the existence of man in remote epochs, just as he accepted that the geological features of the Alps were not the results of the Flood but of extended glaciation in the distant past, but it is interesting to note that he was not at first inclined to embrace Darwin's godless mechanism of evolution by natural selection.

But the idea of evolution by some means, though pushed out of many people's minds by the catastrophic creationism of Cuvier, was kept alive in the 1840s by works like Chambers' *Vestiges of the Natural History of Creation* which, though it again lacked any notion of natural selection, contained the clear idea of species' varying in adaptation to circumstances. Chambers was prepared to countenance human evolution and presciently observed that evolution, which he called here 'the development hypothesis', 'would demand . . . that the original seat of the human race should be in a region where the quadrumana are rife': in other words, the apes and monkeys.

If Neanderthal Man quite comfortably escaped being called Engis Man, thanks to the difficulties involved in recognizing a lone Neanderthal child, then his escape from being called Gibraltar Man was a narrow one indeed and, if there was any

The Gibraltar skull.

justice, that would be his name now. For in 1848, during fortification work at Forbes Quarry, North Front, Gibraltar, one of the most complete of all Neanderthal skulls ever found was turned up, and the heavy brow arches, pulled-forward face and huge nasal opening of the race were so unmissable in this specimen that some of the arguments over the actual Neanderthal find of nine years later might have been avoided if this discovery had been recognized at the time. (The facial area of the Neanderthal skull is absent from the material turned in by the workmen who recovered – and probably broke up – the material from the Feldhof cave.) As it was the Gibraltar woman's skull languished in obscurity in the local museum for many years, finally making its way to London and recognition only after the Neanderthal discovery. One of the English geologists who had supported Boucher then suggested the scientific name *Homo calpicus* (after the classical name, Calpe, of Gibraltar) for the Gibraltar female Neanderthal and, if he had been able to do it earlier, that might more or less be the scientific name of Neanderthal Man to this day: *Homo sapiens calpicus* instead of *Homo sapiens neanderthalensis*.

Back in 1857, when the first scientific assessment of the remains from the Neanderthal were undertaken, it was fortunate that they came into the hands of an open-minded anatomist, Professor Schaafhausen of Bonn University. It is interesting that Schaafhausen had published in 1853 a paper on 'The Stability and Transformation of Species' in which ideas of the mutability of species and of human descent from apes were discussed. Fuhlrott sent him a plaster cast of the cranium in early 1857 and in June they presented a lecture together at the Natural History Society of the Prussian Rhineland and Westphalia, in Bonn. Fuhlrott described the circumstances of the find and set out claims for the great age of the human bones in the light of their location under so much cave deposit and of their fossilized state. Schaafhausen at this stage was able to give a brief description of the Neanderthal bones and already to state his conclusions about their implications, to quote his own words:

1) that the extraordinary form of the skull was due to a natural conformation hitherto not known to exist, even in the most barbarous races;

2) that these remarkable human remains belonged to a period antecedent to the time of the Celts and the Germans, and were in all probability derived from one of the wild races of north-western Europe, spoken of by Latin writers; and which were encountered as indigenous inhabitants by the German immigrants; and

3) that it was beyond doubt that these human relics were traceable to a period at which the latest animals of the diluvium still existed; but that no proof in support of this assumption, nor consequently of their so-termed fossil condition, was afforded by the circumstances under which the bones were discovered.

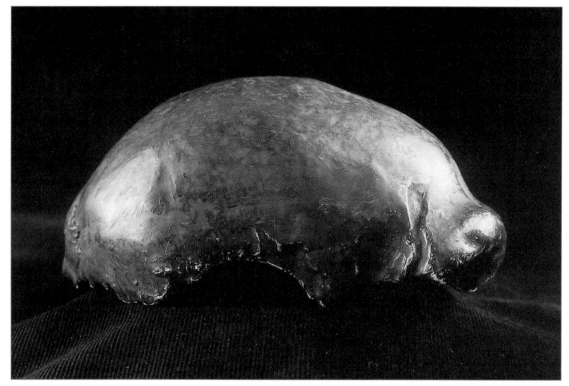

Side view of the Neanderthal skullcap showing 'bun' at the back and heavy brows at the front.

Schaafhausen was clearly stating that the highly unusual shape of the Neanderthal skull, in particular, was not due to disease or injury but represented a previously unmet early form of human being in the natural state of that creature, who must belong to times at least as remote as those of the last of the line of extinct animals.

After subsequent closer examination of the Neanderthal bones, Schaafhausen was able to write up a fuller (and still impressive) description of the find. The cranium, he said, was of unusual size, and of a long elliptical form. Obvious at once was the remarkable peculiarity of the prominence of the brow arches, coalescing completely in the middle and forming a bar over the eyes and nose that was separated from the low-rising forehead by a depression. The rather undomed brain-case was still quite capacious, even in its broken form, with a cranial capacity he estimated at about 1033 ml (rather small for a Neanderthal, but damage no doubt accounts for that). He noted, too, the unusual shape of the Neanderthal skull at the rear, with what has come to be called a bun-like bulge in the occipital area. He went on to describe the postcranial bones: the femurs (thigh bones) of unusual thickness and the evident signs of strong musculature; the robust right humerus (upper arm bone) and radius (one of the lower arm bones) and corresponding broken right ulna; the stunted left humerus and left ulna so pathologically deformed that elbow flexure must have been severely restricted; the fragments of pelvis and scapula (shoulder blade); the rib fragments, some of which suggested in their rounded shape an unusually powerful development of the thoracic muscles. The pathological state of the left arm bones left Schaafhausen in no doubt that the Neanderthal individual had suffered some serious injury during life, leading to both abnormal bone growth in places and general stunting of the left arm; he was emphatic that there was no evidence whatsoever of rickets as a cause of the poor condition of the left arm, or – we might add – the bowing seen in the leg bones, which Schaafhausen did not highlight. Interestingly he did note that 'the greater part of the cartilage is still retained in the bones, which appears, however, to have undergone that transformation into gelatine which has been observed by von Bibra in fossil bones'. It was this situation (together with the varnishing of the bones) that was, nearly 150 years later, to facilitate the genetic determinations on these original Neanderthal bones that have recently promised to settle some of the outstanding controversies over Neanderthal Man's evolutionary status and relationship to ourselves. It is to be hoped that similar genetic investigation may prove to be possible on some of the bones of other Neanderthal people and prehistoric people in general, to create a wider and firmer picture of the evolution of *Homo sapiens* as a whole, but it may be that circumstances were especially favourable at the Neanderthal caves and like genetic information may not be so easy to come by elsewhere. Schaafhausen observed, in his paper of 1858 translated into English for the *Natural History Review* of April 1861, that 'the bones, which were covered by a deposit of mud not more than four or five feet thick . . . have retained the greatest part of their organic substance'.

Schaafhausen, already aware of the tack that would be taken by scholars who disagreed with him about the Neanderthal bones, was at pains in his paper to make clear his conclusion that the strange form of the skull was not the result of pathology or of injury or of deliberate deformation (as still practised in some savage parts of the world in the nineteenth century), but was rather the natural state of the race represented by the Neanderthal find. He had very little to go on, as he was fully aware, when he came to this conclusion, but he was absolutely right about it. While noting that the 'remarkable conformation of the forehead . . . gives the skull somewhat the aspect of the large apes' he also saw traits in the rugged-browed Neanderthal skull that reminded him of features seen 'at the present time in some of the German races, as for instance in Hesse and the Westerwald' and concluded that it might 'fairly be supposed that a conformation of this kind represents the faint vestiges of a primitive type, which is manifested in the most remarkable manner in the Neanderthal cranium, and which must have given the human visage an unusually savage aspect'. In these remarks we see an implicit acceptance of the notions of human descent from ape-like ancestors and of the possibility, at least, that modern populations might still here and there evince physical traits descended in turn from earlier (but human enough) populations represented by individuals like the Neanderthal Man.

Not everyone in the German academic establishment was going to agree with Schaafhausen's view of the matter. The disagreement began with a colleague of Schaafhausen's in Bonn University, who noted the curvature of the Neanderthal limb bones and proposed that this bowing had resulted, on top of the rickets which Schaafhausen had explicitly and correctly ruled out, from a lifetime in the saddle ('typical thigh bones of a man who has ridden horses constantly since his youth'). He concluded that the remains belonged to an unfortunate Cossack (of Mongol descent, presumably to help cover the skull peculiarities) of the Russian army that passed through Germany to fight in France in 1814; wounded, the man had crawled into one of the Feldhof caves to die. The exaggerated state of his brow-ridges was attributed to a habit of frowning to excess. Other opinions saw in the Neanderthal individual: 'an ancient Dutchman', 'undoubtedly a Celt', 'a poor hydrocephalic idiot who had lived like an animal in the forest', even 'a wild cannibal who had somehow been transported to Europe'. The most formidable opponent of Schaafhausen's (and Fuhlrott's) interpretation of the Neanderthal find told Fuhlrott at a scientific convention in Kassel in 1857 that the Neanderthal Man was, after all, a thoroughly pathological specimen, whose brows were the result of injury, whose bowed limbs had been caused by rickets and whose other general divergences from the modern human form could be put down to arthritis deformans. Professor Virchow of Berlin University (one of the greatest biologists of the day) continued with an ingenious, if as we now know unfounded, argument against the attribution of any great antiquity to the Neanderthal Man: since this crippled unfortunate had evidently lived on well into maturity in his diseased and injured state, then he must have enjoyed the benefits of a developed and caring society which, Virchow was sure, could not have existed in the remote past. We shall see that just such care and concern was very likely a feature of Neanderthal society, however different from us physically and mentally these people turn out to have been. Virchow, though a liberal-minded, even radical figure without theological prejudice, was ever an enemy of all ideas of biological evolution (human or in general) and kept up his opposition for the next thirty years, dismissing with ever more contortion every new find of fossil man that came along after Neanderthal as pathological or mistaken. His remarks about the impossibility of a caring society in the remote past do indicate a belief in social if not physical evolution, however.

Neanderthal Man had got off, then, to a start of mixed fortunes in the country of his discovery. He had his supporters as a very ancient and different sort of human being, with a part to play in the evolution of mankind, but had also his detractors who saw in him only a poor freak of whom nothing more would be heard. To establish himself, Neanderthal Man would have to figure in a wider world.

CHAPTER 2

Neanderthal Man Abroad

The work of Fuhlrott and Schaafhausen on the Neanderthal find was not known in Britain until after the publication of the *Origin of Species* in 1859. Those who were won over by Darwin's theory were naturally disposed to accept the Neanderthal evidence more readily than they might have been in 1857. The geologist Lyell, who overcame his initial scepticism about evolution by natural selection, visited the Neanderthal site in 1860 – to him we owe the only attempt at an archaeological section of the find spot now available. He brought back casts of the bones to England. By then, Boucher's finds in the Somme gravels were widely accepted as firm evidence for the remote antiquity of man, especially after the more painstaking work of Rigollot in the 1850s. After fresh explorations, the evidence of the excavations in Devon in the 1820s was reinforced with further clear proof of the presence of humanly-worked flint tools in association with the fossil remains of mammoth, rhino, reindeer, lions, bears and hyenas sealed under unbroken stalagmite; full recognition of this evidence came in 1859.

All this evidence, taken together with the persuasive publication of Darwin's work in that same year, predisposed many in Britain to welcome the news from the Neanderthal. Darwin had rather coyly mentioned at the end of his book that 'light will be thrown on the origin of man and his history' and left it at that, in accordance with his remark to Wallace late in 1857 that he thought he would avoid the whole subject of human evolution 'as so surrounded with prejudices'. But the implications for humanity of Darwin's work were apparent to all who took it seriously, and enthusiasts for evolution fell on the Neanderthal bones with relish. Darwin's champion Thomas Huxley described the Neanderthal skullcap as 'the most ape-like human skull I have ever seen', but, lecturing with the title 'Evidence as to Man's Place in Nature' in 1863, he was at the same time keen to emphasize that the Neanderthal specimen was no ape-man from the earliest times of human evolution: 'though truly the most pithecoid of known human skulls . . . the fossil remains of Man hitherto discovered do not seem to me to take us appreciably nearer to that lower pithecoid form, by the modification of which he has, probably, become what he is.' In other words, Huxley could see that Neanderthal might be just a bit ape-like, but he was nowhere near the bottom end of the progression from ape to man. In fact, with some foresight given the paucity of fossils of ancient humanity, Huxley considered Neanderthal Man to be but an extreme form of *Homo sapiens* – many recent workers have come to the same conclusion, making the Neanderthalers a subspecies with the full scientific name of *Homo sapiens neanderthalensis*. Ironically, *Homo neanderthalensis* was coined in 1863 by Professor William King of Queen's College, Galway, who from the first did not consider Neanderthal Man to be *Homo sapiens* at all, finding him 'eminently simial', and went on later to want to exclude him from the genus *Homo* altogether. That would be unthinkable today, but the new genetic evidence so far available has certainly been interpreted to distance Neanderthal Man far from our own line of descent. King held Neanderthal Man's brain-box in low esteem and 'felt constrained to believe that the thoughts and desires which once dwelt within it never soared beyond those of a brute'. And there were those in Britain too who followed the German academic establishment in dismissing Neanderthal Man as a merely pathological specimen, a rachitic or an idiot. One English commentator on the find came up with a very colourful dismissal: 'It may have been one of those wild men, half-crazed, half-idiotic, cruel and strong, who are always more or less to be found on the outskirts of barbarous tribes, and who now and then appear in civilized communities to be consigned perhaps to the penitentiary or gallows, when their murderous propensities manifest themselves.'

Darwin himself, though he took up the challenge of human evolution in due course, was never very interested in the details of the recent course of that evolution and made little of the Neanderthal remains or those of other Neanderthalers that came to light in his lifetime. He preferred to theorize about the earliest phases of human evolution and was the pioneering advocate of Africa as the likely starting point of the human story, an idea that is well to the fore today.

In 1864 the English translator of Schaafhausen's paper, Professor Busk of the Royal College of Surgeons, resurrected the Gibraltar skull, which had been sent to him a year or two before, after its sojourn of more than a decade in the Gibraltar Museum. This very complete woman's skull closely resembled the surviving cap of the Neanderthal cranium and, carrying as it did the whole facial area missing in the Neanderthal specimen, made it possible to form a better idea of its human status than was the case with the Neanderthal relic alone. Busk, with Falconer who proposed the name *Homo calpicus* for the find, saw in Gibraltar Woman another sort of humanity, different from our own, 'very low and savage, and of extreme antiquity – but still man, and not a halfway step between man and monkey'. In this view, they lined up with Huxley's view of Neanderthal Man. At this stage in the study of the physical remains of human evolution, with so very few specimens to go on and no way of arriving at even relative datings for the material, the now obvious kinship between Gibraltar Woman and Neanderthal Man was not, perhaps, as apparent as it is today, when so many more individuals of the Neanderthal people have been found and studied. (As a matter of fact, Gibraltar Woman is probably an older Neanderthaler than Neanderthal Man himself.) For Busk, Huxley, Darwin, Schaafhausen and all the other scholars of the time, the field was open for fresh interpretations with every new find – a situation that has not altogether ceased even now.

During the rest of the nineteenth century more finds of fossil man and his works were made with increasing regularity as the study of remote prehistoric times was developed. Not all the finds were of the Neanderthal type; not all of them were even genuine discoveries of our forebears. A melancholy fraud was perpetrated on Boucher de Perthes by some of his workmen in 1863, when a completely modern sort of human jawbone (it was a completely modern human jawbone) was 'found' in the usual association with extinct faunal remains and flint tools near Abbeville in northern France. This time, the British who had supported Boucher in the past against his compatriot detractors were the first to smell a rat – French enthusiasts paradoxically stood by him for a long time after the fraud was exposed. In general, it is fair to say that those who consciously or unconsciously resist the idea of human evolution altogether will always favour a modern-looking fossil in an ancient context where they possibly can: if modern human beings can be shown to have existed ever further into the past, then one need not soon face up to the fact of human evolution at all. Those who firmly believe in the fact of human evolution might be expected, by the same token, to greet a little frostily any newly claimed representative of the modern sort of humanity to whom a very remote antiquity is attributed by his discoverers. We shall see that philosophical divergences along these lines have gone on throughout the history of anthropology, and do so to this day. Of course, responsible scholars readily disregard their own prejudices in the interest of scientific objectivity.

A toothless jaw that was altogether a better match for the Neanderthal and Gibraltar skulls was found in Belgium in 1865, in a large cave called le Trou de la Naulette in the Namur province. It was not only toothless, it was chinless as well, and had evidently been so in life in a way not seen in modern specimens. There was also an ulna and a metacarpal bone from the fingerless part of the hand, along with the prerequisite bones of rhino, mammoth, reindeer and bear and stone tools to establish the antiquity of the whole collection, sealed under four strata of stalagmite. The tools were of a distinctive type later recognized as constituting the stone tool kit of the Neanderthal people. That missing chin was easily perceived as a simian trait, in line with the increasingly accepted conclusion since Darwin that man was ultimately descended from something like an ape. At the same time the jaw was clearly human and fitted well, for those who cared to remember them, with the Gibraltar and Neanderthal skulls. Schaafhausen welcomed its discovery. It is interesting to record that a little later in the century the apparent lack of certain bony attachments for the tongue on the la Naulette jaw was the occasion for some researchers to assert that Neanderthal Man could not speak: 'la Naulette says No'. Related claims have gone on being made about other features of the Neanderthal voice-box in recent times, without succeeding in getting Neanderthal Man certified mute, as we shall see.

It was at about this time in the 1860s that scientists working in the Alps established that a succession of glaciations had occurred there in what were, geologically speaking, comparatively recent times in the history of the world. No one knew what dates were to be put upon these glacial episodes, but it was evidently a matter of tens and hundreds of thousands of years. The implication was that the entire globe had suffered periods of glaciation, ice ages, whose geological remains – in the form of moraines and boulder-clays – could be tracked in northern and alpine regions. Later it was recognized that sea level fluctuations during periods of glaciation could similarly be identified in raised beaches and high river terraces. After the first discoveries of the advanced Stone Age tools and art objects of the Crô-Magnon people, with their modern-looking bones, started to be made in the 1860s, it was even possible for a first synthesis of discoveries to date to be constructed. The Frenchman Gabriel de Mortillet proposed a division of the Old Stone Age, dubbed the Palaeolithic period by the Englishman Lubbock, into a later Palaeolithic of glacial times incorporating the finer toolmaking traditions identified at such French sites as la Madaleine, Solutré, Aurignac and le Moustier and an earlier Palaeolithic of the cruder and heavier material of the sort that Boucher de Perthes had been finding in the river gravels of the raised terraces of the Somme. De Mortillet thought that Neanderthal types had made the earlier stuff and modern sorts of human being had made all the later tool traditions. In this he was wide of the mark, since it would quite soon emerge that while modern men had made the Magdalenian, Solutrian and Aurignacian tools, the Mousterian tool kits were distinctly associated with the Neanderthalers, while de Mortillet's Chellean axe material had been produced by men earlier and more primitive than the Neanderthal people. Still, one admires the systematic thinking with which de Mortillet pioneered the correlation of tool types, geological phases and sorts of human being. Essentially, his entire approach is still with us.

Germany was by now by-passing the legacy of Virchow and taking human evolution seriously. People like Schaafhausen and the radical Karl Vogt always had, but Virchow's influence had usually seen to it that any finds suggestive of man's presence in remote geological epochs were written off as intrusions of later, pathological material. Vogt colourfully remarked that: 'Indeed remains of extinct animals intermixed with human bones had already turned up here and there; but these had either been pushed aside or entirely ignored, or explained in a manner that hardly cast a favourable light on the sagacity of the observer.' But in 1868 the zoologist Ernst Haeckel boldly constructed a scheme of the descent of man from an ape ancestor through an intermediate and as yet undiscovered form to which he gave a classificatory name, for all the world as though he had its bones in front of him and sufficient others to compare them with so as to create a new genus and species. The name he gave to his hypothetical missing link between apes and men was *Pithecanthropus alalus*, meaning Ape-man without speech. According to the rigorous scientific rules of modern biology, he had no business creating a name for a genus not yet identified in the fossil record, nor for a species of that genus either, but his name is interesting historically. It posited a creature in which pongid (ape) traits were mingled with incipient hominid (human) ones, and such creatures have been subsequently found, though their form in detail might have surprised Haeckel; it also highlighted at an early stage in the story of anthropology the all-important issue of speech and language that has become crucial to modern discussion of anthropogenesis, the process of becoming human that overtook a line of ape-descended creatures over the past two million years. Two important points should be emphasized about anthropological studies in Haeckel's time: no reputable biologist believed (or has ever believed) that human beings are descended from apes exactly like any of the apes still alive today; and no one thought that Neanderthal Man was an ape-man, for his human likeness was too apparent for all the divergences in detail of his bones. When people conjectured about a *Pithecanthropus*, they were thinking of much earlier days than those of Neanderthal Man.

Moreover, 1868 was also the year in which the vivid Crô-Magnon discovery was made. In a rock shelter that is now behind the garage of the Crô-Magnon Hotel, in les Eyzies in the French Dordogne, railway workers found the remains of five or more individuals, including the bones of four men, a woman and a foetus not quite come to term. The workmen, labouring on the railway line from Paris that still brings stopping trains to les Eyzies, understandably managed to mix up the bones, but it was very clear that what had been found here were fully modern sorts of human beings, with skulls like our own and skeletons if anything more tall and imposing than the average inhabitants of Western Europe could boast in the second half of the nineteenth century. The bones were apparently associated with finely made flint tools and with pierced shells and ivory pendants that evidently constituted items of personal decoration and there were pieces of carved reindeer antler. To establish the considerable antiquity of the human remains there were the bones of extinct animals and geological indications of some long period of time since what appeared to be the

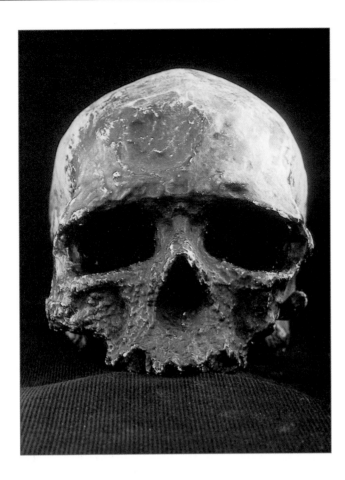

One of the skulls from the Crô-Magnon rock shelter.

deliberate disposal of the Crô-Magnon bodies. People who did not really care for Darwin and the idea of human evolution were pleased to see that, even in remote prehistoric times, human beings had been what they are today (or even better, like Adam and Eve before expulsion from the Garden of Eden); surely these Crô-Magnon types made better ancestors for the human race than some brutally visaged Neanderthaler ever could! On the other hand, the finds from Crô-Magnon puzzled superficial enthusiasts for evolution who expected to see some signs at least of primitiveness in the bones of the shell-wearing savages of very ancient Europe. It needed the sophistication of a scheme like de Mortillet's to picture distinct phases within extreme antiquity when, first, more primitive human ancestors might have made the cruder axes and, later on, more modern types might be the authors of the finer products that were now coming to light.

Those finer products were turning out to include not just delicate flint tools and necklaces, but real works of art not only found in geological contexts of antiquity with associated remains of extinct animals, but also themselves vividly depicting those extinct animals of a vanished ice age world. A world where the denizens of the cold north of today like the reindeer roamed southern Europe alongside species that have since disappeared altogether like mammoths and cave-bears. Stray finds of such ancient art objects in bone and ivory had been made, without acknowledgement, since the middle of the century; after the 1870s such finds were increasingly to be made and recognized, and spectacularly augmented by the discovery of large paintings and engravings in French and Spanish caves that most people could not at first believe to be the products of ice age humanity. The startling paintings of Altamira in northern Spain, first seen in 1879 and published in 1880, were widely condemned as a forgery despite the previous discovery of small pieces of art in the same tradition; people simply could not accept this quality and scale of art in an ice age context, even if its makers now seemed to have been fully modern types of humanity. The wall pictures of Pair-non-Pair in the Dordogne, discovered in 1881, were similarly disregarded till the end of the century. In the climate of opinion of the time, the first discoverer of the engravings at Marsoulas (Rhône Basin) concluded that they must be of recent origin. The revelation that the wonderful reindeer engraving of Kesslerloch on the Swiss–German border had prompted some of the locals to create more in what they imagined to be the same vein (based on drawings in children's books) to keep the discoverer happy only served to bolster the scoffers. Even when the ice age art was recognized not to be of fraudulent origin, it was often put down to the Greeks or Romans.

Meanwhile further remains of Neanderthal Man were being turned up. A skull and teeth unearthed at Taubach in Thuringia were dismissed by Virchow in his familiar style, while fragments of what we now know to be Neanderthal-related individuals were also found at Pontnewydd in Wales in 1874 and at Rivaux in southern France in 1876. In 1880, at Šipka in Moravia, a part of a Neanderthal child's jawbone was found in association with the bones of extinct animals and stone tools of the type called after the French site of le Moustier, which de Mortillet had previously lumped in with the finer tools from other French sites as products not of the Neanderthal sort of humanity but of fully modern types. At Šipka there were also traces of the use of fire. Schaafhausen identified the Šipka child's jaw as of Neanderthal kinship – he was by this time calling his Neanderthalers by the scientific name *Homo primigenius*, meaning Man of the first kind. If we do not call them by that not unappealing piece of scientific nomenclature today, it is because William King of Galway had already coined *neanderthalensis*, with primacy in today's system which tries to avoid the proliferation of new names for genera and species already named. Virchow, predictably, said the Šipka child was not a normal representative of another sort of humanity but again a pathological specimen.

At Spy d'Orneau, again in the Namur province of Belgium, there came to light in 1886, in a cave on a limestone hillside above a small valley, two almost complete

Neanderthal skeletons that afforded both a fuller picture than before of the Neanderthal anatomy and proof positive of the Neanderthalers' association with the Mousterian culture. Just as Neanderthal Man was neither the primitive ape-man that people expected eventually to find low down on the ladder of human evolution nor the fully modern superman of Crô-Magnon, so it now appeared certain that his stone tools were neither the large and sometimes crude flaked axes of the ancient river gravels nor the finely retouched blades of the ice age artists. Neanderthal Man's axes, when he made them, were smaller and slimmer than those from the Somme terraces, and he employed a distinctive set of what we now call side-scrapers and points (and other tools) made on flakes of stone, rarely as slender and systematically formed as the tools of the Crô-Magnons. Fossils and stone tools had been turning up at Spy since the beginning of the 1880s, but the careful excavations of 1895–6 were able to reach into deep and undisturbed deposits – so that the association of Neanderthal Man and the Mousterian tool kit was quite unambiguous. This association in itself made Virchow's rearguard determination, to see in the increasing number of Neanderthal-type finds only an implausibly growing crop of pathological cases, look desperate and impossible. The work at Spy was done carefully and quickly published, and soon all the world had a much better idea of what the Neanderthalers had been like. The Spy skulls were very like the original skullcap from the Neanderthal, while the Spy jaws were very like the la Naulette jaw found in the same province of Belgium in 1865.

Tentative reconstructions sketched by the discoverers of the Spy remains.

The limb bones were robust like those from the Neanderthal cave and these, taken with what could be interpreted as the ape-like features of the skulls, permitted a picture to be presented of a creature not indeed at all close to the apes but a bit closer than any living human being, with a bent-legged ape-like walk. This was an early version of a caricature of Neanderthal posture that is regrettably still around today, having been perfected by a French anthropologist between the world wars.

In 1889 work began at a site called Krapina in Croatia which was, over some fifteen years, to yield up the remains of between two and three dozen Neanderthal individuals, with further stray finds up to about 1970, including those of several children. Fossil animal bones had already been found there in the course of quarrying for sand and a human tooth came to light as soon as proper excavations were begun. The excavations were conducted along first-class lines for the time, producing bones of extinct animals, Mousterian tools, much evidence of the use of fire over long periods of human occupation, and human bones of the Neanderthal type. The Zagreb professor who conducted the work began as a follower of Virchow,

Neanderthal bones from Spy.

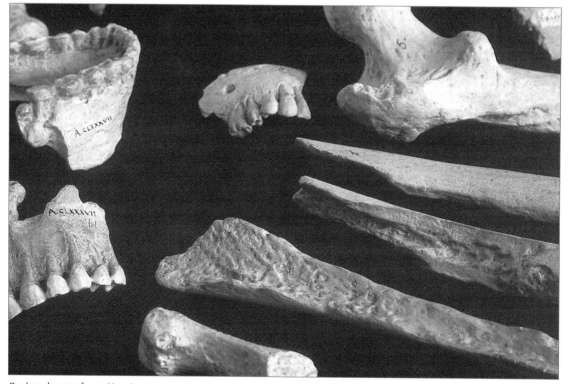

Broken bones from Krapina.

relegating the Neanderthal and la Naulette remains to pathological status, but the many bones he turned up at Krapina convinced him that he was dealing with a natural population of human beings who were simply different from modern men in some respects. (Interestingly, the Krapina Neanderthalers were perhaps not quite as very distinctively Neanderthal as others found to date, having in some cases, for example, more rounded backs to their skulls and other less than fully Neanderthal features.) It was Professor Gorganović-Kramberger of Zagreb who really gave impetus to the idea of cannibalism among the Neanderthalers; it had been mooted before on the basis of the broken jaw of la Naulette, but the excavator of Krapina was faced with a mass of disarticulated and scattered bones, with the long bones split open (for marrow?), many of them those of juveniles, some of them burned. He concluded that these abused bones represented the remains of victims of cannibal practices, presumably on the part of others of their kind. (Others were to propose further that these Neanderthalers had been the Untermenschen losers in a struggle with the Crô-Magnon Herrenvolk – another idea that has never gone away.) Gorganović-Kramberger believed that his Neanderthalers at Krapina, as evidenced by his deep stratigraphic sequence of hearths, had succeeded one another over a long period of time during the warm period before the last ice age and that they were a people directly ancestral to modern man of today, a view already espoused by the German Gustav Schwalbe, whose patient study of all the Neanderthal remains available at the end of the nineteenth century finally put paid to any lingering faith in Virchow's views. An American anthropologist recalled King's coinage of *Homo neanderthalensis* and brought together all the Neanderthal material found by the end of the century under that classificatory name.

By that time the first discovery had been made, in Java, of a type of man older and more primitive than the Neanderthalers. A Dutchman named Dubois had set out there to search for a human ancestor whose speculative existence had been inspired by reflections upon the gibbon, the odd man out among the apes (gorilla, chimpanzee, orang, gibbon) in having a more globular skull than the rest, with a less protruded face, and walking more naturally on two legs like a human being. At the time a gibbon-like ancestry for the human line was not a silly thing to look into. Dubois encountered his first finds in 1891, with a molar tooth and then a skullcap strikingly lower and more massively browed than the original of the Neanderthalers. The next year he found a femur in what seemed to him to be a similar state of fossilization from seemingly the same geological context. He recognized that it carried a pathological bone growth as the result of injury. Interestingly, most anthropological opinion has now come round to the view that the femur does not belong with the skullcap and is of much more recent origin – many subsequent finds of the same sort of human species as Java Man, some of them very complete, have built up a comprehensive

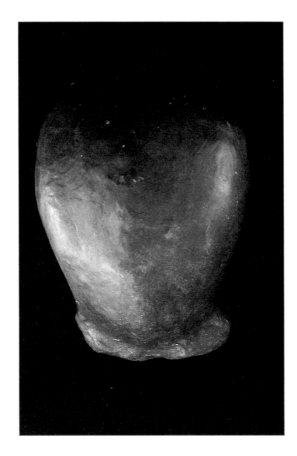

The skullcap from Java, very constricted when seen from above behind the heavy brows.

picture of this stage of human evolution. On the basis of the femur, Dubois invented a species name for his Java find, calling it *erectus* to mark its fully human carriage on long straight legs; if he was wrong about the association of the femur with the skull, he was right about the erect status of this new sort of human being, and the species name remains, in line with both its priority and its aptness. At the same time Dubois adopted a new genus for the moment, calling his Java creature *Anthropopithecus erectus* in a reversal of the components of Haeckel's *Pithecanthropus* – ape-man, man-ape. Neither genus name is still with us – Java Man and his kind are now seen to belong to the genus *Homo* like the rest of us, though they carry the distinguishing species name *erectus* to mark them off from earlier, different and later species. When Dubois established the cranial capacity of his Java find at about 1000 ml of brains, more than double that of any ape, he saw in his discovery less of a man-like ape and more of an ape-like man, and changed to Haeckel's *Pithecanthropus*, keeping *erectus* and dropping Haeckel's *alalus*, with its imponderable implications about speech abilities or lack of them. He was content to find gibbon traits in the Java skull, as he had hoped to do, but he saw that Java Man was even further from the apes than he was from modern

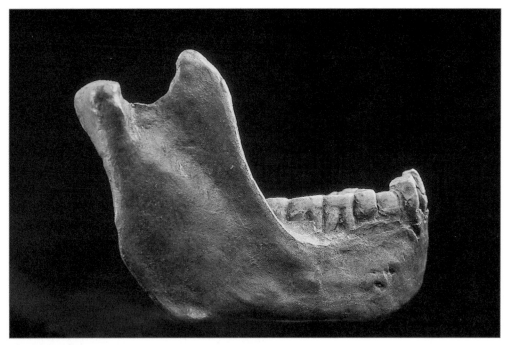

The Mauer jaw.

humanity. (Dubois, incidentally, had scorned all the Neanderthal discoveries as both recent and pathological until news of the Spy remains.) Dubois had a very inadequate grasp of the geological context of the Java finds and no real idea at all of their age, except that they were in a general way very old and more primitive than any human fossils found elsewhere at the time. Most authorities agreed with that: de Mortillet saw Java's foreshadowing affinities with Neanderthal, and many in England with Schwalbe in Germany adopted a simple scheme of human descent from some ape-like ancestor through first Java Man then Neanderthal Man to *Homo sapiens*. Predictably someone said Java Man was just a microcephalic idiot, and some German workers saw in the skullcap the evidence for just a very old species of giant gibbon, but Haeckel – who had previously been happy to dish out genus and species names to a thought experiment – at last turned his interest to real fossils and gave his support to this *Pithecanthropus* made bone if not flesh. He sent Dubois a telegram 'from the inventor of *Pithecanthropus* to his happy discoverer'.

A fossil that more or less matched the jawless Java Man's skullcap came to light in Germany in 1907, in gravel pits at Grafenrein, Mauer, near Heidelberg, at a depth of about 25 m. It was a very massive thing, that could easily be read as ape-like except that its full set of teeth were not ape-like at all but eminently human. Like the Neanderthal jaws, it had no chin. Its discovery at a very great depth in the earth suggested a high old age for the specimen which in turn suggested, along with its larger size, that it belonged to a skull more like that of *Pithecanthropus* than Neanderthal Man's. This interpretation put *Pithecanthropus* in place in Europe as well as the Far East, as a likely ancestor to Neanderthal Man in the way that some anthropologists already expected. In the same year the skull from Gibraltar was again studied, after what can only be rated an incomprehensible obscurity since the early 1860s when one recalls that it had possessed all along a better preserved face and skull base than any other Neanderthaler found during the nineteenth century.

In the last years of the century the authenticity of the ice age cave art was gradually established with the discovery of engravings under a stalagmitic layer at la Mouthe in the Dordogne in 1895 and the further finding in the same region of convincing engravings at Font de Gaume. As the artistic achievement of the Crô-Magnon sort of people, to all intents as modern in physical type as ourselves, became apparent, archaeological excavation was at the same time frequently revealing a sterile hiatus between the deposits containing Mousterian material (associated with Neanderthalers) and the deposits above with Upper Palaeolithic material (associated with the Crô-Magnon peoples). This sterile gap encouraged the thought that the Neanderthalers had not, after all, gone on to turn into the modern types in the simple line of human evolution from *Pithecanthropus* to Neanderthal to Crô-Magnon as many had come to believe. People who were uneasy with such a ready realization of the fact of human evolution, people who would rather not face up to the fact too soon and too clearly (with its inevitable reminder that we are, in the end, descended from something like apes and monkeys), such people were relieved to think that the Neanderthalers had perhaps already faded away even before the arrival of the Crô-Magnons, from points comfortingly unknown, with no call for a fight let alone the possibility of any intermingling that might taint the modern human line with a more animal heritage. Even so, there were sites like Grimaldi on the Riviera where the red-ochred burials of the Upper Palaeolithic people seemed scarcely separated in time from the underlying Mousterians. In the end, of course, the whole situation has turned out as is usual with human affairs to be much more complicated than anyone originally thought; it is likely to be more complicated than we think nowadays, too.

CHAPTER 3

Neanderthal Man
in the Twentieth Century

Some of the most significant finds of the Neanderthal people were made in the years between the turn of the century and the First World War, particularly in France. In 1908 the well-preserved skeleton of a young male Neanderthaler was unearthed at le Moustier near les Eyzies in the Dordogne, the site which had already given its name to the stone tool kit so often found in association with Neanderthal physical remains. The le Moustier skeleton was examined by the German anatomist Klaatsch, who was an enthusiastic supporter of the idea of the Neanderthalers' extermination at the hands of the Crô-Magnon people; he was not willing to credit Neanderthal Man with much in the way of culture, believing that he had lived as 'an animal among animals'. Klaatsch developed the view, distasteful and ominous as well as wrong, that the Neanderthalers lay on a line that led from the gorilla to the negro, while the Crô-Magnons graced a lineage from the orang to the modern European. None the less it was Klaatsch who spotted the Neanderthal kinship of the le Moustier adolescent. The young man of le Moustier had a very chequered career after his discovery, incidentally, which involved being sold to a museum in Berlin, facing the threat of air raids there during the Second World War (some said, actually being blown up by a bomb) and then being stolen by the Russians at the end of the war, turning up in Leningrad in the 1950s, minus his postcranial skeleton. The casts that archaeologists and anthropologists make and circulate among themselves have more than once stood them in good stead when the originals have, for one reason or another, become unavailable. But you cannot, for example, get genetic material from a cast.

The body of the le Moustier adolescent had evidently been laid in the earth on its right side in a sleeping posture, the right arm supporting the head with cheek on elbow; it lay on a bed of flints and a fine Mousterian hand-axe was found just before the skeleton appeared, to go with what might have been other grave-goods in the form of reindeer and ox bones. It is always difficult to determine, especially with older excavations, whether finds like these were purposefully associated with Neanderthal burials by the mourning party, as it were, or whether they are just

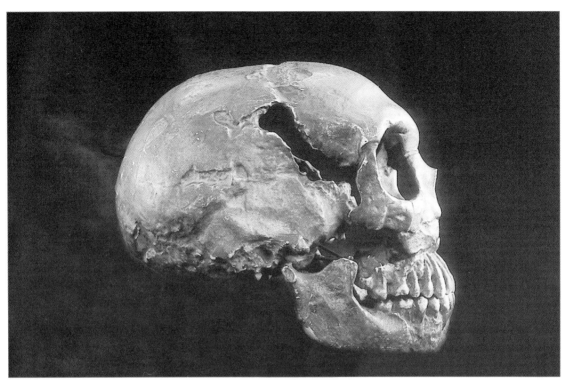

The much-travelled skull from le Moustier.

Excavator's section at la Chapelle aux Saints, with the Neanderthal grave.

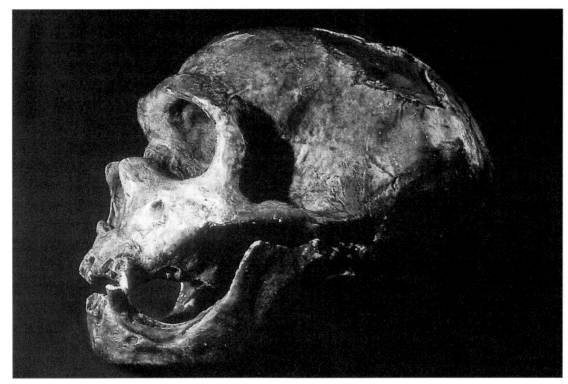

Skull of the 'old man' of la Chapelle.

elements of the clutter of Neanderthal sites that ended up close to the interments. Opinions veer to this day as to the validity of such evidence of 'provisions for the afterlife' and so forth. We shall see that, time and again, the evidence recovered by excavation and laboratory examination can be variously interpreted and that hypotheses, however attractive, sometimes lack the force of inevitability that their protagonists confidently attribute to them. Marcellin Boule's work on the la Chapelle skeleton, as set out in his monograph of 1911–13, is a case in point.

When it was found in 1908 the skeleton of the old man of la Chapelle aux Saints – he was forty or so – was the most nearly complete Neanderthal skeleton to date and was to be the basis of a most influential, and partly misleading, reconstruction by Boule of Neanderthal Man's physique and deportment. Parts missing at la Chapelle were supplied by bones from another fairly complete Neanderthal skeleton discovered at la Ferrassie in 1909. (Astonishingly, the la Ferrassie skeleton has recently turned out to carry unmistakable evidence that this Neanderthal adult male was a victim of lung cancer.) In 1910 an adult female was found at the same site, and subsequently the remains of five children, all buried together with the male in a sort of family vault: what Neanderthal burials can tell us about these people we shall discuss in a later chapter. Boule was sure that his reconstruction of Neanderthal Man, based on the la Chapelle skeleton, distanced the Neanderthalers far from modern humanity, to whom they could not be ancestral. The discovery of a fully modern human type at Combe Capelle, also in 1909, in apparent association with Upper Palaeolithic flint tools but only just above Mousterian levels, seemed to confirm his belief that the Crô-Magnon people must have arrived on the scene fully formed, with no time to have evolved out of their Neanderthal predecessors, whom they quickly supplanted. (The Combe Capelle skull also made the journey to Berlin and probably Leningrad too, but has never turned up again.)

While Boule was working on la Chapelle, in 1910 evidence came to light at the French site of la Quina, which he clearly soon heard about, that overturned one of his several misrepresentations of Neanderthal Man's physique and posture, but he ignored it. Ankle-bones were found at la Quina which proved that the Neanderthalers most certainly did not have divergent big toes, as the apes do, but Boule went on to incorporate the claim that they did into his report on the Neanderthal man from la Chapelle aux Saints. The, admittedly somewhat impressionistic, statue of *Homo neanderthalensis*, firmly based on Boule's work, that stands on the terrace of the museum in les Eyzies sports an unambiguously diverged big toe (see colour plates).

Boule was one of those nineteenth-century people (often, but by no means exclusively, French – and the type has persisted into this century, too) who never really embraced Darwinism, with its matter-of-fact mechanism of continuous evolution. Such people, with what degree of conscious choice we cannot always say, at heart preferred the catastrophism of Cuvier, with its succession of unrelated Creations and no continuous evolution of forms. Where Man was concerned, it was comfortable for them to be able to dismiss any and every candidate (like Neanderthal Man) that came along promising to embody the transition from a lower form to the higher form of modern mankind. They liked to think that some essential streak of modern humanity, if not full-blown moderns themselves, could always be tracked back into the remote past, bypassing all the unwelcome claimants for

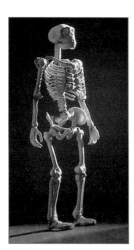

*Homo sapiens
neanderthalensis.*

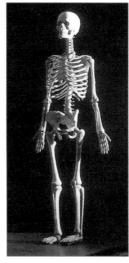

*Homo sapiens
sapiens.*

transitional evolutionary status. In this way the 'presapiens' idea was born (though the term was not coined till the 1930s): the idea that, in particular as regards brain size and skull shape, there would always have been some sort of modern men around to put the Neanderthalers and for that matter, if you wanted to push the issue, the *Pithecanthropi* in the shade. As long as you could posit the existence of such presapiens types far enough back into the very obscure past, preferably flourishing in as yet unexplored regions, you might never need to face up to human evolution at all. It was this sort of thinking, together with maybe ambition or revenge or a perverse sense of humour, that spawned the Piltdown hoax (in 1912), where an ape's jaw, in a nod to evolutionary thinking, was mated with a fully human, big-brained, in fact modern cranium – to pick out just that streak of essential humanity, in the form of man's higher mental powers, that was supposed to run like a silver thread through all the murky business of human evolution. (Interestingly, Boule thought, on the basis of brain anatomy as understood at the time, that the la Chapelle skull indicated that Neanderthal Man lacked the mental capacity for speech.)

One fears overdoing the matter of Boule's prejudices, for he was a distinguished scientist working within the limitations of his time, as all must, and he chanced with

The man from la Chapelle as envisaged by the *Illustrated London News* in 1909.

the old man of la Chapelle to be working with a diseased specimen whose pathology he did not fully recognize. It is an irony that Virchow, another and more open anti-evolutionist, saw pathology where there was none in order to dispose of inconvenient data, and Boule failed to see it where it was present (or at least failed to appreciate all its effects on the object of his study), to the same end.

In order to sidetrack Neanderthal Man and get him as far away as possible from the noble line of human descent, Boule had to make him as ape-like as he could. The divergent toe was one such stratagem. The long spines he found on the neck vertebrae he interpreted as a simian trait which would prevent their owner from carrying his head held high like a proper human being – Boule did not in his day appreciate how variable the modern human population can be in respects like this but in fact such long spines can occur in perfectly upright people today. In Neanderthal Man's backbone as a whole, Boule saw no properly S-shaped curve and concluded that his subject, and all his kind, must have gone around permanently bent forward. The ends of the shin-bones seemed proof to him that Neanderthalers could not straighten their knees, condemned to a shuffling gait which, taken with their lowered heads and sloping backs, must have looked as ape-like as you could wish. Again, modern populations contain individuals with the same sort of knee joints as the Neanderthal people, who do not shuffle on account of them. And while Boule was not unaware of the arthritic state and advanced years of the man of la Chapelle, he played down the effects of age and disease, in part with the honourable intention of producing a general description of the Neanderthal type and not just a characterization of one particular, damaged individual. But some of the specific effects of arthritis and age on the la Chapelle skeleton were thereby added to the misapprehended evidences of stooping and shuffling to reinforce the picture of an ape-like creature who could not possibly be ancestral to modern man. When Boule recalled the stratigraphy of the Grimaldi site where, as seemed to be the case at Combe Capelle, Mousterian remains were overlain almost without hiatus by the quite

Neanderthal vertebrae.

different Upper Palaeolithic material with Crô-Magnon bones, he felt content to conclude that the Neanderthalers had indeed been abruptly replaced by incomers for whom they were simply no match.

People who espoused the idea of superior invaders into Western Europe, bearing the Upper Palaeolithic culture of sophisticated stone tools and works of art and displacing the Neanderthalers, were not of one mind as to where these invaders had come from. Some thought it might be Eastern Europe, some thought it was Asia and some already favoured Africa as the first home of modern man. In the year when Boule completed his account of the Neanderthal people as evidenced by la Chapelle and la Ferrassie, the German Hans Reck put forward for consideration a modern sort of human skull he had found at Olduvai Gorge in East Africa in presumed association with the fossils of a long-extinct fauna. This was the first of many claims for the very early appearance of modern humanity in Africa and, like some other such claims since, it turned out that Reck's Oldoway Man was nowhere near as old as he thought, being a recent burial intrusive into the context of the very early animal bones. Today, too, there are key human fossils from East Africa about whose significance as very early examples of the modern human type there is considerable doubt along just the same lines as there was with Oldoway Man. At the same time there is a growing conviction among anthropologists, based on some soundly dated fossils, that modern man did indeed appear at a very early date in Africa and it would be ironic if the sort of thinking that Reck was expressing back in 1913 on the basis of the wrong fossil currently looked like turning out to be correct. It seems unlikely that Boule himself could ever have seen Africa as the likely home of anything so exalted as his presapiens humanity.

The year 1914 saw the first discovery of what would come to be seen as a strain in the Neanderthal camp of people who were clearly not as Neanderthal, if you like, as the classic Neanderthalers of la Chapelle, etc. Krapina had already hinted at this situation. At Ehringsdorf in Thuringia, not far from Taubach where Neanderthal remains had been found over forty years before, a child's skeleton was discovered in the year of the outbreak of the First World War. Even young children's bones can already display unmistakable Neanderthal features, but in the case of the Ehringsdorf child and of the woman whose skeleton was found at the same site in 1925, the Neanderthal traits were less distinct. In time, many more of these less-than-classic Neanderthalers were found, especially outside Western Europe, prompting new theories about the evolution of both the classic Neanderthal type and of modern man. It is pleasant to report, incidentally, that it was Virchow's son Hans who correctly identified the Ehringsdorf woman's character as a form of Neanderthaler, albeit less distinctly Neanderthal than most discovered to date.

Between 1917 and 1923, at a cave called Drachenloch in the Swiss Alps, a series of discoveries was made which promised to rescue Neanderthal Man from the extreme depths of simian degradation to which Boule's interpretation of his physical remains had condemned him. At this site Neanderthal Man was credited with nothing less than a cave-bear cult, collecting and artfully arranging the skulls and long bones of these huge and rather man-shaped animals on natural shelves of rock or in an artificially constructed box of stone slabs. He might have been, on the basis of Boule's anatomical work, a brutish fellow, but evidently he was capable of some sort of magical or even religious sentiment that inspired these non-utilitarian provisions. This interpretation of the Drachenloch finds has not altogether stood the test of time, though there is other evidence suggestive of a bear cult, as we shall see.

In 1921 something like a Neanderthaler was found in Africa for the first time, at a place then called Broken Hill in Rhodesia, and now called Kabwe in Zimbabwe. Mining for lead and zinc on a limestone hillside turned up a skull whose general resemblance to Neanderthal Man's was immediately obvious, though the brow-ridge over the eyes outdid anything seen on any Neanderthal specimen. The teeth, on the other hand, were of a fully modern kind. There was also a femur and fragments of a tibia and pelvis, which are now considered likely not to belong with the skull, but

The discovery at Broken Hill.

which at the time could be interpreted to suggest that a basically primitive form of man might have survived in Africa to a late date, having acquired a modern sort of postcranial skeleton but retaining a backward skull. This was all of a piece with colonial attitudes towards African culture in general. In fact, dating a find like that of Broken Hill was no easy matter at the time: we nowadays regard 'Rhodesia Man' not as a late surviving primitive but as a very early step towards the modern, and older than the classic Neanderthalers of Europe.

The picture of human evolution that could be envisaged in the mid-1920s was still a simple one: there were only the Neanderthalers and Java Man to go on. You could easily plump for a simple unilineal descent from some remote and undiscovered ape-like ancestor through *Pithecanthropus* (Java) then Neanderthal Man to ourselves, which at least had the merit of making the most of the evidence to hand; or you could posit an as yet untraced line of more sapiens-like humanity, again from an undiscovered ape-like ancestor, including *Pithecanthropus* in the scheme or not (probably not, he was too rough a customer) and definitely excluding Neanderthal Man as a doomed byway of human evolution. The gaps in the latter hypothesis were glaring, indeed it was all gap, but those in the former were clear enough too – no remote ape-like ancestor, no transitional forms to *Pithecanthropus*, and none from Neanderthal to modern. In the decade-and-a-half before the Second World War, those gaps started to be filled in, but in complicated ways that fuelled controversy.

In 1925 the first of the South African ape-men put in an appearance, in the form of an ambiguously infantile skull of debatable geological age that could not be definitely characterized to everyone's satisfaction. The 'Taung Baby', so named after its find site, was a curiously distorted and damaged fossil, with part of its brain exposed as a naturally mineralized cast. Emphasizing their human affinities, its discoverer interpreted its teeth as indicating an age of about five years at death – he considered the brain, too, to be suggestive of the first steps towards humanity taken by a basically ape-like animal. Dart called his baby ape-man *Australopithecus africanus*: the African species of Southern Ape. But most workers in the field of human evolution concluded that this was simply a new sort of fossil ape whose immaturity had fooled Dart into thinking it showed signs of humanity when it did not. As the geology of its find spot was not well documented, it might not be as old as Dart hoped either. In fact, Dart was amazingly right in his interpretation of the Taung Baby's significance and only wrong about its date in not being able, at the time, to see that it was even older than he thought it might be. From 1936 onwards finds of adult Australopithecines were made in various South African caves, but it would not be until after the war that due recognition could come to *Australopithecus* and his kind with postwar finds that established, moreover, the bipedalism of the Australo-pithecines: walking on two legs like human beings and quite unlike the apes.

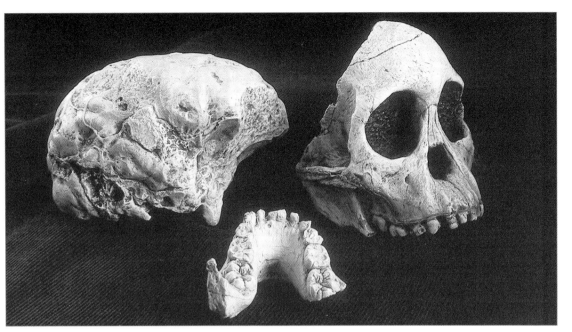

The separated skull, jaw and brain cast pieces of the 'Taung Baby'.

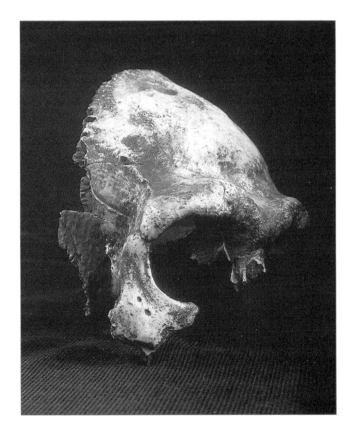

Skull fragment from Zuttiyeh.

Also in 1925 the upper facial portion of something like a Neanderthaler was found at Zuttiyeh in Galilee, harbinger of all the important finds to be made subsequently in the same area, while the skull of a juvenile Neanderthaler came to light on Gibraltar. The year 1929 saw the start of Neanderthal discoveries in Italy, and in 1931 another site in Java produced eleven jawless skulls that at first glance looked very much in the Neanderthal mould, though their dating was obscure. And then the puzzling picture of Neanderthal intermixture with modern types at Mount Carmel in Palestine began to take shape; associated with Mousterian tools, there were found bones from some dozen individuals that included a clearly Neanderthal woman and some robust but equally clearly non-Neanderthal skulls. Any simple scheme of human evolution was now faced with complications and the Levantine region remains to this day of critical importance in the discussion of modern human origins and the fate of the Neanderthalers, with startling new finds and datings at the forefront of anthropological research.

In 1933 a skull was found at Steinheim in Germany. Apparently pretty old, it was neither quite modern nor patently Neanderthal in form; it was heavily brow-ridged but seemingly rounder like a modern skull, and it was for this skull that the term 'presapiens' was coined, though the essential idea of a presapiens line of descent was already in currency, as we have seen.

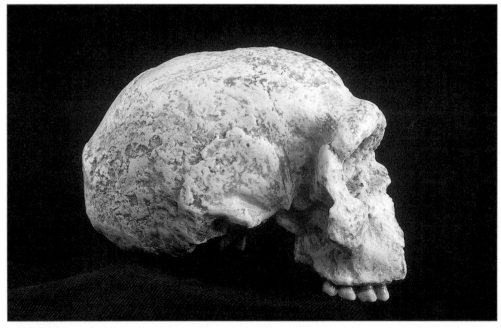

The Steinheim skull.

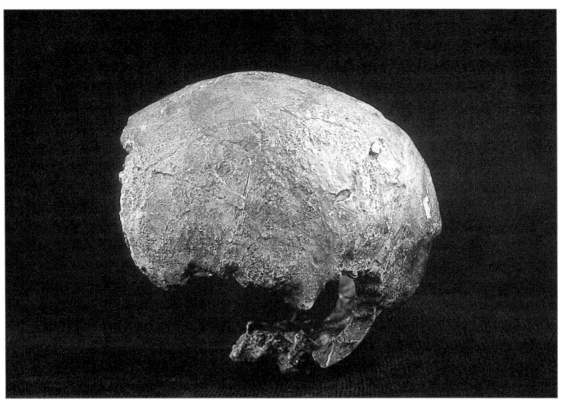

The Swanscombe fragments.

The excavations at la Ferrassie, which had already turned up an adult male and female, were concluded in 1934, having additionally revealed the burials of two children and three small infants in what looked like a regular graveyard under the rock shelter. There were various indications of grave-goods and ritual practices at la Ferrassie which have resisted subsequent debunking much better than has been the case with some other claimed pointers to Neanderthal spirituality and we shall consider them fully in a later chapter.

Pieces of a skull were found in 1935–6 (and astonishingly added to in 1955 with the finding of another piece belonging to it) at Swanscombe in England. It resembled the Steinheim find, neither full sapiens nor Neanderthal, but evidently older than both the last ice age to which the classic Neanderthalers were seen to belong and the warmer interglacial period before the last ice age in which the more generalized Neanderthalers of, say, Krapina and Ehringsdorf apparently found their place. (It was in 1936, too, that the child's cranium found just over a hundred years earlier at Engis in Belgium was finally recognized as belonging to a Neanderthal child.) The recognition that the classic Neanderthalers were a human species of the last ice age, its earlier phases at least, and that their antecedence might be traced back into the preceding interglacial period prompted the American anthropologist Aleš Hrdlička to theorize that the Neanderthal type with all its physical ruggedness represented an adaptation to extreme cold, rather like the physique of the Eskimos of today, only more so and starting from a pre-modern ancestor of the last interglacial. This idea, too, is still with us, having been taken on by several distinguished anthropologists since the Second World War. On the eve of the war, at a place called Monte Circeo in Italy, a further and very intriguing Neanderthal find was made, which the discoverer interpreted as the ritual placing of the skull of a Neanderthal individual, with the opening in its base for the spinal cord brutally enlarged, at the centre of a small circle of stones. It was a speculative picture of ceremonial brain-eating and cultic practice at some sort of shrine that, however barbarous, brought the Neanderthalers closer to ourselves in this apparent display of 'religious' concern. The Neanderthal people of Krapina may have looked like cannibals, or the victims of some other people's flesh-eating propensities, but the Monte Circeo find, at least as interpreted by its discoverers, was suggestive of belief and ritual. This side of the Neanderthalers, real or imagined, was to be played up to a peak of enthusiasm for their spiritual potential in the 1960s and 1970s which has since, it has to be said, rather faded in the light of harder-hearted interpretations of the evidence of places like Monte Circeo, just as the bear cult notion born at Drachenloch has similarly been revised. And a like fate has overtaken the spiritual implications once seen in the circle of wild goat horns around the burial of a Neanderthal boy at Teshik Tash in Uzbekistan, discovered at about the same time as the Monte Circeo skull. (Teshik Tash retains, however, the distinction of being the most eastern, and most mountainously remote, outpost of the Neanderthalers.) Still, while he lasted, the spiritually enhanced version of Neanderthal Man came as a welcome contrast to the merely ape-like Australopithecines and the clearly brutish Pithecanthropines: compared with them, he was practically one of us.

Pithecanthropus had meanwhile been given a boost before the Second World War by the spectacular discoveries made at Zhoukoudian (formerly rendered Choukoutien) near Beijing (formerly Peking) in China. The first fragments came to light in the late 1920s, in the form of teeth and pieces of skull, in association with faunal remains of extinct animals and some rather undistinguished stone tools. By 1937 there were the parts of fourteen skulls, eleven lower jaws, assorted teeth and a few limb bones. The study of them was conducted by Franz Weidenreich, who had previously worked on the Ehringsdorf material, and he made excellent casts of the original finds. At the end of 1941, with the Japanese on the doorstep, the Zhoukoudian material was packed up to be sent to America, under guard of a party of US Marines, for safekeeping. The Marines were captured by the Japanese and nothing has ever been seen since of the

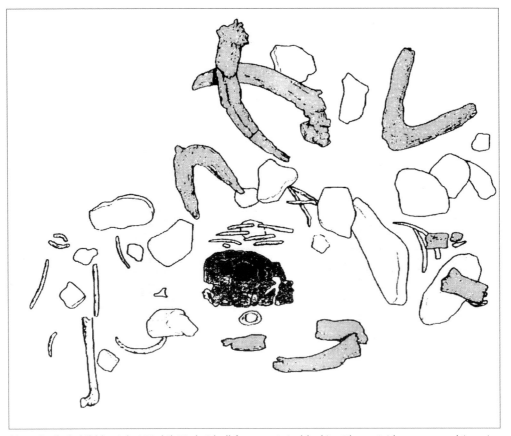

Neanderthal child burial at Teshik Tash (skull fragments in black) with goats' horns around (grey).

original finds of 'Peking Man', or *Pithecanthropus erectus* as he came to be known in light of his obvious kinship with the Java Man discovery of half a century before. (All such material, since found more widely, is now scientifically called *Homo erectus* as these people plainly belonged to the human genus.) There have been tales of boxes of bones in New York apartments and the like, but none has stood investigation. The original 'Peking Man' is now available to science only in the form of Weidenreich's excellent casts, photographs and notes. And, of course, the further discoveries of *Homo erectus* have reduced our reliance on the Zhoukoudian material in arriving at an overall characterization of this phase of human evolution. Interestingly, Weidenreich thought he had followed the cannibal trail back well before Krapina at Zhoukoudian, noting that there were many more skull parts than limb bones on the site, with evidence of smashed faces and enlarged basal holes in the skulls, suggestive of brain extraction.

After the Second World War the accumulated evidence of human evolution that had been raggedly piling up for almost a century was subjected to a more rigorous classification than had been thought necessary before. Evolutionary thinking in

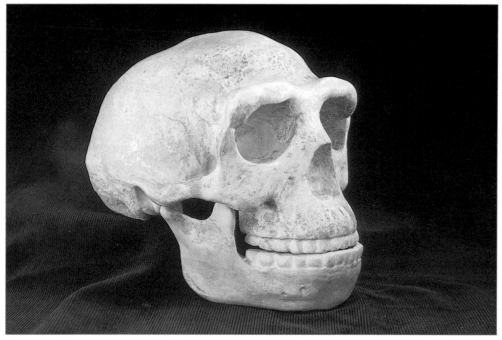

Reconstruction of the skull of 'Peking Man'.

general had moved on and it was seen to be no longer good enough to hand out fresh scientific-sounding labels as little more than nicknames to every new fossil that came along, though the habit was not abandoned overnight. In time, only two genera were allowed to survive – *Australopithecus* and *Homo*, doing away with *Pithecanthropus* and many more that had been recklessly coined for new fossils as they appeared. Neanderthal Man, Crô-Magnon Man and the modern populations of the world were seen, in this spirit, to be all of the same species, *Homo sapiens*, with subspecies distinctions into *Homo sapiens sapiens* and *Homo sapiens neanderthalensis*. It was Ernest Hooton of Harvard who formalized the division of Neanderthal-type finds into an earlier generalized form (as seen at Krapina, Ehringsdorf and Saccopastore in Italy) and the later classic expression of la Chapelle, la Ferrassie, etc. Weidenreich developed the idea of humanity as a single worldwide genus *Homo*, with strongly localized (i.e. racial) variations, that has gone through a sequence of species–phases (*erectus*, *sapiens*), not necessarily in strict synchronism and always preserving local lines of descent with distinctive variations at the same time as remaining interfertile across its global range. He thought that the common pressures of natural selection, and interbreeding across the borders of populations, have kept humanity advancing in a broadly similar way all over the world. This view was in marked contrast to that of the majority, perhaps, of anthropologists who have believed that new forms of humanity have arisen in particular places and spread out to outdo and replace the representatives of older forms. These two conflicting ideas of human evolution are still with us and nowhere does their clash reverberate so loudly as in the study of Neanderthal Man and his part (or lack of it) in our own origins and our potential part in his downfall. Weidenreich himself was undecided about the Neanderthal question – for him, the Neanderthalers might or might not have been the direct ancestors in Europe of the modern Europeans, but in any case in his view the general sort of stage of human evolution to which they belonged was one that humanity everywhere must have gone through, even if the European Neanderthalers as such were a race vanished without descendants.

In the 1950s the American anthropologist F. Clark Howell took up Hrdlička's pre-war suggestion that classic Neanderthal Man's distinctive features might well be seen as an extreme adaption to the severe cold of the last ice age, or failing that as a pronounced genetic drift into certain exaggerated physical traits that was possible in a small-numbered and climatically isolated population in Western Europe. On this basis, he proposed that classic status could be attributed to those West European Neanderthalers of the first half of the last ice age like la Chapelle, la Ferrassie, le Moustier, Spy, Gibraltar, Monte Circeo, and the original Feldhofer find, while the more generalized form would include what he called the 'progressive Neanderthals' of Krapina, Saccopastore, Tabun (the Mount Carmel Neanderthal woman), Teshik Tash and so forth, who belonged to the warmer interglacial period before the last ice age got under way. To these progressives, he granted the potential to evolve further towards the classic type in Western Europe but also, in Western Asia and the Levant, the potential to become modern *Homo sapiens sapiens*, as seen in some of the Mount Carmel individuals. He envisaged the possibility that it was from this source that what we call the Crô-Magnons arose, taking their chance to get into Europe when a milder interstadial within the last ice age let them through. In essence, this idea, too, is still with us, though the Middle Eastern *Homo sapiens sapiens* component is nowadays more likely to be thought to owe its appearance to evolutionary events within Africa on the ultimate basis of something like 'Rhodesia Man', who admittedly shares general traits with the Neanderthalers but could not now be considered to be in detail any sort of Neanderthal as encountered in Europe (nor to be as recent in date).

In 1947 (but not published until 1957) a skull was found in France that afforded a final outing for the idea of a presapiens entity in Europe. The Fontéchevade skull (actually there were fragments of two skulls, but one of them may not be as old as the other and is of a juvenile individual) does not conclusively exhibit heavy brow-ridges, for the simple reason that it is broken at the point where it would do if it originally possessed them. (The Swanscombe skull of 1935–6 and 1955 is in the same boat, only more so.) This situation permitted a reconstruction of Fontéchevade II to be made without any suggestion of brow-ridges (backed up by the childishly browless fragments of Fontéchevade I) and so for Fontéchevade (and Swanscombe) to be advanced as just the sort of presapiens intruder into the primitive world of the Neanderthalers and their ancestors that the disciples of Boule wished to see. But the geology of Fontéchevade was shaky, with no firm evidence as to its age, and while the Swanscombe skull was certainly of great antiquity it was entirely possible that it had originally sported marked brow-ridges and so was a poor candidate for presapiens status anyway. Since the 1960s enthusiasm for the presapiens idea as a European phenomenon has faded, and people of what we might call a presapiens disposition now look above all to Africa for the first appearance of early *Homo sapiens sapiens* traits at a time when the rest of the world was struggling through the Neanderthalers or other local varieties of similarly backward types.

We may conveniently end our review of historical developments in the field of human evolution, as particularly relevant to the Neanderthal issue, in 1960: not because no more Neanderthalers, to say nothing of earlier and very important fossils, have been found – indeed crucial Neanderthal discoveries have since been made in the Levantine region and in France, too, along with many more routine finds – but because by 1960 the main themes of Neanderthal controversy were clearly established and the detailed work of reinterpretation is part of the current state of the subject and needs to be discussed as such.

The year 1960 saw the end of the excavation at Shanidar, in Iraqi Kurdistan, that had begun in 1953, in the hands of Rose and Ralph Solecki for the Smithsonian Institution in Washington. Mousterian tools were found to a depth of 5.5 m in a huge cave overlooking a river. In 1953 the flexed skeleton of a very small child was found there and then in 1957 those of three adults, with clear Neanderthal features. In 1960 five more Neanderthalers were dug out of the cave deposits. Of the nine persons now discovered, five seemed to have been deliberately buried and four accidentally killed under rock falls. There are probably more to be found at Shanidar, but in the present political situation the cave cannot be explored further. One of the bodies was found to be accompanied by a very high intensity of flower pollens, which suggested at the time the touching possibility of a mourning gesture at the graveside but has since been prosaically interpreted as the result of the blowing wind or burrowing rodents. One of the victims of rock fall had had a particularly harrowing life, even for his times: a blow to the left side of his head had fractured his skull and damaged the eye socket, almost certainly causing blindness in the left eye; at some time in life his right arm had been so badly injured that it withered away and it was eventually either removed by surgery or even came off; probably in the course of the same injury, his right foot and leg were wounded with permanent damage. He was evidently a severely crippled case who nevertheless lived on with healed wounds to die somewhere between the advanced age of thirty and the great age of forty-five. It

Neanderthal Man washed and brushed up
for the New York subway in the 1930s,
according to Professor Carleton S. Coon.

is impossible, as with the cripple of la Chapelle, to imagine an old and rather useless individual like this being able to survive without some care and attention from his fellows, with all the implications for emotional attachments and social structure that thought brings. Taken together with the vignette of grieving Neanderthalers casting wreaths on the grave of one of their own, this revelation of Neanderthal humanity for a while brought the Neanderthalers closer to ourselves and further from Boule's apish caricature. Boule's work had by now been reassessed and his distortions removed from the image of Neanderthal Man, at least as far as anthropologists were concerned. There was a tendency to think that, washed and brushed up and in a collar and tie, Neanderthal Man might not arouse undue curiosity in the London Underground or the New York Subway. But the best joke ever made about Neanderthal Man has it that, if a Crô-Magnon Man came and sat next to you on a train, you would change seats – if a Neanderthal Man sat next to you, you would change trains! For the huge brow arches and heavy, pulled forward, chinless face would startle anywhere. Even if elements of a modern sort of behaviour, taking in grief and compassion, could be attributed to the Neanderthalers, it still remained for even the least classically featured of them to reduce their great and surely, to us, ugly faces in order to look like ancestors of ours. Whether they were our ancestors or not has been one of the burning questions of anthropology, which genetic studies now look set to help answer. If they were not, then the question of the humanity of their behaviour remains crucial to discussion of the origins and significance of our own.

CHAPTER 4

Neanderthal Types

We know the Neanderthal people from the remains of a few hundred individuals, not more than perhaps four hundred, from about eighty sites, even when stray finds of just the odd bone are taken into account as well as more complete skeletons. This may sound like a small number, but it is considerably higher than the numbers of earlier forms like *Homo erectus*, of whom we have about 150 specimens. Of the Neanderthal individuals known, about half are children.

The Neanderthal children are interesting because they demonstrate that many of the noticeable physical distinctions of their people, like the heavy brow arches and the general robusticity of their bodies, put in an early appearance in the life of each and every Neanderthaler. Teeth studies, moreover, indicate that they matured rapidly during infancy; their brains, in particular, seem to have achieved nearly full size at an early age. The molar teeth of the Neanderthal children are already well developed and it has been possible, by counting layers in the surface enamel of the front teeth, to arrive at close estimates of age at death for many of the infant skeletons and skulls, with results that have been surprising in relation to determinations of brain size for the same specimens. The four-year-old Neanderthal child from Gibraltar, for example, already carried a brain of 1400 ml (as large as many fully grown adults today) in its young head. The Teshik Tash nine-year-old had reached 1500 ml.

It might be said that the historical accident whereby it was the bones of Neanderthalers that first came to the attention of the scientific world in the nineteenth century got the search for human origins off to a skewed start. Neanderthal skeletons, in general, are not quite like those of any modern human beings, nor in some respects those of our remoter ancestors: their skulls, in particular, are very distinctive, but so in many ways are the rest of their bones. People who wanted to find human ancestors just like ourselves in the distant past were able to put the Neanderthalers aside as, if not freaks, then surely not on the direct line of human descent. People who expected to find a veritable 'missing link' sort of ape-man in our own evolutionary lineage were inclined to see Neanderthal Man as more simian than he really was and assumed that his traits would be found, more or less pronounced, in all other finds of fossil men. And so there were some researchers

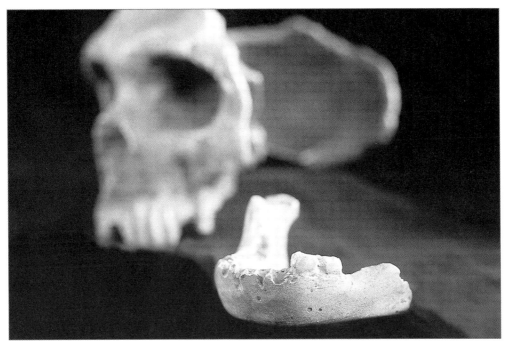

A Neanderthal child's jaw from Gibraltar, with the Gibraltar woman's skull in the background.

looking for human fossils as unlike Neanderthalers as possible, and others seeing Neanderthalers everywhere as new finds went on being made in Asia and Africa. The situation was complicated further in that, however racially distinctive and localized the Neanderthalers might be, they certainly represented a general stage of human evolution that might be tracked elsewhere in the world even where the particular distinguishing traits of the Neanderthalers were absent; and the Neanderthalers themselves turned out to show a considerable range of variability within their own type, with time and geography.

The classic type was realized in the la Ferrassie couple as well as anywhere, and the description that follows of their traits (supplemented by details from other finds where necessary) paints the definitive portrait of the *echt* Neanderthaler. Facially, you could never mistake a Neanderthal person, male or female, for any modern human being from anywhere in the world, and if no single postcranial feature of the Neanderthal anatomy is wholly outside the modern human range, it is none the less true that the entire package of Neanderthal traits below the neck similarly adds up to a type not seen anywhere today. There is a general impression of robustness and heaviness of build, of squat compactness of body with short, powerful and slightly bowed limbs. The leg bones, for example, are noticeably curved, probably on account of strong attached musculature, and thickly rounded in section, with large slanting

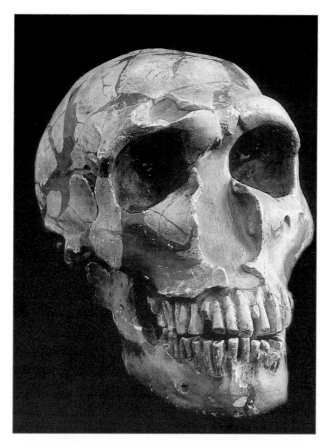

The male Neanderthaler of la Ferrassie.

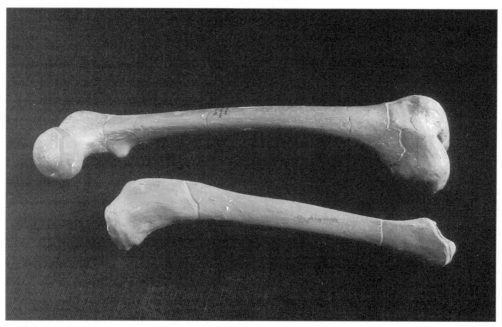

Limb bones from le Moustier.

A Neanderthal footprint from Italy.

joints at the knee that must have made for a knobbly appearance if not for some slightly less than straight-leggedness. The massive shafts of Neanderthal thigh bones lack the oval section, front-to-back, seen in the same bones among modern hunting peoples, which results from a lifetime of purposeful forward motion; some researchers have seen in the Neanderthal pattern a clue to an indeed less purposeful way of life, with more random scrambling about than motivated walking and running. Neanderthal feet have no ape-like divergent big toes, but their toes in general are fat-boned, adapted again to barefoot scrabbling over rough ground rather than much in the way of a sustained walking gait. But the toes are not elongated like apes' phalanges and the feet are well arched like our own. A Neanderthal footprint from a cave in Italy reveals, as would be expected, a broad foot. Neanderthal legs were short in proportion to trunk size, and shins were short in proportion to thighs, but not in a way that puts them outside the modern human range. Indeed, these physical proportions recall those of people today, like the Eskimos in particular, who live in cold circumstances where conservation of body heat would be compromised by long, lanky limbs. Some Neanderthal shin-bones are reported to carry the 'squatting facets'

Neanderthal hand-bones from la Ferrassie.

seen on the same bones today among people who habitually crouch down, in the absence of chairs by the fireside or shooting-sticks in the field.

Neanderthal chests were thick-ribbed and barrelled in shape, with strong backs and spines, where the cervical vertebrae often carried longer spines than are usually seen today, presumably in connection with powerful musculature. The broad scapulae of the shoulders, again with marked bony muscle-attachment ridges, saw to it that the arms would not twist under heavy loading. The big hands were clearly capable of a powerful grip, with large and rounded finger tips and thumbs made up of two

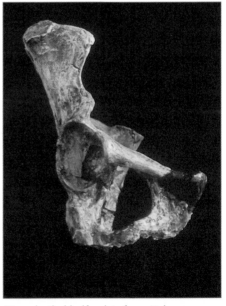

Neanderthal half pelvis from Kebara.

bones of equal length (where ours have a shorter distal phalange), but anatomical study has shown them to be as adept and manipulable as our own. Taken all round, Neanderthalers have rightly been described as 'bear-like' individuals!

The Neanderthal pelvis was a little different from that of modern people. The sexes were more alike in pelvis shape than men and women are today and, until a complete pelvis with a birth canal of similar size to modern examples was found at a site in Israel, it was conjectured that the wider pelvis of the Neanderthalers might point to greater head size (and brain development) of Neanderthal babies at birth. This was thought to reflect a situation wherein Neanderthal children were more fully formed in terms of brain development at birth than children are today, with consequently less scope for flexible and fruitful brain improvements through long years of childhood. Neanderthal children may well have matured faster than ours do, achieving the large brains of their adulthood much more quickly, but not because they were born with bigger heads through Neanderthal birth canals that were any larger than those of women today. The differences of the Neanderthal pelvis are probably witness to differences of gait and locomotion, with the centre of gravity of Neanderthal bodies forward of our own and falling more over the hips, with inferior shock absorption at the hip joints.

Neanderthal males stood at about 1.65 m on average, as against the modern European average height of about 1.75 m. Females were only a little shorter, with the shortest known (la Ferrassie) at 1.55 m. The tallest male was found in Israel at a site called Amud, and he stood at nearly 1.8 m. He also sported the largest brain of any fossil man, at 1740 ml.

Neanderthalers in general had bigger brains than we do. When we review the steady increase of brain size throughout human evolution, we might well be impressed by the size of Neanderthal brains. The Neanderthal people certainly belonged to a stage of human evolution that had fully achieved big brain status – but the brain was housed in a different skull architecture and belonged to a body that was, all in all, ruggedly and heavily built. In part, the Neanderthalers' exalted brain size relates more to their body weight and concomitant metabolic processes than it necessarily does to mental ability. And the Neanderthal brain was differently shaped, and differently developed in some respects, from modern brains, partly because it was carried in a skull very different from our own. People today are less confident than in the nineteenth century that brain shape and relative degrees of development in different parts of the brain can tell us so very much about the mental capacities of the individuals to whom the brains belong. Boule thought that areas of the brain then firmly identified as concerned with speech

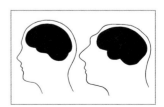

The different shapes of modern (left) and Neanderthal (right) brains.

capacity were less well developed in the Neanderthal type than they are in our own brains, but most workers today eschew rigid phrenology of that kind. Perhaps the one significant thing we can record about the Neanderthal brain in the present state of research is that the Neanderthal neocortical ratio was lower than it is on average with modern populations; in other words, the extent of the outer neocortex of the brain, which we think plays an important part in the complex bioelectrical switching of brain messages, was smaller in relation to the total brain size than is the case with ourselves, and the evolutionarily 'older' parts of the brain were correspondingly larger in proportion. It is interesting to note that Eskimos possess large brains, to go with their stocky cold-adapted bodies, but their brains are rounder than most and certainly rounder than the long, low, top-flattened brains of the Neanderthalers.

Neanderthal brain size ranged from about 1200 ml to 1740 ml, where modern brain capacity usually falls between 1200 ml and 1500 ml, though there have been perfectly normal people – for what that is worth – with brains of 1000 ml and 2000 ml at the extremes. The average Neanderthal woman had a brain of 1300 ml and the average man of 1600 ml, both in excess of the average woman and man today. Their brains do, incidentally, indicate that, like us, most Neanderthalers were right-handed, with larger areas to the right at the front and to the left at the rear; evidence from their teeth reinforces this conclusion.

The skulls in which the Neanderthal brains were housed are the most strikingly different thing about these people. Unlike any people living today, including those that live in very cold places as the classic Neanderthalers did, they had long and low skulls with a sort of bun-shape at the back, which look like slightly flattened globes when viewed from the rear, in clear contrast with modern skulls which appear higher and more rounded seen from the sides and look like steep-sided loaves from the back. These differences from our own crania might have been disguised by good heads of hair (of what colour we do not know, any more than we can know their skin colour) but the Neanderthal face presented a quite unmistakable picture of divergence from the modern human type, even when we acknowledge the range of our type today that can include quite heavily browed individuals and populations. Neanderthal brow arches were much bigger than anything seen in the modern world and of different form from the brow-ridges of earlier forms of fossil men like *Homo erectus*. In Neanderthal Man the bone of the brows did not form a single bar over the eyes but was separated into two rounded arches, seemingly of great solidity and heaviness but in fact lightened by the presence of sinuses within them. Most of our fossil ancestors possessed prominent brow-ridges, but the arrangement of the Neanderthalers was distinctive: at least it would have served to keep their hair out of their eyes! Such brow-ridges and arches are seen to have played their part in a general skull architecture adapted to strong jaw musculature to facilitate the workings of massive jaws with large teeth. The Neanderthal jaw usually

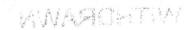

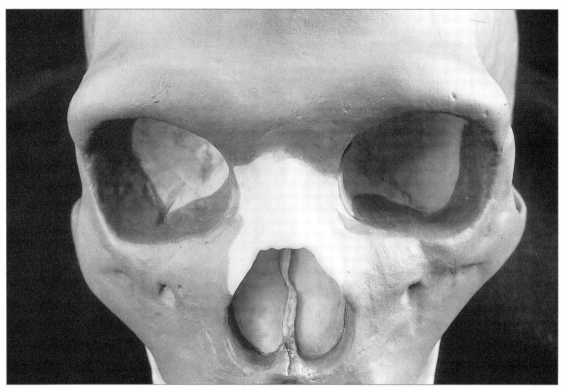

The heavy brow-ridges, swept-back cheeks and broad nasal base of the Neanderthal face.

had little or no chin, having perhaps no need of one in its generally rugged state, and the part of it reaching up to articulate with the cranium was broader than it is with us. The angle made by this piece with the arcade holding the teeth was more acute, closer to a right angle, so that instead of an effect of a delicate jaw tucked in under the skull, the Neanderthalers presented a picture of a huge jaw thrust out. The front teeth were very large by our standards and the top incisors were often rather shovel-shaped, a Neanderthal trait seen at lower frequency in later European populations. The front teeth are usually worn from heavy use and sometimes carry marks suggesting that they were used like a vice to clamp meat, sinews or hides while these materials were being cut with stone tools: scratches on the teeth show that the tools were worked very close up to the teeth, by right-handed persons. Front and back teeth show exposed dentine and pulp cavities, indicative of heavy wear, and the Neanderthalers exhibit a high incidence of a genetically determined dental pattern called taurodontism whereby root fusion creates enlarged pulp cavities, a useful stratagem of nature that permits prolonged use of badly worn teeth; some Eskimos show this trait today and it is found elsewhere in association with the presence of extra X chromosomes. These traits in common between the Neanderthal people and inhabitants of the cold north today

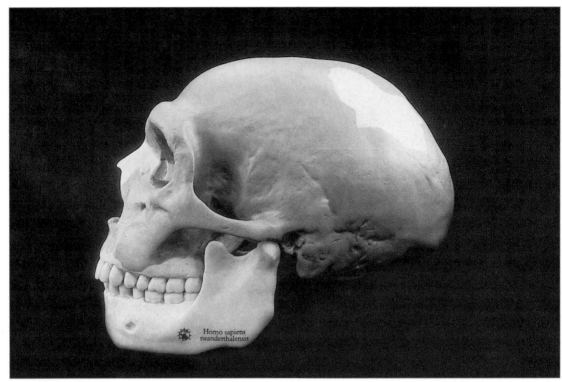

A teaching model of a Neanderthal skull illustrates, along with brow-ridges and bun, the mid-face prognathism and chinless right-angled lower jaw of the type.

imply no genealogical link between them – rather both peoples have adapted, along sometimes similar lines, to similar environmental conditions. The Eskimos, too, use their front teeth as vices and shears and pull skins through them in the course of preparing hides for clothes. In the la Ferrassie male's lower jaw, it is the left molars that are most worn while in the upper jaw the right side teeth have suffered correspondingly and teeth marks indicate a lifetime of heavy horizontal working. Neanderthal back teeth often display additional cusps, and there is almost invariably a gap between the last molar at the back and the ascending ramus (the upright portion of the jaw that hinges with the cranium) which relates to the length of the jaw thrust forward under the projecting Neanderthal face.

For the whole mid-face of the Neanderthal type was, as it were, pulled forward, as though one had got hold of the nose and somehow stretched the face towards one on the median line running from the 'chin' to the gap between the eyes. This prow-like mid-face is really the most distinctive feature of the Neanderthal countenance, after the brow arches. The pulled-forward mid-face resulted in an appearance of swept-back cheeks and eye sockets that is simply not seen in any modern people, an effect

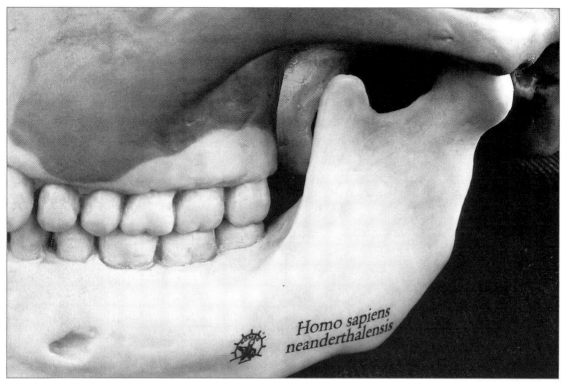

The Neanderthalers' typical retromolar gap.

made more obvious still by the lack of any hollowing in the cheek-bones above the eye-teeth (called canine fossa) of the sort that we display. It has been suggested that the inflated and swept-back cheeks might have reduced the chances of frostbite in freezing winds, but modern dwellers of the frozen north do not exhibit this condition. And it should be noted that the 'mid-line prognathism' of the Neanderthal face is not the same condition as the projecting mouth and teeth region seen in some people today, which does not involve the whole face, cheeks and eye orbits. The Neanderthal nose was evidently huge, with large nostrils as indicated by the low floor of the nasal opening. This represents another departure from the Eskimo pattern, where narrow noses conserve internal heat and moisture in the dry cold conditions of the north today. The big Neanderthal nose has been proposed on the one hand as a mechanism for heating air in proximity to the brain's blood supply and, on the other, as a cooling radiator for people working hard, harder perhaps than anyone does today, and in danger of overheating inside in externally cold conditions. On both accounts, the nose is plausibly seen as some sort of adaptation to a hard life in the cold, until one recalls that ancestral Neanderthalers of the warm interglacial period before the last ice age also displayed the large noses.

The mouth and throat region of the Neanderthal type has been of particular interest to anatomists since it promises to throw some light on the Neanderthalers' physical capacity for speech. It may not be possible, on the basis of brain details as evidenced by the interior form of their skulls, to draw firm conclusions about speech capability in any sorts of fossil men, so study of throat and mouth conformations at least opens up the possibility of determining whether the Neanderthal people, for example, were physically capable of speech (always supposing they were mentally disposed to it). Apes can be taught to wield a certain amount of 'linguistic' ability (how much is a matter of controversy) in the form of sign language, but only with the greatest difficulty can they be encouraged to utter even a very few more or less recognizable words like 'mama', 'papa' and 'cup'. The truth is that they are simply not physically equipped to come out with a range of consonant and vowel sounds. In the wild, chimpanzees employ a repertoire of a dozen or so calls with absolutely no signs of anything we might call a pre-language tendency.

Neanderthalers were a very long way from chimpanzees, with admittedly distinctive but none the less basically modern human skeletons and full-sized brains. They made a range of tool types and thrived in very adverse conditions, with a panoply of behavioural accomplishments that included co-operative hunting and burial of the dead. The use of language, though it might well have been less complex and developed, looks like a certain Neanderthal attribute. But in the past, and not just in the nineteenth century with people like Boule, serious doubts have been raised as to Neanderthal Man's physical capacity for speech. We are able to produce the large range of consonants and vowels that we do because our vocal tract is a complicated instrument with several components acting upon each other. The basis of the system is the larynx, the voice-box containing the vocal cords, originally evolved in our remote animal ancestry perhaps to prevent food from getting down into the lungs. Above the larynx is the supra-laryngeal tract consisting of the section of windpipe called the pharynx and then the oral and nasal cavities. Sounds are produced as air is forced through the closed vocal cords, vibrating at different frequencies with different degrees of force of air and closure of the cords. Clearly breath control is a basic factor in producing the sounds, requiring complex nervous regulation of the chest muscles – it has been thought that older forms of man like *Homo erectus* may have been deficient in this respect, judging by the size of the holes in the thoracic vertebrae through which nerves controlling breathing pass, but the Neanderthalers were as well endowed in this area as ourselves. The various frequencies of sound produced by the vocal cords are extensively modified thereafter by tongue position, by routing or not through the nose, by opening or closing the mouth in conjunction with different lip shapings. Tongue control seems to have been as well developed in even *Homo erectus* (or at least the latest manifestations of the

H. erectus type) as in Neanderthal and fully modern people: the hypoglossal canal through which pass nerves to the tongue is as capacious in 400,000-year-old fossil men as it is today, providing similar capacity for tongue control in speech, but the Australopithecines of a couple of million years ago show no more nervous provision for tongue control than do the chimpanzees.

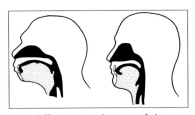

The differing vocal tracts of the Neanderthalers (left) and moderns (right).

In modern humans the supra-laryngeal tract is long, with much scope for subtly modifying the sounds coming off the vocal cords, by virtue of the low position of the larynx itself in the throat (lower than in the apes). With a low-placed larynx, the pharynx is almost as long as the oral cavity above it and these two compartments, at a right angle to each other, offer in combination many opportunities for sound modification. In the Neanderthalers, judging by the conformation of their skulls and jaws, the windpipe section was not as long in relation to the mouth cavity as it is in moderns and the conjunction of these two parts of the supra-laryngeal tract did not form so much of a right angle; these effects were exaggerated by reconstructions like Boule's that made the Neanderthal skull base too flat and put the larynx too high in the throat. This in turn suggested a reconstruction of the shape of the hyoid bone of the back of the throat (the human body's only free-floating bone, not articulated with any of the rest, and – until the 1980s – never recovered among Neanderthal bones) that would have rendered Neanderthal Man not only incapable of forming several important vowel sounds, as the protagonists of this reconstruction hoped to demonstrate, but also of swallowing or even opening his mouth. When a Neanderthal hyoid was eventually found, it turned out to be just like a modern one. It probably remains true, all the same, that the Neanderthalers were not as subtle in their vowel distinctions as we are and perhaps could not utter the G–K consonantal sounds either. It might be thought that this would not matter very much, since modern human speech covers such a wide spectrum of sounds, with many vowels unstable in pronunciation, but it is possible that even slight ambiguities of speech, slightly greater difficulties of interpretation in tricky hearing situations, might have helped to take the competitive edge off the Neanderthal people if and when they found themselves on the same patch as more fully modern humans. There are certain vowel sounds that all known languages like to keep stable and, it has been contended, these may have been beyond the powers of the Neanderthalers. In short, physiology does not deny the Neanderthalers a voice, but it holds out the possibility that that voice was not quite as useful as our own, and as yet it has little to say about the mental capacities that might have driven any Neanderthal speech.

It is possible to imagine an evolutionary scenario in which the achievement of the fully modern sort of human skull shape and vocal tract went hand in hand with the development of language capacity and improved technology. Better tools and better cooking methods might be seen to reduce the Neanderthal use of the mouth as vice or shears or hide-scraper, doing away with the need for heavy jaw and face with brow-ridges and bun, shortening the skull and allowing the skull base to arch upwards to a greater extent, permitting the extension and angling of the pharynx, enhancing powers of speech, putting a premium on individuals who could speak well and think well, promoting the incidence of clever people in the population, leading to the adoption of better technology, doing away with the need for heavy jaw and face . . . and so on, in an interactive feedback that led from something like Neanderthal Man to ourselves. But to many it looks increasingly as though the unique idiosyncrasies of the Neanderthalers mark them off as a European peculiarity of the story of human evolution and that we evolved from people who, while they were once at the same general stage of evolution as the Neanderthal type, were not themselves distinctively Neanderthal. Still, something like the feedback process just described must have happened to those direct ancestors of ours.

There are further detailed idiosyncrasies of Neanderthal anatomy, like the suprainiac fossa at the back of the skull, where neck muscles were attached to a depression rather than the protuberance commoner in other forms of humanity, the

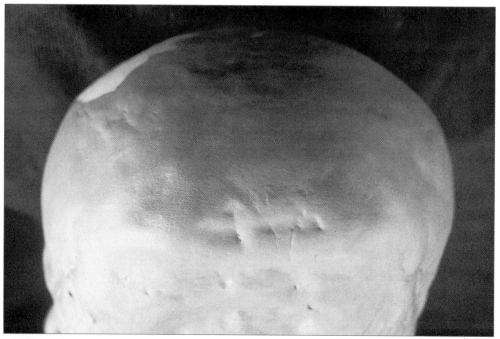

The back of a Neanderthal skull, showing the depression of the suprainiac fossa where neck muscles were attached.

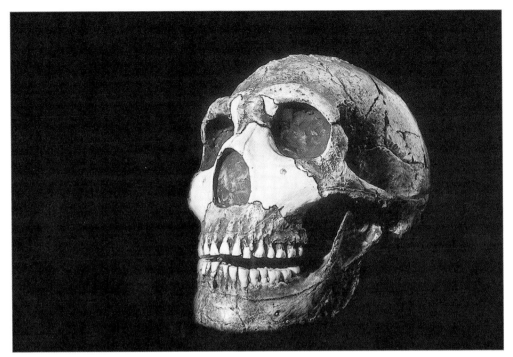

The adult male Neanderthaler from Amud.

large juxtamastoid process (in relation to the mastoid) where the muscles of the lower jaw were anchored and details of the inner ear, that both mark out Neanderthal Man's distinguishing features and help us to trace them back into general human evolution. Those distinguishing features, as we shall see, evolved over time and not all at the same time, and were less in evidence even among the immediately ancestral Neanderthal types of the last interglacial period before the ice age heyday of the classic Neanderthalers.

Those less-than-classic Neanderthalers have been dubbed 'generalized Neanderthal' and 'progressive Neanderthal'. The people of Krapina belonged to this grouping: they were more lightly built and their faces, though large, were more lightly made, sometimes with higher foreheads, while their limb bones were more like those of moderns, less stout, less curved. But they were unmistakably Neanderthal in their projecting mid-faces, their taurodont teeth, their retromolar gaps at the back of the mouth, their barrel chests, their brow arches and buns at the back of their heads. While the classic Neanderthal type is associated with the last ice age and most individuals of the type probably lived between about 80,000 and 50,000 years ago (though there are some important finds of later dates), the Krapina people were probably living at around 130,000 BP (Before the Present), at the end of the last interglacial or during a warmish interstadial after the slow onset of the last ice age. Similar dates and earlier ones apply to other finds of this more generalized type. In the Near East, even within the period of the ice age but well away from the glaciers of course, there are some non-classic Neanderthalers who do not so much look back to the generalized Neanderthal type of the last interglacial as (conceivably) forward to modern humanity. The tall (for a Neanderthaler) and big-brained male of Amud in Israel, though massive of jaw, exhibits relatively light brow arch development and less inflated cheeks, with a larger mastoid process than most Neanderthalers show and something approaching a chin. The cranium, though long in side view and globular from the back, has not the rear bun that classic Neanderthalers sport like a counterbalance to their heavy faces. Some details of the Amud skeleton are matched in other finds, both of early and late ice age date, from Israel and Iraq.

The evolutionary relationships of all these Neanderthal types with each other and with both our common ancestors of earlier times and ourselves has always been a matter of fierce debate. We have seen the widely varying interpretations of the Neanderthalers in the nineteenth century, ranging from Neanderthal as direct ancestor of modern man to Neanderthal as simian byway of human evolution – from father and mother to hardly a cousin. The debates of the second half of the twentieth century have been even more acrimonious, with good work, sound points and plausibility on both sides of what is essentially the same argument as that between Schwalbe and Boule. Anatomical comparisons of specimens, dated as closely as can be, can only get us so far. We can arrange the meagre fossil material we have on genealogical lines of possible descent, with informed conjectures as to how one form might have evolved into another. We have seen that a picture can be built up of reducing faces, flexing skull bases, better brains and improved vocal tracts, all interacting with culture and technology, to promote rapid evolution from something like a Neanderthaler into modern man. A biological process known as neoteny has been advanced as another mechanism by which modern man might have evolved out of something like a Neanderthal type: neoteny sees an immature stage of a creature's life cycle become capable of reproduction without ever reaching the adult form seen previously in its ancestors. There are numerous examples of neoteny at work in zoology and it has been suggested that slender, smooth-browed, mentally adventurous modern humanity might have evolved quite quickly out of heavy, big-faced, stick-in-the-mud Neanderthal Man, when natural selection favoured the fresh type. There are detailed reasons, both on biological grounds and arising out of study of the record of fossil man, why this idea has not continued in favour, but speculation like it is inevitable and only right and proper while we are faced with making sense of our fossil record of a relatively few bones from sometimes doubtfully dated contexts. So the application of genetic studies to the problems of human evolution and the human fossil record has been welcomed by many anthropologists and archaeologists (if not by all those with a talent for comparative anatomy) as a way of taking the study of our ancestry on beyond what the physical comparison of the bones can tell us. We shall see later that genetically grounded estimates of the dates of various phases of human evolution, arrived at by genetic analyses of modern human populations, have been the basis of much contention among anthropologists in recent years. Meanwhile, direct genetic work on Neanderthal remains has also produced dramatic results to date, with the promise of more to come. And so we are able to round off our characterization of the Neanderthal physical type with some details of these people's genetic type too.

Aptly, it is upon the very bones of the original Neanderthal Man that the first published work on Neanderthal genetics has been done. The upper arm bone of the skeleton from the Feldhof cave in the long since vanished Neanderthal, kept these 140 years in Bonn Museum where Schaafhausen first examined it, was recently tested to see if enough mitochondrial DNA (mtDNA) was left in it to allow the extraction of genetic information. Thanks perhaps to the long preservation of the specimen in the mud of the cave and then to the varnishing by Fuhlrott and Schaafhausen, the bone turned out to make some genetic determination feasible. About one-fortieth of the entire sequence of every cell's mtDNA, 378 bases of mitochondrial DNA, was available for study in comparison with the same sequence of modern humans and chimpanzees. Within this run of the sequence, modern populations show variations among themselves at up to about eight places, with chimpanzees differing from humans at some fifty-five places. The mtDNA from the Neanderthal revealed variation from the average modern count at twenty-seven places, markedly more than the widest range of variation among modern peoples and halfway to the chimpanzee rate of variation. On the strength of this degree of variation, the geneticists who did the work concluded that Neanderthal Man was not at all closely related to us, and that indeed his line might be calculated to have diverged from our own at about 600,000 years ago – before Neanderthal or modern forms of humanity had distinctively evolved out of the lattermost manifestations of *Homo erectus*.

It may not be so easy to extract mtDNA from other specimens of Neanderthal Man or other early humans; the important Neanderthal finds from Israel, for example, preserved in much warmer circumstances, may not afford the necessary organic material without loss and contamination. So this particular approach to the genealogy of the Neanderthalers might be limited, with only a few instances among the hundreds of fossils where information is forthcoming – but even a few instances will certainly throw much light on the question of the relationship between Neanderthal and modern humanity. If further mtDNA determinations (and it seems that the Krapina and Gibraltar remains are already under study) confirm the distancing of the Neanderthalers, both classic and generalized, from modern types, then the tendency of both comparative anatomy and archaeology to remove the Neanderthal people from the line of our descent will be reinforced. But the situation is a complicated one. There always remains the possibility that some modern people might turn out to carry more of the Neanderthal sort of mtDNA sequence than any so far tested (and the tested sample is not that large, inevitably). There is the distinct possibility that the Neanderthal people themselves showed a considerable variation in their mtDNA constitutions. And it must always be remembered that mtDNA only charts one line of genealogical inheritance in the cells of the human body; the same cells also carry nuclear DNA that has come down by other lines of descent and it may be that, while modern humanity carries no distinctively Neanderthal pattern of mtDNA inherited from Neanderthal women, we may display a partly Neanderthal inheritance in our nuclear DNA. Studies of worldwide variation in DNA patterns, especially of mtDNA, have in the last decade been used to suggest that modern humanity everywhere is all descended from a relatively small population of modern *Homo sapiens sapiens* individuals who evolved in Africa by 'about 100,000 years ago' and then spread all over the world, replacing (by fair means or foul) all pre-existing local populations of Neanderthalers or late *Homo erectus* or whatever. The date at which all this might have happened has been disputed even among proponents of the theory, but is largely based on estimates of the rate of mutation, of mtDNA in particular, that might have produced the current variations in human populations today. We shall return to this topic later – for the moment, it is enough to note that Africa is often nowadays posited as the cradle of modern humanity, not so much because it has a clear and well-dated fossil record of evolving forms as because its modern peoples show more genetic variation than do people in the rest of the world, suggesting that African moderns have been there longer (and in larger numbers) than modern types anywhere else, with more time and numbers in which to develop and maintain more mutations, whereas in the rest of the world we are all descended from small numbers of moderns who spread out of Africa after the modern type evolved there, with less time for accumulated variations. Much can and, needless to say, has been said about the assumptions and methodology that underpin this idea and its dating implications, as we shall see.

Neanderthal people, then, and especially the classic form of them did look very different from any modern peoples of the Earth, and were probably genetically very different too. If we put together a picture of their distinctive physical traits, we can readily see them as something so particular to their time and place (to which they seem to have been heavily adapted) that no modern people look likely to be their direct descendants, especially when the time of the last of the Neanderthalers is seen to be so close to the time of the first Crô-Magnon people, with no duration during which the latter could have evolved, however quickly, out of the former. At the same time, downplaying the very distinct peculiarities of the Neanderthalers, we can conclude that they basically belonged with other fossil finds from Africa and the Far East to a certain (and important) stage of human evolution when modern brain size was achieved in a skull architecture still strongly adapted to powerful facial musculature for heavy working of the jaw and teeth. It was out of that general stage of human evolution that modern people evolved, with teeth and jaw reduction, lightening of the skull architecture, change of cranial shape and flexing of the skull base, to the accompaniment of cultural changes that included better-made and more versatile tool kits, more competitive hunting skills, and very likely more sophisticated use of language and better organized minds than had gone before. It is possible that the Neanderthal people of Eurasia did not play any part in the further evolution of mankind, remaining only an isolated and perhaps terminally overspecialized human species until the better-endowed Crô-Magnon people came along to out-compete them into oblivion. This is a common view of the matter among anthropologists and archaeologists today. On the other hand, it is possible that even the classic Neanderthalers contributed something to the genetic make-up of the modern people of Europe, since some of their peculiarities – like the shovel-shaped incisors for example – do occur at higher rates among Europeans today than elsewhere in the world. One may point to some apparent continuity of physical traits between the Neanderthalers and the Crô-Magnons, like (among some other traits) the bony lip to a nerve hole in the jaw that two-thirds of the Neanderthal sample and one-quarter of the Crô-Magnon share in common, which is sometimes seen in Europe today but is otherwise rare, and unknown among earlier forms of men and the apes. And some anthropologists hold to the view put forward by Weidenreich before the Second World War that envisages a worldwide sequence of stages of human evolution whereby mankind, having spread over Africa, the Middle East, Europe and the Far East by at least a million years ago, went on to evolve in the same direction everywhere as a result of both common selective pressures and uninterrupted sharing of genetic improvements by constant interbreeding between the spread-out populations. In this way, it is proposed, all the peoples of the world could come on together through broadly the same stages of evolution while retaining locally distinctive characteristics through many generations. Nowhere are the implications of this theory, when taken neat, more vivid than in the case of the Neanderthalers, for it requires us to consider the possibility that some of them at least, with all their peculiarities, evolved in short order into the Crô-Magnon people and so on into the modern populations of Europe.

Not only genetics but also the archaeology of the behavioural patterns of the Neanderthalers and their contemporaries (their tools, their food debris, their dwellings) have a bearing on the questions thrown up by the bones of the Neanderthal and Crô-Magnon people and their successors and predecessors. In later chapters we will follow the Neanderthalers into their own prehistory, tracing their evolution out of earlier forms of Man and seeing how their evolution relates to that of other types in other parts of the world. Before that, having seen what the Neanderthal people looked like and how they differed from ourselves, we will consider the world in which they lived and how they managed to live in it.

CHAPTER 5

The World of the Neanderthalers

The classic type of the Neanderthal people lived in the world of the last ice age, or latest ice age as we should perhaps say while we await the seemingly inevitable onset of another one. Not all the classics, whose range was quite large, from Western Europe into Central Asia with a southerly outpost in the Levant, lived in glaciated circumstances but all of them lived in times that were affected in one way or another by the freeze-up. Most of the more generalized sort of Neanderthal folk lived in the warmer times of the interglacial period that came between the last ice age and the one before, and their evolving ancestors take us back into previous interglacial and glacial phases. The past seven million years or so, in which the human line arose out of an ape ancestry, have been a period of relatively cold conditions in the long history of the Earth, albeit with substantial warmer fluctuations within it. In fact, colder times have gripped the Earth since much earlier than that: until about 55 million years ago (mya), the world was enjoying stable warmth with little difference in conditions between the poles and the equator; a slow fade over millions of years reached a temperature low (but still not as low as today's) between about 35 and 25 mya. An improvement thereafter peaked at about 16 mya, to be followed by further drops at about 12, 10 and 7 mya, after which a more severe drop in temperature heralded the epoch of fluctuating ice ages in which we still live, with permanent ice in Antarctica. The earlier drops probably resulted as much as anything from changes in the configurations of the continents, but the potential factors leading to subsequent climatic deteriorations, especially over the last few millions of years, include: changes in the output of solar heat, which goes up with sunspots and down with less stormy times on the Sun; variability in the Earth's reception of solar heat as a result of the overlapping effects of variations in the Earth's orbit around the Sun and the angle (and the wobble of that angle) of its axis to the plane of the solar system; and further variability in the strength of the Sun's heat at the Earth caused by blocking from interstellar or volcanic dust in the Earth's atmosphere. With the exception of the random effect of vulcanism and interstellar dust, there are cycles in all the other factors which mesh together in interactions too complicated to model with any certainty. Fortunately, the Earth's geology contains a detailed record of the climatic changes of the long period during which human evolution has so far taken place, so that a reasonably sure framework of climatic change, with details of changing vegetation and animal life, is now in place, decked out with dates arrived at by means of various scientific techniques. By the early twentieth century a relative chronology of the ice ages had been worked out for the still glaciated Alpine region, with four glaciations (during which the Alpine glaciers had expanded beyond their present extent) and three interglacials (during which the glaciers had shrunk in size), but the scheme was flawed because it carried no real dates in years, no single site could record all its phases and the evidence was damaged by the inevitable fact that successive glaciations had advanced over the moraines left by earlier ones, obscuring and confusing the details. The worldwide application of the scheme was not easy to make.

Nowadays, the basis of our glacial chronology is provided by deep sea cores from the oceans' beds. These cores, of great length in some cases, can be correlated to provide a scheme covering the entire span of human evolution. They chart, most significantly, the changing volumes of the oceans during the epoch of ice ages. During an ice age, ocean volume contracts with the cold and precipitation fails to find its way back into the oceans in full strength, since much of it becomes locked up at the poles and in the mountains as ice, with the result that sea levels fall all over the world. Evidence of low sea levels is evidence of ice ages and evidence of high sea levels is evidence of interglacial periods. When the volume of the world's oceans is low, the heavier oxygen isotope Oxygen 18 is more richly present in the water in proportion to the lighter Oxygen 16, which evaporates more readily than when the seas are full, and the ratio of these two isotopes is reflected in the composition of the shells of the sea's foraminifera. Determination of the oxygen isotope ratio can tell us whether sea volume was low or high, and so whether the tiny creatures were living in an ice age or not. Up to a point, the species of these micro-organisms also indicate in themselves whether they were warm- or cold-sea types. The deep sea cores, then, constitute a detailed record of the fluctuations of the ice ages. The convention is to call our own postglacial (or interglacial) period by the number 1, with odd numbers representing the warm interglacial episodes and even numbers the periods of glaciation. The heyday of the classic Neanderthalers was thereby Stage 4 of the scheme, and the generalized Neanderthal type belonged to Stage 5 or earlier, but it has to be said straightaway that fluctuations within the main stages, denoted by the addition of small letters, require us to keep in mind a much more complicated picture of climate changes and the human comings and goings which have been heavily influenced (perhaps crucially for human evolution) by them. Warmer episodes within glacial periods that do not merit the full-blown status of interglacials are called interstadials.

Putting dates to the phases evidenced in the deep sea cores relies, as far as the cores taken by themselves are concerned, on estimates based on depth of deposits forward and backward from a fixed point, dated by other means in terrestrial rocks, at which the Earth is known to have experienced one of its periodic reversals of magnetic polarity: at 730,000 BP, or perhaps as far back as 790,000 according to the latest determinations. The top of the deep sea core sequence can additionally be dated by the radiocarbon technique, which does not reliably go back beyond about 40,000 BP.

The data from the deep sea cores is buttressed by physical evidence of altered sea levels at different times during the ice age epoch, which can in some cases be dated by one or more scientific methods. Coral reefs and terraces in New Guinea and Barbados, with dates by the radiocarbon and uranium series techniques, are the principal source of information, but evidence of higher than today's sea levels is also available round Mediterranean and Atlantic coasts. Britain, of course, was connected to the European mainland during periods of glaciation (and during interstadials within them) and the Atlantic coast of France extended some 30 to 40 km to the west when the sea level was low.

Another chronological scheme is afforded by the deep deposits of loess that are found across northern Europe from Brittany in the west into Central and Eastern Europe, and in China. Loess is a loamy deposit of wind-blown origin which, during the ice age, built up to great thickness in some places when howling winds blowing off the glaciers carried away loads of material from river margins or beaches or maybe glacial outwashes, areas with little or no vegetation to prevent it, and deposited them far away – to deepen during glacial times and weather during interglacials. For the past three quarters of a million years, the loess deposits show the same subdivisions of cold and warm phases as the deep sea cores, with the addition of faunal remains and archaeological deposits that can sometimes be dated – not that anyone lived in the loess areas during their periods of deposition, when they must have been fearful places indeed. They would have been deserts at the best of times, and only habitable during weathering phases of the interstadials and interglacials, when they resembled steppe country today.

Other lines of evidence that throw light on the glacial chronology of the ice age epoch come from polar ice cores, Andean lake bottoms, the study of the pollen sequences in archaeological sites and the succession of animal life – some of it extinct nowadays – from similar sources. Again there are the alternations of warm- and cold-loving forms, shading through all the intermediate situations.

The evidence taken as a whole builds up a detailed picture of the environmental circumstances of human evolution. After about 5 mya worldwide temperatures recovered a little from the cold spell that saw the formation of the Antarctic ice-cap and the aridification of parts of Africa in which our ape ancestors had been flourishing – globally, cold times are also dry times because, with so much moisture locked up in the ice, evaporation and precipitation are reduced. But after about 3 mya the cold returned and glaciers this time formed in the northern hemisphere, establishing a still-ongoing pattern of relatively longer cold spells and shorter warm ones, with seriously cold episodes at about 2.5 mya, 1.7 mya and 800–900,000 years ago. There have been more than twenty glaciations in the last two-and-a-half million years, averaging perhaps 100,000 years in length apiece, with interglacials running to much shorter durations of about 10,000 years each. At their worst, glaciations have seen ice sheets covering up to one-third of the present land surface of the Earth, though in areas of presently shallow seas more land was exposed by the lower sea levels of the ice ages, notably between Siberia and Alaska and in the region of Indonesia, Papua and Australia. Temperatures fell by perhaps 3 °C even at the equator, and by as much as 16 °C in higher latitudes, with enormous impact on the flora and fauna – to say nothing of the humanity – of these regions.

Climate will continue to be an important factor in the whole story told by this book of human evolution from our ape-man ancestors in Africa to Neanderthal Man and beyond. For the moment, we need a more detailed picture of the world in which the Neanderthal people in particular emerged, thrived and, somehow, disappeared. That all happened in the world of the last interglacial and the first part of the last ice age. The pattern of glacial-interglacial fluctuation involves possibilities of changes in temperature, in wind force and direction, in precipitation, in animal life and vegetation, and in sea level and coastline. Taken as a whole, such changes in the environment must have had a great impact on the career of the Neanderthalers (as they did on earlier forms of humanity, and as they may yet do on us).

The Last Interglacial followed a previous ice age of intense cold, probably every bit as cold as the final phase of the most recent ice age which reached its severest at about 18,000 BP, long after the last of the Neanderthal people had disappeared. The Last Interglacial began in about 130,000 BP and, like our own postglacial times which date from about 13,000 years ago, it probably came on rather quickly, with swift warming and melting of the glaciers at the poles and in the mountains of Scandinavia and the Alps. There seems to have been a sharp increase in solar radiation at the start of the Last Interglacial, with temperatures that went markedly higher than those we enjoy today to begin with, settling down to perhaps some 2 to 3 degrees higher; the glaciers retreated to at least their present positions, if not further back, and with similar sea levels coastlines assumed about their present configurations, though there is evidence of raised beaches at 5 to 6 m higher than today's which may only mean that some spreading of the ocean floor with continental drift has since been a factor in lowering our present sea level below that of those Last Interglacial times. As with the end of the last ice age, the Last Interglacial saw the recolonization of areas at high latitudes and altitudes by plant and animal life that had been driven south, or in some places downhill, by the cold weather of the previous glaciation. Typically, pollen sequences in the stratified levels of north European sites of the Last Interglacial show a progression through a brief episode of birch and pine, on to elm and oak, then alder, hazel, yew and hornbeam, finally indicating the beginning of the return to cooler conditions with pine, spruce and silver fir as the interglacial period drew to a close. Open and relatively treeless conditions obtained only at the beginning and end of the interglacial. By 125–120,000 BP conditions were a little warmer than they are today, with a warm fauna of rhino, hippo, elephant, lion and hyena even in northern Europe; but this range of animals need not imply that things were equatorially warm in our own terms, for the details of land connections and migration routes and even perhaps of human activity or comparative lack of it were factors in the spread of the wildlife. All in all, the world of the interglacial Neanderthalers was not unlike today's, except that the animals they might want to avoid or hunt if they could were a very different lot from the present Eurasian complement, and for that matter from the fauna they would encounter in the ice age that was to ensue.

The evidence of the cores suggests strongly that the Last Glaciation came on not quickly, as the previous one had gone out with a rapid thaw, but rather gradually with a sequence of shortish cold spells of varying intensity over a period of about thirty thousand years, until things got really harsh again at about 80,000 BP. The many interactive factors that can reduce the strength of solar radiation at the Earth's surface produced during those years a basic fluctuation of two cold and two warmish phases: the warm times probably not much colder than today, but perhaps wetter, and the cold spells some 10 °C lower in temperature, with stronger winds (evidenced by sand in Atlantic cores taken near North Africa). The cold periods were not as severe as the fully glacial times to come, but even so the glaciers must have extended somewhat, and climatic zones were shifted everywhere so that the conditions previously seen further north in Europe (or higher up the mountain slopes) were brought south and down the valleys. In Europe, during these early cold phases of the Last Glaciation, patches of pine, birch and willow survived against a background of steppe-like conditions, or even tundra, with more woodland conditions in the south.

Even in the warmer interstadials, the glaciers made their presence felt with colder winds and icy waters in the North Atlantic, producing in northern Europe an environment of pine and birch woods in place of the open or shrub tundra of the cold phases, and in south-west Europe, at best, of elm, oak, hazel and hornbeam, until pine and spruce reasserted themselves with the next cold phase. So the interstadials were not so much worse than today in southern Europe, while they were a bit colder in the north. Even so, there could be shocks: there appears to have been a very cold, if brief (one to two thousand years) episode within the first interstadial.

Even away from the ice sheets, in Africa, temperatures were cooler during the opening phases of the last ice age than they had been, and more significantly they were drier, with shrinking areas of forest and woodland shading into patchily wooded grassy plain. Deserts spread in Africa like glaciers in Europe. These were circumstances, both in Africa and Eurasia, that could lead to a degree of geographical isolation, for humans as well as animals, with real possibilities of quite rapid evolutionary change in small populations that had ceased to be a regular part of larger breeding groups. The Neanderthal people look like one such evolutionary tendency in Europe, while some scholars believe that Africa was the scene of the debut of modern *Homo sapiens*, out of a stage of humanity roughly equivalent to the Neanderthal people but not distinctly of the Neanderthal type. The Levantine region at the eastern end of the Mediterranean could well have offered refuge from both the cold of northern Eurasia and the aridity of North Africa, so it is not surprising that we find a coming and going, perhaps a meeting, even a mating of Neanderthal and more modern types at sites in this region: some would say it was simply the scene of one big, if variable, family of evolving humanity.

After 80,000 BP it became too cold to live north of the Alps, except during further interstadial warmings, down to about 60,000 BP. Temperature evidence from the cores makes it clear that the glaciers would have extended beyond anything seen since the onset of the Last Glaciation. It has been suggested that an unparalleled explosion of a volcano in Sumatra, the worst in 450 million years, was the last straw that brought on the full rigours of the Last Glaciation after 80,000 BP, blocking the already diminished sunlight with ash and sulphur fumes. Pollen records demonstrate that the area of Holland, Denmark and North Germany became at this time just treeless tundra, even polar desert in places, with temperatures well below freezing for much of the year. The Scandinavian and Alpine ice sheets spread to perhaps within 500 km of each other in Germany. In Central and Eastern Europe the loess storms made occupation impossible outside of any warmer interstadials when the deposited loess could weather. The Neanderthal people of Western Europe could only adapt their way of life, and perhaps (under pressure of natural selection) their own physical type too, and try to hang on where they could in a world that for the time being no one from anywhere else would want to come and share with them.

The exact limits of the ice sheets of this first fiercely cold phase of the Last Glaciation are not known since they were subsequently overridden by the final extension of about 18,000 BP. All the same they brought much of the character of the frozen north today to what in our times are the temperate regions of northern and not so northern Europe, but with some important differences. The tundra in the proximity of the ice sheets, though utterly barren in places, still received the hours of sunlight through the seasons of northern Europe today, not the limited periods of daylight seen in the Arctic winter, and the sunlight's angle was the same as it is now in these latitudes, however diluted it was in strength. Air temperature was low and winds were strong, but the summers could still be long and warm, if drier than today's, and sheltered spots would have supported stands of trees. South of the tundra-like conditions there was something like steppe, with a dry 'continental' character in south-west Europe whose coasts were now extended out into the Atlantic by the lowering of the sea level. Hardy trees like pine and birch were commoner here and sheltered valleys might be quite wooded. All in all, even in the severest times, circumstances were set fair for a rich wildlife on which the European Neanderthalers could prey. And after about 60,000 BP conditions on the whole improved, with fluctuating but generally slightly milder times. There were some short but other quite long interstadials, up to perhaps 4000 years in duration, but they were evidently not as mild as the interstadials of the earlier part of the Last Glaciation. Whether these interstadials resulted from subtle details of the combined astronomical cycles or perhaps from shifting patterns of the Atlantic currents as icebergs were shed into the sea, decreasing salinity, is difficult to determine now. By 45,000 BP it was pretty cold again all round, and then there quickly followed another 15,000 years of fluctuation with an overall improvement towards warmer conditions, with oak-mixed forest replacing more open conditions. It was during this time that the Crô-Magnon people and the superior technology of the Upper Palaeolithic put in their appearances in Europe, and the Neanderthalers and the Mousterian tool traditions bowed out. By 30,000 years ago it was colder again and 18,000 BP saw the very worst of the ice age, and the biggest challenge to human beings who lived – and thrived – through it. By then, the Neanderthal people were long gone, but they too had managed to prosper well enough through the harsh conditions of the middle reaches of the Last Glaciation.

Harsh though the Neanderthalers' ice age may have been in weather conditions, it was a time of ample wildlife and opportunities for good hunting, or at least good scavenging. The tundra conditions close to the ice sheets were a particularly rich area for animal life, as was the taiga with more, if stunted, trees that it sometimes incorporated. Here there were reindeer, musk ox, wolf, arctic fox, glutton, ermine, stoat, many rodents and breeding birds. There were the warm-coated elephants, too, that we call mammoths, and woolly rhinos, which like most of the birds and the reindeer, followed by the wolves, would have migrated further south in winter – to the fringes of the forests, with subarctic species like pine and spruce, that were the world of red deer, brown bear, lynx, marten, mice, voles, lemmings, beaver, hyena, bison and aurochs. The forest fringe was not, in fact, so well stocked a world as the teeming tundra and it was more difficult to hunt and scavenge in. The windy, dusty world of the loess-steppe was worse still in glacial times, with nothing like it in the world today, but in the summers of the interstadials its parched grass cover could support many rodents and some large fauna, too, including horses, hyenas, even reindeer, mammoths and predatory lions. Away from the loess deposits into Eastern Europe, steppeland with horses, carnivores, rodents, maybe seasonally mammoth and rhino, extended into Asia.

Though earlier human forms had spread into northern Europe during previous interglacials, the Neanderthalers were the first people to inhabit the periglacial regions of full ice age times, living relatively close to the ice sheets in the bare world of harsh-wintered tundra and taiga that predominated even in France and northern Spain in their time, as well as across Germany into Central Europe. They shared that world with a range of animals which would be regarded as quite exotic if encountered outside of a zoo in the same places today, and in some cases inside the zoo as well. The woolly rhino, the mammoth, the cave-bear and the cave lion are no longer with us at all, and it may be that men – later than the Neanderthalers – had a hand in their demise. The lion may seem an unlikely component of the ice age fauna, though lions are living through our winters in northern zoos and safari parks today. The cave lion version, at least 25 per cent bigger than the African lion today, was probably the biggest cat that has ever lived on earth and must have been both a serious competitor and a real threat to the Neanderthal folk. The cave-bear was commoner, and, at about 2.7 m long, bigger than a grizzly bear. While the lions used caves as their lairs, the bears also hibernated in them and probably more frequently disputed occupation of them with man, with victory going either way. One Austrian cave contained the remains of 30,000 bears, representing long and secure tenancy. The cave-bears were primarily herbivores but probably ate more meat than bears do today, just as the Neanderthalers almost certainly depended more on meat in their diet to keep them fed through the seasons of their harsh world than people do in milder times and places. Bears might on occasion have been a source of meat for humans, or at least their skins and fat may have carpeted or heated and lit the Neanderthalers' cave homes and camps. How far we can believe in some bear cult on the part of the Neanderthalers we shall consider later on. The cave-hyena was another numerous animal of the last ice age, if more interstadial than glacial in preference, and found on the steppe during the cold. It too was bigger than its modern counterpart and its dens show that it scavenged widely, putting its teethmarks on bones in a way that provides evidence in discussions for and against cannibalism and big game hunting as we shall see.

The woolly rhino and the mammoth were both cold-adapted species of genera from warmer climes. The 3.6 m high mammoth was not to survive the end of the ice age, at about 13,000 years ago, making its last home in the grazing grounds of Siberia and North America. The woolly rhino went out with the ice age too and its presence on an archaeological site or in a geological context is a sure indicator of cold; it is thought that it used its 'horn' as a snow shovel as it grazed the stubby vegetation of the tundra near the glaciers' edge, and its teeth were well adapted for a tough vegetable diet. The European bison went the same way as the mammoth and the woolly rhino, in Europe at least, disappearing as woodlands spread north again with the great thaw. The reindeer went north in Europe in the same situation, not into extinction but into the new lands to which they are presently confined: they require a tundra lichen to stay healthy. Red deer were denizens of the more southerly and sheltered temperate woods and parkland found well away to the south of the tundra of ice age Europe, and only came into more northern territory in interstadial times, as did the giant aurochs, ancestors of domesticated cattle, formidable horned creatures 3.5 m long. Horses roamed the dry grasslands of the steppe regions in the warmer interstadials.

The often cold and sunless world of the Neanderthal people of the last ice age was a harsh place to live in. Their remains bear witness to the hardness of their lives and to the stress and ever-present threat of injury and disease to which they were subject. They were not as well equipped technologically, or most probably mentally either, as the people who came after them, but they pioneered the habitation of these cold and forbidding regions, extending the range of human occupation significantly beyond that of their predecessors, but not penetrating as far as we can tell into the fastnesses of Siberia, or on into the Americas. Their range runs from Gibraltar in the south-west to southern Britain in the north-west, across northern and central Europe and down into Italy and Greece, north of the Black Sea and just north of the Caspian into present-day Uzbekistan and south of those seas across Western Asia into the Middle East, with that important southerly outpost in the Levant. Some of these places were quite warm even in the ice age and certainly so in the preceding interglacial, but life looks to have been always hard for the Neanderthalers. Fire they possessed and the shelter of caves where there were any and, we have evidence to suggest, of some sort of tents and huts on occasions. They surely wore clothes, though physical evidence for such is naturally lacking. Even in the later times of the Crô-Magnons, direct evidence for clothing is encountered only in the form of patterns of bone toggles and beads that the Neanderthalers did not sport. They probably went in for wraps of animal skins held together with rawhide strings and thongs to be more or less airtight. Some of their flint scrapers fit the bill for hide preparation and, as we have seen, they used their teeth to work on skins and sinews too. In the relatively unsunny world they lived in, their own skins may well have been pale as are those of indigenous Europeans today, to maximize the value of ultraviolet radiation in producing Vitamin D. There is at the same time no reason to think that, with the blessing of warm clothing and fire, the Neanderthalers need have followed the lead of the mammoths

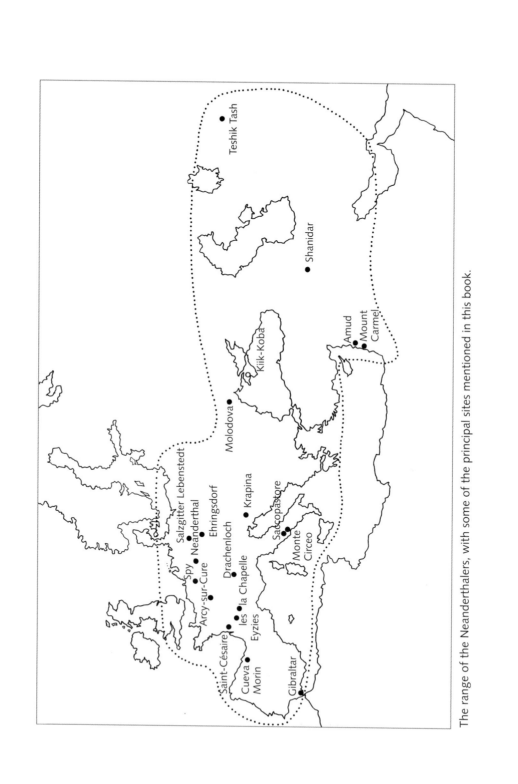

The range of the Neanderthalers, with some of the principal sites mentioned in this book.

and woolly rhinos in developing very hairy skins of their own, though many reconstruction drawings and models have shown them so — we simply do not know about this.

We do know that their lives were hard, perhaps the hardest ever lived by human beings outside the forced labour camps of the ancient empires and the modern tyrannies, when their living conditions are considered alongside their technological, social and mental resources. Their world was one of abundant animal life, if perhaps less well endowed with plant foods, but it was a harsh regime that permitted them to survive in it. And the demands upon the Neanderthal people were quite changeable, too, requiring periods of major adjustment: first from interglacial to ice age conditions and then to the ups and downs of the interstadials. They were to meet all these requirements with a technology vastly inferior to that of the Eskimos in recent times. Many if not most Neanderthal remains show signs of stressful living. We have already seen that their skeletons all over show a robusticity suited to hard labour with pronounced ridging for muscle attachment; we have seen that their leg bones attest to a life of scrambling over rough terrain while their shoulders, arms and hands are suited to grasping and lifting heavy burdens. Judging the ages at death of the known Neanderthal individuals (by microscopic examination of the fossilized cells in their long bones, by noting the closure of sutures and symphyses, by study of their teeth), we can see that infant mortality was higher than it was among their Crô-Magnon successors and among foraging peoples today and that fewer than 20 per cent of adults reached the age of thirty-five, against a figure of 50 per cent for modern hunter-gatherers. It has been said that in general Neanderthal skeletons show patterns and degrees of stress comparable with those of rodeo riders.

Degenerative disease and injury are plain on many Neanderthal remains. The original Neanderthal skeleton shows a deformed elbow joint, probably resulting from a badly healed fracture. The old man of la Chapelle (not much over forty, remember) suffered from degenerative joint disease that showed its effects on skull, jaw, spine, hips and feet. Serious arm injuries are in evidence on some of the Krapina and Shanidar material. Shanidar, as we have seen, reveals an appalling history of injury to several individuals. Shanidar 1 had been blinded in the left eye, among other head injuries, and suffered crushing of the right side of the body during life, with evidence of post-traumatic infections, and yet he lived on, to be laid low in the end by a rock fall from the roof of the cave (in an earthquake zone) where he and his fellows lived. Shanidar 3 had probably died of a stab wound (delivered, apparently, by a right-handed assailant) which badly damaged a rib. Shanidar 5, like Shanidar 1 and one of the Krapina people, survived severe head wounds. Life was fraught with perils, one can conclude, but it is also apparent that some individuals like the la Chapelle and Shanidar wounded could survive with the tolerance, at least, of their relatives and very likely their active care too. Of course, injuries occur in all walks of life and the Crô-Magnons who came after the Neanderthalers also show signs of often similar wounds and diseases, but not so frequently – as though they may have been better at avoiding trouble and making the best of ice age life. Certainly the Crô-Magnons of Europe lived in larger numbers than their Neanderthal predecessors. It is hard to estimate population sizes for these remote times, but it is certain that there are many more sites of Crô-Magnon Man and his Upper Palaeolithic tool traditions than of Neanderthal Man and his Mousterian tools.

A recent medical discovery about an old archaeological find has shown that some things have sadly not changed in the long history of disease. The male from la Ferrassie, excavated between the world wars, has now been revealed to exhibit signs of lung cancer. Lesions in the lower ends of the thigh and shin bones, where new surface bone has formed in response to inflammation below, constitute a pattern of affliction specifically associated with cancer centred in the lungs. Certain cancers may have increased in frequency in the human population with the invention of ways of life that Neanderthal Man can never have followed (there was no tobacco in the last ice age of Europe, for example), but our predecessors could on occasion suffer in ways that, perversely, seem to bring them closer to us than fights with cave-bears ever could.

If the world of the Neanderthal people was a tough one as a whole, with a struggle for life in circumstances of hardship and heavy labour, there were particular times and places where things were more congenial. Putting together both the finds of Neanderthal bones and of the Mousterian tools that are commonly associated with them, it becomes clear that there were two centres of Neanderthal life where occupation of sites was well maintained by local populations of some numbers: south-west France, with its abundance of classic Mousterian sites and Neanderthal remains, and the Levantine region in the Middle East, with long sequences of Mousterian occupation and important discoveries of Neanderthal types (and, importantly, of non-Neanderthal types, too, as we shall see). Elsewhere in the Eurasian range of Neanderthal Man, occupation was more intermittent, with fewer finds of both tools and bones, in a way that suggests that these regions were inhabited when climate and food supply encouraged it and abandoned when resources thinned in unfavourable times. In Europe and Western Asia (not including the Levant), the long years of the Neanderthal heyday from the Last Interglacial into the first phases of the last ice age, do not show evidence for other types of human being than the Neanderthalers or for other types of tool kit than their Mousterian tradition until the arrival of the Crô-Magnon people and the main traditions of the Upper Palaeolithic at around 40,000 BP. But, of course, the rest of the world was not all empty (though parts of it still were, like the Americas). In Africa and the Far East, other descendants of *Homo erectus* and related forms were continuing on their way, with different toolmaking traditions. For much of the time in Africa, the contemporaries of the Eurasian Neanderthalers were making tools of broadly the same sort as the Mousterian (with differences of detail), and we can usefully lump all such tool types into the category of the Middle Palaeolithic, to distinguish them from the Upper Palaeolithic tools of the Crô-Magnons (and their close relatives in the rest of the world) and the Lower Palaeolithic ones of the sort that we saw were being found in ancient river gravels in Europe in the nineteenth century. But there were episodes during Middle Palaeolithic times in Africa (called Middle Stone Age by African specialists) when different tool types foreshadowing the blade techniques and bone-working of the Upper Palaeolothic put in various appearances and when human types generally judged to be more like modern *Homo sapiens sapiens* than the Neanderthalers also occur in the (admittedly meagre) fossil record. In the Levantine region we sometimes encounter during the millennia of the Neanderthal ascendancy in Europe forms of humanity much closer to *Homo sapiens sapiens* but still in association with thoroughly Mousterian tools, indicating if nothing else that the linkage between Neanderthal Man and the Mousterian is not a simple matter. While the ice age raged in northern Europe, North Africa and the Levant experienced cooler but, more significantly, drier times than before, as did the rest of Africa and the world in general. If the Neanderthal people were a local adaptation to cold conditions, then equally the rest of the world's human populations were profoundly influenced by the global climate of the ice age, which played a crucial part in the evolution and spread of modern humanity. In later chapters we will piece together the evidence for the evolution of *Homo sapiens sapiens* and review the rival theories as to how that evolution came about. Before that, the Neanderthal way of life and the achievements of these people deserve to be described.

CHAPTER 6

Neanderthal Technology

We think of the Neanderthal folk as people of the ice and snows, living in caves, and for many of them that is a just picture of their life. The west European Neanderthalers did occupy caves which we may call their homes, even if some of them also set up temporary camps in the open air from time to time. Where there were no caves, further to the east on the Russian steppe, for example, open-air sites with some sort of constructed shelter were the only option. We know much more about the cave sites than the open-air ones because, historically, it was the cave sites of Western Europe that were first explored by archaeologists and also because open-air sites are harder to find. Many of them have disappeared under deep loess deposits or under the rising postglacial seas and, in any case, are less likely to come to light than archaeological evidence in inviting caves. Caves, moreover, aid the survival of archaeological material and are long-lasting repositories which can preserve the record of remote millennia for millennia more. At least, the limestone caves of Europe are relatively long-lasting and good for preservation – in other parts of the world, caves can be positively destructive of bone, for example, or be more quickly eroded away in themselves.

In south-west France the limestone caves of the Périgord region made ideal homes for the Neanderthal people, as they did for their Crô-Magnon successors. There were good supplies of flint to hand and the caves were often sited in small river valleys that offered protection against the worst of the weather. The Neanderthalers liked south-facing caves, for obvious reasons of sunshine and wind avoidance, and caves at some height above the valley floor offered refuge from floods and good game-watching vantage points. The Périgordian region during the last ice age was, in fact, an exceptionally benign place in which to live. Being nearer to the Atlantic Ocean, even when sea level was low, than northern and central zones of Europe, it enjoyed a rather maritime climate with cooler summers that permitted an extension of tundra and steppe over its higher plateaux; thanks to its latitude, its year-round high levels of sunshine favoured the growth of the ground plants needed by reindeer, bison and horse as the overall climate came and went from full glacial to interstadial conditions. Winters were mildish for the ice age, with good forage for large herds. Up on the plateaux it might be tundra, but the sheltered valleys could be quite wooded, while the east to west slope of France's Massif Central down to the Atlantic coast made for a rapid gradient of ecological change, so that animals never needed to migrate far from summer to winter and men never needed to travel far from home to find an abundant supply of meat. In the valleys, they could watch from their caves for the coming up and down of the seasonal herds, literally sitting on their migration routes: it was like shooting fish in a barrel.

In France, too, many open-air sites of the Neanderthal people have been discovered, particularly up on the plateaux, but they never yield as much archaeological material as the caves. In Central and Eastern Europe, where caves were unavailable, such open-air sites as have been discovered were mostly located near water – both because water was a good place to be for people and animals, and also because the sedimentation potential of lakes and stream courses has aided archaeological preservation – whereas erosion has presumably blown away other sites out in the open. Some of the open-air sites from Germany through Central Europe across to Russia have provided valuable information about Neanderthal Man and his way of life. From Molodova, for example, in the Ukraine, comes evidence that has been interpreted as the remains of wind-break structures, or even a large tent: a ring, up to about 8 × 5 m in size, of mainly mammoth bones enclosing a dense concentration of stone tools, animal bones and ash. A suggestion of an entrance structure on the east side of the ring has been detected, and more ash was reported on the north side of the enclosed circle of debris, suggesting the possibility that this was where people slept, close to a fire. It is unlikely, perhaps, that the mammoth bones of Molodova were the anchorage of some completely roofed-over tented structures but wind-breaks seem likely, though we must always be aware of the possibility that accidents of arrangement as a result of nature (like slope wash in floods) might partly account for features like this. Three similar circles of mammoth bones covered in loess, found near Cracow in Poland, have been attributed to Neanderthalers. At Ripiceni-Izvor in Romania an oval structure of stones and mammoth tusks with Mousterian tools has been interpreted as perhaps a hut emplacement of some sort, or a symbolic collection of objects that meant something to the Neanderthalers of the place. At Rheindahlen in Germany a shallow pit in loess deposits that probably date to the early part of the last ice age contained burnt Mousterian flints and evidence of post holes, and a 5 m diameter setting of stones with ash and Mousterian tools is reported at Il'skaya in the Caucasus. At Salzgitter-Lebenstedt in Germany a structureless bivouac in a gully is evidenced by the finding of Mousterian flint tools together with an apparent club of reindeer antler (a rare find of a non-stone artefact for a Mousterian context) in association with the bones of reindeer, mammoth, bison and horse, to the accompaniment of pollen remains indicating a subarctic environment with few trees.

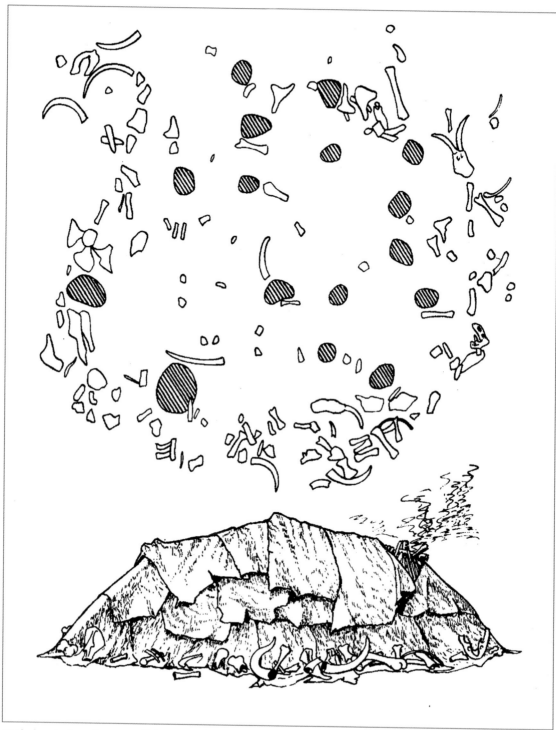

Molodova's ring of mammoth bones, with reconstruction drawing of a possible tent represented by the archaeological remains; with thanks to Dr John Wymer.

From the west European caves more evidence of built structures is available, and some of it goes back a long way in time. In the Grotte du Lazaret, near Nice, at a date during the last ice age but one (and so before the Last Interglacial times of the first real Neanderthalers), claims for some sort of skin tent within the cave have been advanced, on the basis of arrangements of large stones out from the cave wall that might have supported timber struts for a covering of skins up to the rock face above. Such structures are entirely plausible and have possible antecedents from even earlier times in the history of man, as we shall see; the shelter afforded by any cave could be enhanced with man-made alterations and, no doubt, often needed to be. At Lazaret what might be openings in the hypothesized tents seem to point away from the cave mouth and finds of wolf and fox foot bones, without the rest of the skeletons, inside these 'tents' have been thought to indicate the use of animal pelts as bed coverings. (Similar finds elsewhere, including beaver, cat and rabbit foot bones, may also point to the use of pelts in clothing.) The two patches of ash at Lazaret that mark ancient fires, with stone tools around them evidently made and used on the spot, are edged with small marine mollusc shells, prompting the excavator to suggest that seaweed had been used as bedding around the fires, with its inevitable concomitant of these tiny sea creatures. Another early site, the Grotte Vaufrey in the Périgord, affords evidence suggesting that people worked by day in the lighted area of the south wall of the cave and slept out of the draughts along the dark north wall by night, with areas of burnt bone remains to show where they cooked. The cave of Baume-Bonne in the Basses-Alpes, another early site (of the penultimate ice age), boasts 10 sq m of cobbles brought up from the local river and laid down, for all the world as though to take care of a puddled area in the cave, with the smoothest and roundest surfaces of the stones uppermost, and there are other similar cases. On sites that do strictly belong to Neanderthal times, further evidence of built structures has been claimed. At the Cueva Morin in Spain collapsed piles of stones have been interpreted as a low dry-stone wall constructed across a narrow part of the cave mouth, delineating a dense area of debris, including Mousterian tools, resulting from human occupation. At Pech de l'Azé I, in the Dordogne, a dry-stone wall of 2 m in length but only 25 cm high, has been discovered. La Baume des Peyrards has a similar 'wall', but higher at up to 70 cm, delimiting an area against the rock face, with ash and Mousterian tools behind it. A semicircular wall of interlocked reindeer antlers has been claimed at the Mousterian site of Roc en Paille.

The ash encountered in concentrations at Mousterian sites testifies to the Neanderthal people's use of fire: not surprising, since use of fire was by Neanderthal times an already ancient accomplishment of evolving humanity, and survival in the subarctic conditions faced by the Neanderthalers is inconceivable without control of fire. Fire gave warmth, light, heat for cooking and defence against predatory animals.

A charred piece of birch from Krapina is thought to be the remains of a fire-making twirl stick. But Neanderthal hearths in the sense of specially constructed places for fire are fewer and harder to identify with certainty than the mere ash piles that are a regular feature of their sites. They seem often to have just lit a small fire (40–50 cm across) on the existing ground surface of the cave, without preparation and of short duration to judge from the shallow penetration of heat effects under the ash. Sometimes the fires were larger, up to 1 m across, and quite irregular in shape. It is not always easy to decide how much additional structure some Mousterian fires possessed: claims of stone circles to contain the fire run up against the fact that stones tend to litter the cave floors everywhere and those around a fire can quite accidentally look as though they were arranged in a circle. Paved and stone encircled hearths have been reported in pre-Mousterian, pre-Neanderthal contexts, let alone Mousterian ones. Certainly, the hearths of some of the latest Neanderthalers we know of, at Arcy-sur-Cure, do seem to have been artificially constructed, at about 37,000 BP, but these were Neanderthal folk who had somehow progressed beyond the Mousterian culture – we shall return to them and their special status later.

Deliberate scooping out of a depression to make a hearth has been claimed at Pech de l'Azé II, with a lead-in vent for a flue, but the example was very small – only 15–25 cm in diameter – and looks like a fire for light rather than heat or cooking, deep as it is in the cave. Limestone slabs around a shallow fire-bowl are reported at la Grotte de Hauteroche, Charente, and stones were found around a hearth on a Mousterian site at Vilas Ruivas in Portugal. At Kebara in Israel, hearths were at best bowl-shaped depressions, but interestingly the ash (of local oak) contained the remains of carbonized wild peas. In contrast, recent claims have been made for a Spanish site at Capellades, about 55 km north-east of Barcelona, with rudimentary furnaces for the shaping of utensils (in clay, presumably) which so far outshine any other Neanderthal provisions for the use of fire that judgement on them must be withheld pending full archaeological report. Wooden items of manufacture are also reported on this site, which are rare but not wholly absent in other Mousterian contexts. Certainly, the 'hearths' of the Neanderthalers in general do not display the technological advances of those of the Upper Palaeolithic people who came after them in Europe, and who regularly built their fire in stone-lined and flued hearths. There is, moreover, no good evidence that the Neanderthal people employed rock-heated pits in their cooking, so their cuisine found perhaps only limited use for fire in the preparation of the meat they ate, despite the presence of burnt bones on their sites. It was perhaps not only the development of better tools that did away with the need for powerful chewing (and vice-like) jaws as humanity evolved towards modern *Homo sapiens sapiens*, but also the invention of better cooking techniques. It has been further suggested that the Neanderthalers used fire in their caves to create defrosting chambers just as much as to cook (and give light and comfort), thereby exploiting a subsistence niche all of their own among the carnivores of their world: based on their unique ability to thaw out frozen carcasses, useless to their animal competitors, of large meat-bearing creatures that they did not need to hunt, only to scavenge. Use for long-term food storage has been proposed for a few pits discovered on Mousterian sites in France like Combe Grenal, where the feature was 90 cm wide and 40 cm deep, and le Moustier and la Quina – in some cases apparently covered over with limestone slabs. Human burial, or the intention of it at least, might be the explanation of these pits, but meat storage over winter is as likely in the light of the absence of human bones. Such pits must have been hard to dig in the consolidated cave deposits and digging sticks of bone or wood, not preserved or discovered, are indicated. A post hole for a wooden post was excavated at Combe Grenal, 4 cm in diameter and 20 cm deep, in a Mousterian context containing many of the so-called 'denticulate' tools that we conjecture were for woodworking purposes, or for cutting meat into strips. The wooden post of the hole at Combe Grenal may have been part of a drying rack for strips of meat.

Studies of the spatial distribution of features on Mousterian sites in France suggest that relatively small numbers of people were living on them, able to conduct separate activities in different areas. There is no consistent pattern of placing for hearths, though Combe Grenal does show large centrally located fireplaces. Both the knapping of flint tools and the use of these tools seem to have been carried on close to the hearths, where the concentrations of animal bones also occur, though large bones are sometimes encountered at the margins of the living areas centred on the hearths. There is some evidence to suggest that simpler tools, like the notched denticulates, were used close to the hearths and better tools were employed on the margins, perhaps to process the bigger pieces of meat whose bones are found there. (All of this quite lacks the sophistication of arrangements found in the later Upper Palaeolithic contexts in the same region and sometimes in the same caves.) The caves of south-west France can be seen as the homes of the Neanderthal folk of the region, provided that we do not load too many sentimental associations on the word home; the open-air sites of the same area were probably kill-sites (or scavenging places) and camps for the acquisition of raw materials, of limited duration. The same situation obtained in the Levant and the Middle East with cave occupations and open-air sites, but in Central and Eastern Europe open-air sites were the only homes they had, a circumstance that strengthens claims for shelters and perhaps more complicated structures in these regions. Where there were caves, the Neanderthalers seem to have been rather sedentary folk, content to eke out whatever living they could (and, in some areas like south-west France, that living could be pretty good) without continually moving on or fetching in their resources from very far away.

Most of the tools and weapons used by the European Neanderthalers were made of stone acquired close to home, usually within only a few kilometres of the sites where the archaeologists find them, as far as south-west France is concerned. There is evidence that the best raw material for the most elaborate items might have been fetched from a little further away than the stone used for more run-of-the-mill products and on the plains of Central and Eastern Europe fetching distances were greater, but even then do not compare with those travelled by raw material in the Upper Palaeolithic. Stone tools are, of course, the most easily and therefore best preserved of all the productions of our remote forebears. They constitute the absolutely unmissable remains of archaeological sites of these remote epochs, and were collected and classified from the earliest days of archaeology in the last century, when much other evidence was ignored and unrecognized. Wood cannot often survive from the times of the Neanderthal folk and items made of bone or antler have not been frequently recovered from Mousterian sites, but stone tools survive in abundance and quite naturally have become the basis for archaeologists' attempts to subdivide the overall Mousterian tool tradition into recognizable 'cultural' packages with geographic or chronological identities. If such distinct communities of toolmakers could be shown to have existed in certain times and places, then a broad picture of Mousterian development through time and space might be painted, with implications for the evolution of Neanderthal Man and his relationship to what has come after him in his former homelands. Quite legitimately this sort of typological study of tool forms can be, and often has been, carried on without any concomitant study of what the tools were used for, however interesting that might be. In fact, microscopic study of the wear on the edges of Mousterian tools seems to indicate that many of the tools, of whatever type, were used for woodworking – an interesting finding in itself, if correct, for reminding us of the likely importance of wood in the overall technology of the Neanderthalers. Some Mousterian 'points', a technical term for a certain sort of pointed flake of stone, bear tip breakage consistent with use as projectile points, as well as facets at their bases that look like provision for hafting, while others suggest themselves as butchery tools; all this we might expect among the tools and weapons of a people dependent on the acquisition of meat. Some of the various 'scrapers' of the Mousterian can readily be seen as tools used in the preparation of animal skins though microwear studies do not suggest that very many of them specifically were; the notched and denticulated pieces certainly look like woodworking and plant processing items. Points, side-scrapers (often called 'racloirs' after their French name) and notched/denticulated pieces, all made on flakes struck from cores of raw material, are the stock-in-trade of the Mousterian, but in different places and at different times other tool types feature in the assemblages of tools found together on Mousterian sites: there are sometimes small bifacially worked hand-axes

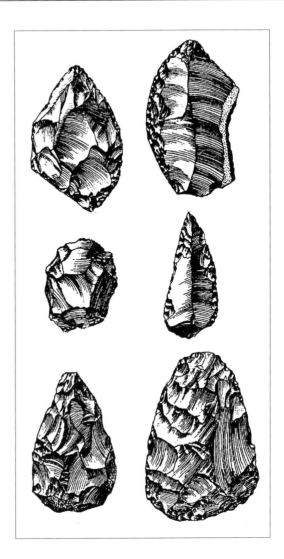

Mousterian stone tools.

not unlike the hand-axes of much earlier times found in Africa and Europe – apart from their size; there are occasionally backed knives, longer for their width than most Mousterian flakes, blunted along one edge to make them safe to hold; there are sometimes chisel-tipped burins, more common in the Upper Palaeolithic; there are scrapers in many forms and a few items definitely distinctive of certain geographical areas. There are also differences in techniques of manufacture, particularly with regard to the preparation of the lumps of flint from which the basic Mousterian flakes were to be struck, and differences too in the degree of 'retouch' employed to arrive at the various tool types. Thus any given layer of any given Mousterian site will not produce the same tools as are found in another layer and elsewhere – though it may only be a striking difference in percentages of types, rather than sheer presence or absence of certain forms, that encourages us to distinguish between one sort of Mousterian and another. What these different sorts of Mousterian mean has been the subject of debate; some have seen in them the products of different families or tribes, while others see only the results of special tool kits' being run up for particular jobs by the same people in different circumstances, perhaps according to season, for example. The former is a 'cultural' interpretation, the latter a 'functional' one. Some extremists have even proposed that most of the variation among Mousterian assemblages arose out of constant reuse, damage, modification and retouching of a simple set of flake forms that all started life as pretty much the same all-purpose tool – the archaeologists simply finding them at various stages along the way to ultimate reduction to uselessness. Probably there is some truth in all these explanations of Mousterian variability but not as much in any single one of them as their proponents would like to think. The cultural explanation still holds water, if not as hermetically as some of its supporters have argued. It is hard to think that, say, five distinct cultural groups of Neanderthalers, each one staunchly committed to its particular line-up of tool types and tool percentages, came and went over tens of thousands of years in the relatively small area of south-west France, occupying the same sites by turns, without culturally coalescing and losing their particular identities. One or two of the five sorts of Mousterian that were proposed in France, defined more by the absence of distinctive forms than by any positive traits, are probably statistical constructs resulting from the lumping together of random occurrences of functionally limited assemblages, but when these are removed it is still possible to identify three different sorts of Mousterian in south-west France, in stratigraphical (i.e. chronological) relationships with each other. The la Ferrassie variant of the Mousterian, named after the place at which it was first identified, antedates the la Quina variant at a number of sites; both have high percentages of racloirs, with steep retouch, and slug-shaped double side-scrapers called 'limaces' as well as points, but in the earlier variety there is much more evidence of a particular preparatory technique called 'Levallois', after the Paris suburb where it was first noted on flakes and cores much older than the Mousterian. The Levallois method calls for the preliminary striking off of a number of large flakes from the lump of raw material to prepare its shape to the point where the final decisive blow will bring off the desired flake in one go, with only the need for finishing retouch thereafter. It is, from the point of view of human mental evolution, an interesting early technological invention since it requires even greater prevision of the finished product in the mind's eye, and the intermediate steps necessary to achieve it, than does simply knapping away to produce the tool. The Levallois technique was first employed in Africa well over 200,000 years ago: perhaps it was reinvented in different places at later times, or the idea spread around the world to reach people like the ancestors of the Neanderthalers at about 200,000 BP. Whatever its merits, the la Quina variant that followed on from the la Ferrassie exhibits much less in the way of Levallois technique. On some sites there is a steady loss of Levallois features rather than an abrupt changeover. These two Mousterian variants can be brought together under the name Charentian; they flourished, one after the other, up to about 60,000 BP. Very interestingly, it is with the Charentian Mousterian that many of the French finds of Neanderthal bones are associated, in company with faunal remains including many reindeer bones and witnessing to the coldness of the times. But at le Moustier, the youth's skeleton was accompanied by a more weakly characterized Mousterian called, rather unsatisfactorily, Typical Mousterian, whose main feature is its low percentage of racloirs and absence of any distinct forms other than points: it may well be a statistically generated will-o'-the-wisp. Later than the two Charentian variants on many French sites comes a Mousterian with small hand-axes that seem to relate back to the Acheulian hand-axe culture of pre-Mousterian, pre-Neanderthal times. Where this Mousterian of Acheulian Tradition (MAT) is found it is either at the top of a Mousterian stratigraphy, above la Ferrassie and/or la Quina types, or directly beneath Upper Palaeolithic levels; radiocarbon dates of about 40,000 BP have been obtained for it, and its faunal associations are interstadially warm with red deer, aurochs and bison. It is characterized by its small heart-shaped axes (in addition to points, racloirs and denticulates), but itself comes in two varieties: an earlier one with more axes and racloirs and a later one with more blunt-backed knives. This latter sort of Mousterian looks forward to the very beginnings of the Upper Palaeolithic in an intriguing way, for it seems to be the basis of the Chatelperronian culture of south-west France and northern Spain that, before the 1970s, people thought was simply the earliest of the Upper Palaeolithic manifestations, and therefore the work of Crô-Magnon Man – until a classic Neanderthal skeleton was found with it at Saint-Césaire! The Chatelperronian, whatever its origins, is not a mere Mousterian variant and its implications will be of great importance when we come to discuss the ultimate fate of the Neanderthal people.

The remaining variety of the Mousterian, according to French classification, is the Denticulate, marked out not so much by its notched and tooth-edged pieces as by its generally mediocre character with the near absence of most distinctive tool types like axes, back knives, even racloirs and points. It is easy to see in this a functional aspect, perhaps along seasonal woodworking lines, with no cultural suggestions about it (though what racloirs there are do differ from those of other Mousterian assemblages). The Denticulate and the Typical Mousterian have no clear chronological positions in Mousterian stratigraphies, though the Typical is pretty well confined to the early phase of the Last Glaciation, with the Denticulate cropping up within the Typical and then again at the end of the la Quina.

Some of the Mousterian variants identified in France do occur elsewhere – the MAT and the la Quina, for example, in Belgium – but the chronological scheme from la Ferrassie through la Quina with MAT at the end has not so far been demonstrated outside France. In the wider world of the Neanderthalers, across Europe to Western Asia with the Levant, the Mousterian shows considerable variation. Flint itself, taken from chalk cliffs and river beds, can be of variable quality and in some places only inferior stones were available, limiting the technological expression of toolmaking. Different regions promoted different ways of life, and climatic changes through the long career of the Neanderthalers demanded changes in their behaviour; no doubt there were random 'cultural' variations too in different times and places. So there is variety within the Mousterian throughout its range, but – even when the complexities of the French sequence are taken into account – it is worth noting that neither geographically nor chronologically does the Mousterian exhibit the rich variability and innovativeness of the Upper Palaeolithic cultures that succeeded it, with their much more rapid turnover of styles with strong local flavours. It is apparent that with the Mousterian (and its world contemporaries and predecessors) we are facing a different sort of cultural situation from that of the Upper Palaeolithic and all the productions of modern *Homo sapiens sapiens* ever since. In Central and Eastern Europe the local Mousterians often show small and spindly pointed axes and bifacially worked leaf-shaped points. In Russia there are bifacial knives, while in north-west Greece large blade-like flakes appear at about 80,000 BP and are then superseded by levels with very small scrapers made on flakes. A Mousterian of sorts has been identified even as far east as Afghanistan, but there is nothing distinctly Mousterian in India and Pakistan, and certainly not in China. The Levantine Mousterian does show a similar range of tool types to France's, with something very like the Charentian facies, sometimes with small axes too. The Amudian, seen among other places at the same site as the Neanderthal skeletal remains discussed in Chapter 3, is a Mousterian richer than most in blades, backed knives, end-scrapers and chisel-tipped burins (all rather Upper Palaeolithic elements in Europe). Levallois technique tends to be common in the Near Eastern Mousterian, among whose latest manifestations are the bifacially thinned Levallois points of the Emiran which were very probably hafted on to shafts. In the Negev there are hints of technological progress from Levallois points to true blades of Upper Palaeolithic type after about 50,000 BP. The Mousterian of Shanidar in Iraq is less Levallois in character, probably because raw material here came in smaller pieces that did not lend themselves to the expensive preparatory work of the technique. It is worth noting at this point that in the Near East, the elsewhere quite strict linkage between the Mousterian and the Neanderthal physical type breaks down, for the Mousterian stoneworking tradition is also associated with very much more modern human types at sites like Skhul and Qafzeh as well as appearing with Neanderthalers at Amud, Kebara, Tabun and Shanidar; moreover dating methods applied at these sites strongly suggest that, for example, the Qafzeh moderns at about 90,000 BP predate the Kebara Neanderthalers by tens of thousands of years, though the Tabun Neanderthal woman might be at least as old as the Qafzeh moderns. This complex and puzzling situation is one of the keys to the questions of modern human origins that we shall discuss later in this book. Along the coast of North Africa there is a Levallois sort of Mousterian (with neatly stemmed or tanged pieces) and a hint in places of influence from the Spanish Mousterian – remember the Neanderthal discoveries on the Rock of Gibraltar. In sub-Saharan Africa something essentially akin to the Eurasian Mousterian, in being based on medium-sized flakes struck from cores of raw material, is widely encountered, with about the same date range. Made on poorer quality raw material, often quartzite, the African equivalent of the Mousterian shows Levallois technique but lighter retouch in general, with fewer of the distinctive racloirs of the European Mousterian. In Africa this sort of thing is called Middle Stone Age rather than Mousterian, but both manifestations are so fundamentally alike, as representing a broad stage in the development of stone technology, that they can be lumped together and conveniently called Middle Palaeolithic. Thus they find their place between the earlier Lower Palaeolithic (called Early Stone Age in Africa) of big axes and crude flakes and the later Upper Palaeolithic (African Late Stone Age) of smaller stone products including blades as well as bone tools and weapons of all-round sophistication. It is rather like the situation with human fossils: there are African contemporaries and rough equivalents of the Neanderthalers but, if the word Neanderthal is to carry any strictly distinct meaning, then there are no Neanderthal types in Africa (or in the Far East, either). The Neanderthal people and the Mousterian culture with which they are so almost entirely associated are not African phenomena, but they do belong to roughly the same stages of human evolution and development of stone technology as their African contemporaries.

The Middle Palaeolithic to which the Mousterian culture belongs does show an advance over the Lower Palaeolithic in terms of efficient exploitation of raw material if not altogether in eye-catching sophistication of tool types and innovatory turnover. Middle Palaeolithic technology was securing more cutting edge per bulk of raw material than the Lower Palaeolithic did. More flakes with more useful edges were produced by Middle Palaeolithic techniques and styles than by Lower Palaeolithic ones – but to nothing like the extent of Upper Palaeolithic styles and techniques, where the reliable manufacture of long straight-edged blades had been perfected. The Upper Palaeolithic technology embraced, moreover, the extensive use of bone and antler in the fashioning of very sophisticated items like barbed harpoons and, ultimately, needles.

Bone items of manufacture have rarely been found in Mousterian contexts, partly (but not wholly) because they were not expected or looked for very carefully in the earlier excavations. Modern excavation techniques would certainly reveal them if they were there. In Mousterian levels on two Spanish sites large numbers of animal bone pieces have been found that resemble some of the stone tools of the time: denticulate, notched and scraper-like pieces, along with bone hammers and punches. It has to be said that it can be hard to distinguish some of these from the products of animal activity in chewing and crunching bones, but there do appear to be signs of percussion flaking on some animal long bones of the same sort as was used to flake stone. Elsewhere animal bones in Mousterian contexts quite often carry cut marks made by stone tools in the course of butchery and food preparation, so one might think that the idea of working bone would have occurred to the Neanderthalers more often than it seems to have done. It is as though their minds were rather rigidly programmed for certain accomplishments, like stone and presumably woodwork, and often unable to make the connective leap across the boundaries of mental domains to link up the idea, say, of animal bones with the idea of toolmaking. We shall return to the matter of Neanderthal mentality in the next chapter. Whatever their limitations, they did produce a few bone items that have come down to us, including a bone point at Combe Grenal in France and points made on mammoth rib at Salzgitter-Lebenstedt in Germany. The latter site also produced the antler club mentioned earlier and one well-made barbed point of mammoth bone, a significant find for its time. With one spectacular exception, barbed points and harpoons have only otherwise been found in Upper Palaeolithic contexts, to which it is easy to think they naturally belong in their sophistication of forethought and execution. That exception is an important, if contentious, piece of evidence for the evolution of modern mankind in Africa and we shall look into it in Chapter 12.

In contrast to the paucity of bone manufactures on Mousterian sites, all the signs are that wood played a considerable part in Neanderthal technology. We simply cannot expect many wooden items to have survived from Neanderthal times, but there is the evidence of the microwear on Mousterian flints, which points above all to their use in woodworking. There is the post hole at Combe Grenal and the hut emplacements from various sites that necessitate the idea of trimmed poles in the construction of shelters. From Lehringen in Germany comes a yew wood spear, 2.4 m long, which might have had a fire-hardened tip and was found in the ribs of an elephant of Last Interglacial times (about 130,000 BP), bolstering not only the case for Neanderthal woodworking but also for Neanderthal big game hunting, about which some archaeologists have been sceptical. In fact, even older wooden spears are known: the sharpened front portion of a spear was found at Clacton in Essex in 1911, dating back to about 450,000 BP, but sometimes reinterpreted as a digging stick;

recently three very well-made throwing spears, heavier at the tip (which was formed from the denser and harder root end of the wood) and tapered to the back, were found in a German coal mine and dated to about 400,000 BP. These and the Clacton spear well predate the appearance of Neanderthal Man and show that woodworking and ambitious hunting were established accomplishments long before the arrival of big-brained people like *Homo sapiens neanderthalensis* and *Homo sapiens sapiens*.

The thinned butts of some of the Mousterian points and bifacials suggest that the Neanderthalers could wield wooden spears with sharp flint tips and it may be that Neanderthal hunting habits made more use of spearing than had been seen in the world before. A Levallois point was found in a mammoth skeleton at Hounslow in England. The Mousterian tool and weapon kit may not look so much more sophisticated than the Lower Palaeolithic one does in terms of workmanship, style and standardization, but it helped the Neanderthalers to extend the range of humanity beyond the borders of the old Lower Palaeolithic world, on to the North European Plain and into Eastern Europe and Western Asia where the Lower Palaeolithic people had not gone, and to hang on there in climatic circumstances of the harshest kind. (The Upper Palaeolithic people did better still, as we shall see, penetrating Siberia and reaching the Americas, and occupying Australia.) Population numbers among Neanderthal groups all over their range can never have been large, even in the favourable environment of south-west Europe (though they were evidently up on Lower Palaeolithic numbers), and their environment was often hostile and changeable; they must meet their circumstances with a limited Middle Palaeolithic technology with which there was only a limited

Wood spear tip from Clacton.

number of things that could be done (which is one reason why a basically similar range of tool types shows up all over the Mousterian range, in contrast with the flexibility of the Upper Palaeolithic). For all that, through two major climatic phases and many more minor, the Neanderthal people endured for 80,000 years or so from Spain to Uzbekistan with a way of life that harked back in most respects to the long past history of evolving mankind but looked forward in just a few intriguing ways to the future of humanity.

CHAPTER 7

The Neanderthal Way of Life

Next to the flint tools left behind in the places occupied by the Neanderthalers, it is the bones of wild animals – the faunal remains, as archaeologists call them – that are the most obvious features of Mousterian sites. We have seen that the faunal evidence can tell us about the climate of the times in which particular levels of particular sites were accumulated – reindeer bones, for example, from very cold periods, red deer from warmer ones; the faunal remains also tell us, of course, something about the subsistence of those times – what animals or parts of animals were brought to their sites by the Neanderthal folk, what age those animals were, perhaps on occasions whether they were hunted or scavenged. Plant remains, particularly pollen grains, can also tell us much about climatic conditions, but direct evidence as to plant food – highly perishable or wholly consumed without residue – is hard to come by. In general, it is likely that in most times and places (especially in the cold periods) the Neanderthal people relied more on meat than plant food, but for all that vegetable matter must have been of some importance to them and sometimes, perhaps, the main part of their diet. It has been suggested, for example, on the basis of pollen traces on some of the simpler (but abundant) types of flint tools, that at Combe Grenal the staple foodstuff of the Neanderthal inhabitants might have been aquatic plants from the stream below the site! At Gorham's Cave on Gibraltar there were found charred pine cones in the Mousterian levels, but these may have been used as fuel for the fire; a Spanish site near Barcelona did yield carbonized seeds of sea-beet and wild vetch, while the Kebara site in Israel showed burnt peas among its ash deposits.

But the evidence for plant food on Mousterian sites is thin and, for the most part, it was clearly meat of some sort that kept the Neanderthalers going in their hard-working way of life. As with their largely local acquisition of stone, the Neanderthal people appear not to have gone far for their meat, exploiting the fauna to hand, which varied from place to place and time to time. Whatever was around in the largest numbers and was easiest to acquire is what we find in the debris of the Neanderthalers' sites. The question is, whether they came by their meat mostly by hunting or by scavenging. People with a poor opinion of the Neanderthalers' capabilities (in which they may be justified) *vis-à-vis* our own and those of our Upper

Palaeolithic ancestors, play down Neanderthal hunting prowess and credit them with frequent recourse to scavenging of animals that had died of natural causes or been brought down by various carnivorous rivals of humanity. Scavenging is not in general a good strategy for human beings and is avoided as far as possible by foraging peoples in the world today, certainly in warm climes where bacteria see to it with quickly generated toxins that dead meat belongs as much as possible to them rather than appealing to scavengers. Even so, creatures like the hyena and vulture have made a career out of the scavenging way of life. And in the cold world of the Neanderthalers of the last ice age, scavenging may well have been an attractive proposition, equipped as they were with fire to thaw out frozen carcasses and sharp (and if necessary heavy) tools to break them up – things that none of their animal competitors could do.

The marks of scavenging animals' teeth and/or humans' flint tools can help to decide whether hunting and butchery, or intervention at scavenging sites, or just the activity of hunting and scavenging carnivores accounts for the animal bones found in the occupation layers of caves and among the debris of sites in the open. The nature of the bones themselves, the species, sexes, ages and parts in question, also contribute to the assessment. There seems no doubt that the Neanderthalers did hunt in some circumstances, on a large scale and successfully. Cave levels at Combe Grenal accumulated during the second cold phase of the Last Glaciation, after about 80,000 BP, show many bones belonging to the main meaty part of reindeer – the top parts of the legs in particular – and relatively few from the less rewarding parts in terms of meat yield, like lower limbs and heads. It looks as though young and female or sickly reindeer were being killed on the calving grounds in late spring and early summer, probably with the sort of thrusting spears we know to have been developed by this time. This may not have been exactly the thrill of the chase with long-range weapons but it is a step, at least, in the direction of real hunting. (The spear-thrower and the bow were not to be invented till long after Neanderthal times.) On the other hand, the predominance of horse heads and jaws in most levels of the Combe Grenal sequence has been interpreted to represent the human scavenging of horse parts that the carnivore killers of these animals had left behind after feasting on the meatier portions. In this picture, the Neanderthalers would have brought back to their caves the only horse meat they could come by – the unrewarding heads; but it might equally be that they dealt with the meat-rich portions like the upper legs swiftly and efficiently out in the wilds, bringing the good meat back off the bone and the heads to toy with at their leisure. It is not so clear, either, whether red deer were hunted as opposed to scavenged in the first and less severe cold phase of the last ice age, since upper limb bones are relatively lacking from these levels of Combe Grenal; but horses probably were hunted during that early part of the Last Glaciation, to go by the greater frequency in those same levels of their upper leg bones, which moreover do not display heavy cut marks caused by the dismembering of dried or frozen carcasses with flint tools. It is worth noting that Mousterian sites like Combe Grenal do not show faunal remains in great abundance when we take into account the great duration of occupation at some of them (Combe Grenal covers some 75,000 years) and the large numbers of flint tools they yield. At the sites of recent and modern foraging peoples, animal bones usually greatly outnumber abandoned tools, but at Combe Grenal over 17,000 stone tools are matched by fewer than 7,000 bone fragments which have been deemed to add up to no more than about 125 reindeer, 90 red deer, 70 horses and 20 bovids (aurochs, bison, etc.). This situation suggests several lines of interpretation, not mutually exclusive: populations of Neanderthalers must always have been very small (even in relatively comfortable areas like south-west France); Neanderthal folk may have been prone to live for the day, indeed cut out by Nature for nothing else, casually discarding their tools without a thought for the morrow; their diets must always have been poor and plant food must sometimes have been more important than the evidence can now indicate; meat may have been largely consumed away from 'home' (by hunting males?) and only a small proportion of it brought back on the bone (for the women and children, otherwise faring meagrely?). In all the Combe Grenal sequence only one salmon vertebra was found: a rich and handy source of food in the river below the site was being ignored by these Mousterians, presumably because they could not exploit it on account of technological and intellectual shortcomings on their part. No fish-hooks, gorges, harpoons or pronged points have ever been found among the generally rather paltry bone products of the Neanderthalers. But fish bones are sometimes found on other Mousterian sites, of trout, carp, tench and eel. At Mousterian sites on Gibraltar mollusc shells have been found in accumulations that may be the result of Neanderthal activity and, in one case, it has been suggested that mussels were lightly cooked in hot ashes to open their shells. The bones of marine birds were also found in Mousterian contexts on Gibraltar, while partridge and pigeon bones have been found at French sites. At the site near Barcelona rabbit bones were numerous. But on the whole the remains of prey best taken in snares and traps are lacking on Mousterian sites, a situation which suggests that devices like sapling springs or running nooses (which would not survive in the archaeological record in any case) were not employed by the Neanderthalers. Finds of bird and small animal remains may well represent the rival activities of the carnivores (like foxes, wolves, hyenas, even cave-bears and lions) with whom the Neanderthal folk shared, or more likely disputed their caves and rock shelters. The bones of these carnivores themselves are rare in Mousterian contexts, for obvious reasons.

In some instances, the hunting capacity of the Neanderthal people is not in doubt. There are open-air sites where more than 90 per cent of the animal bones belong to one species, like aurochs or bison, found in association with denticulate flints and heavier chopping tools in a way that strongly suggests the conduct of specialized butchery procedures at kill-sites. Other sites with indications of heavy specialization in certain species of prey include Mauran in the Pyrenees with bison, Vogelherd in Germany with horses, Teshik Tash in Uzbekistan with mountain goats, though one must always remember that in some cases it may have been a matter of limited choice of quarry. At some sites there is evidence of mass slaughter by driving herds of animals over cliffs. At la Quina horse, reindeer and bovid bones were accumulated at the foot of the limestone cliff, while the Cotte de St Brelade site on Jersey shows that woolly rhino and mammoth were driven to their deaths on occasion, clearly in herds with no selection for age or sex. (From this site, too, comes evidence of damage at the tips of Mousterian flint points consistent with their use on the end of thrusting spears.) Massive animals like the mammoth and woolly rhino were no doubt welcome sources of food at times, but their huge bones could also be used for constructional purposes, as we saw at Molodova in the Ukraine (and even for fuel to burn). The commonly consumed animals like reindeer, red deer, horses and bovids also provided materials as well as food, particularly in the form of hides for the clothing the Neanderthalers must have worn, however untailored that was in the absence of bone needles.

An opportunistic mixture of hunting and scavenging was probably the usual way of the Neanderthalers. In Italy one can find a site that shows only horse heads and hooves and can be interpreted as evidence of scavenging, and another site where more complete remains of red and fallow deer suggest hunting as such. To want the unrewarding heads at all only serves to emphasize the potential hardships of Neanderthal life. Interestingly, the site with the fuller animal remains showed many small sharp flints with fresh edges to butcher the hunted meat while the site with the poorer pieces of meat showed flints that had been subjected to more retouch and were often heavier, to work on the scavenged material and perhaps on a greater quantity of plant food to supplement the meagre meat ration.

It is possible to speculate about sexual division of labour among the Neanderthalers, with implications for their social arrangements in general, on the basis of the tool types and faunal remains found in different parts of Mousterian sites or on different sites. It has been noted that, at Combe Grenal, the simple denticulate tools are not only made on locally acquired flints but also found around the big hearths inside the cave in association with paltry faunal remains, while the more complicatedly flaked or retouched points and butchery tools are made on flint fetched from further away and are found closer to the cave mouth, away from the main fires (though there are smaller ones) and in association with more in the way of meat-bearing bones. In all this, it is possible to see a picture of women and children around the cave fire preparing plant food and animal scraps with their simple tools, and of men dropping by with proper cuts of meat acquired by hunting with their thrusting spears tipped with Mousterian points. The males, moreover, may have often eaten much of their meat out in the wilds and not brought so much back with them to share out when they looked in at 'home'. In this view, of course, it would not really be appropriate to speak of 'home' as we know it, for family life, with nuclear families and extended kinship relations reaching out into the wider world, would not have existed for the Neanderthalers. It would have been a world of small groups in which males and females lived largely separate lives, spread thinly across the Neanderthal world with individuals rarely travelling far from base and interacting very little with individuals from other groups. With no sort of even semi-permanent mating arrangements, there would have been no in-laws, no marrying into other groups, no larger society, no alliances, no help from distant relatives when it might be needed. In keeping with this picture, the Neanderthal women would have understandably remained rather robust specimens, used to looking out for themselves and their offspring, more like their males than the women of *Homo sapiens sapiens* are: an important area of sexual dimorphism would have been much less marked with them than it is with us – as their fossil bones attest. Sex might have been a less prominent, certainly less routine, aspect of Neanderthal life and some people have speculated that the concealed ovulation of modern *Homo sapiens sapiens* females might not have evolved in the Neanderthalers. Concealed ovulation does away with the phenomenon of signalized fertility at narrowly focused times, when male competition for females can reach dangerous proportions in a fashion inimical to monogamous mating; it also means that females do not themselves know when they are at their most fertile, and so remain receptive to sex for more of the time, enhancing the capacity of regular sex to cement monogamous relationships. Among the living primates, it is human beings only who have pair-based sexual relations at all times, and only human males provision their families of wives and offspring on a regular basis – indeed, husbands and wives and families constitute a purely human situation. It is possible to see in meat sharing by hunting males with 'wives' at 'home' a fundamental condition of family life and all that grows out of it in terms of social complexity and cohesion: it has been rather directly called the 'sex-for-meat' contract. If Neanderthal life really did not include features like regular more or less monogamous matings, meat sharing with wives and children and relatives, 'home life' (even if mobile), 'marriage' into other groups, larger social groupings and webs of kinship and lineage, then the Neanderthalers would indeed be much closer to our ape ancestors (who also, like the living apes, can have had none of these things) than to us in terms of behaviour, if not in terms of general physique and brain size. Everything about the life of the Upper Palaeolithic successors of the Neanderthalers (as indicated by the archaeology of their tools, shelters, food detritus, demography, burials and art) demonstrates their affinity with recent and modern foraging peoples in displaying evidence of the distinctly human traits we have been discussing. How far the

Neanderthalers and other and older precursors of modern humanity exhibited these traits (and, to the extent that they did not, why they didn't) is a question close to the entire problem of modern human origins, involving issues of language, mental organization and sentience that we shall try to explore towards the end of this book.

All we have to go on in attempting to assess the likelihood of such and such behavioural traits in the remote past is the archaeology of the material remains left behind by long dead individuals, with all the effects of selective survival and discovery involved. We have seen that the evidence surviving from Neanderthal times can be used to paint broad pictures of speculative sexual and social relations, to the detriment by our standards of their status as fully human beings. But, useful and suggestive as these pictures can be, we have to recognize that they are based on pretty exiguous data where, often, only a matter of relative percentages of types of tools or faunal remains in incompletely known spatial relations nudges speculation one way or another. (Most stone artefacts, it is worth remembering, were probably quickly made, general-purpose tools – as they have been among recent 'Stone Age' peoples.) The associations of simple tools with bits of bone poor in meat by the main fireside and better tools with meat-rich bones at the cave mouth at Combe Grenal might only be the evidence of sensible domestic demarcations among a group actually living together on a permanent basis with no implications about mating patterns or wider society. There are open-air sites where the simple tools that have been attributed to women's work at Combe Grenal have been found among what is apparently the men's work of butchery; children's remains have been found on these 'male preserves' too. It seems likely, in any case, that the sheer hardship of life in the last ice age, with its emphasis on the need to secure nourishing and energizing meat, would have prompted the organization of male hunting (or intensively scavenging) bands that retained their attachment to their females and offspring. And some evidence certainly seems to go against the resolutely subhuman characterization of the Neanderthalers reviewed above. There is the strong suggestion of care and concern carried by the crippled skeletons from, for example, la Chapelle and Shanidar – individuals who could not have survived their wounds and diseases as far as they did without provisioning by their fellows. Perhaps their survival can be attributed relatively more to toleration than to active concern, for poorly individuals can scrape along even among chimpanzee groups, but still tropical Africa is not the northern ice age and it is difficult to see the old man from la Chapelle as anything but a real charity case. On the other hand, the almost total lack of anything suggestive of personal decoration among Mousterian remains does argue against social complexity, for the wearing of decorative distinctions is a mark of complex social relations among modern human beings.

Above all, it is in the matter of the disposal of the dead that the humanity of the Neanderthalers seems to be evinced, especially in those cases where some tinge of cult and belief appears to be present. Even the probable cannibalism at some Neanderthal sites can be classed as a form of disposal of the dead (though it requires that the dead be brought to be dead in the first place), and one most likely of ideological import since cannibalism except in very extreme situations is not a very practical thing to do. 'Long pig' (as some recent cannibal societies have called human meat) is nothing like as rewarding as the flesh of hunted wild animals and cannibalism is vanishingly rare as a source of food – it is a cultic practice to do with subduing one's enemies' spirits and perhaps absorbing their qualities (located in brain and marrow) to one's advantage. The long-term cannibalism that some see, probably correctly, in the Krapina sequence is hardly likely to have been undertaken as a regular method of food provision over many generations and so points to some sort of 'spiritual' notion, though we cannot now imagine what exactly that was, and might be dismayed to find out. It would be comfortable to dismiss the Krapina evidence as casual burial of the dead around the site with subsequent interludes of disturbance by cave-dwelling carnivores and scavengers, like the cave-hyena whose teeth marks are said to have been found on some of the bones. On the other hand, the burning of some of the bones and the apparent breakage of long bones at marrow-rich points and smashing of skulls does look like cannibalism, and the nearby site of Vindija seems to show the same sort of evidence, as does Hortus in France. If not cannibalism, then post-mortem defleshing might be a possible interpretation, which would amount to another sort of cultic disposal of the dead.

Cannibalism (or post-mortem defleshing) followed by random scattering of the bones is a far cry from deliberate burial. The relatively frequent discovery of fully articulated Neanderthal skeletons (among them the delicate remains of children) shows beyond doubt that the Neanderthalers did deliberately bury their dead and the fact that they did it in the soil of their cave homes strongly implies that such burial somehow went beyond the mere practicality of getting rid of potential nuisance. If that was all their concern, chucking into ravines or uninhabited caverns would have served their purposes better – shallow burial at home, as was often the case (only about 30 cm below ground level), could not even have removed the possibility of nuisance very decisively. The way they buried their dead does confirm that the Neanderthal folk had some ideas behind what they did in this respect, but evidence for precisely what those ideas were has proved to slip through the fingers when looked at hard. But it is to the bearers of the Mousterian culture that the distinction belongs of being the first people we positively know to have buried their dead at all – we cannot say that that distinction strictly goes to the Neanderthalers, because among the earliest and most clearly spiritually coloured burials of Mousterian times are the graves of some Levantine early *Homo sapiens sapiens* individuals of Mousterian toolmaking habits who were clearly not Neanderthalers: more of them later. And it is worth remembering that the caves, especially of south-west France, in the northern latitudes of Europe – with frost-broken soil and good conditions of preservation – have afforded us Neanderthal burials in numbers that we cannot expect to find for their contemporaries in Africa of Middle Stone Age times, where caves with different chemical properties would often have destroyed any bones that came to rest in them; our sample of these African contempories of Neanderthal Man is small and burial is not clearly evidenced. Even in Europe stray finds of fragmentary and isolated Neanderthal bones outnumber clear burials.

But clear burials there most certainly are. The original Neanderthaler of the Feldhof caves was probably deliberately interred, and so most likely were the Spy remains discovered later in the nineteenth century. The male from la Chapelle was buried in a rectangularly cut pit at the bottom of the Mousterian levels and a whole 'family' of Neanderthalers were buried in six graves at la Ferrassie. The le Moustier youth was accorded deliberate burial, and so was the very late (after 40,000 BP) Neanderthaler discovered at Saint-Césaire in association with not Mousterian but primitively Upper Palaeolithic tools. Interestingly, all the Neanderthal burials of Western Europe are accompanied by Mousterian of the Charentian (Quina-Ferrassie) variety except for the above case from Saint-Césaire and the youth from le Moustier who seems to have belonged to the so-called Typical Mousterian, itself an ill-defined category. No Neanderthal (or other) remains have been found with the Mousterian of

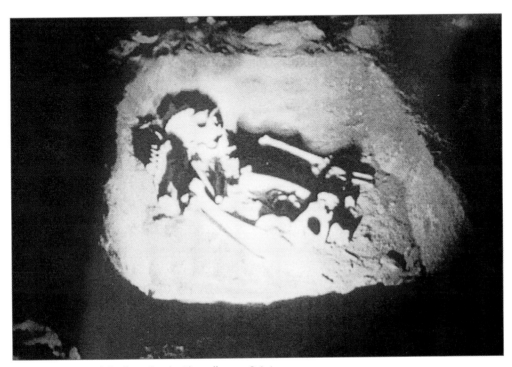

Reconstruction of the burial at la Chapelle aux Saints.

Acheulian Tradition (characterized by the presence of axes and backed knives) but it seems likely this tradition was the handiwork of Neanderthalers since it clearly forms the basis of the Chatelperronian Upper Palaeolithic of Saint-Césaire and a few other sites in France and Spain. Perhaps it is cultural custom that explains the presence of graves in the Charentian Mousterian and their absence in other Mousterian contexts. The Charentian belonged to a very cold time in the career of the Neanderthalers and it is possible that death was both commoner and more calamitous to the group in Charentian times – and perhaps that the dead were more difficult to dispose of in those times, except in the frost-broken floors of the home caves. Outside of Europe, Neanderthal burials are known at Shanidar in Iraq, with perhaps as many as five 'graves', at Kiik-Koba in the Crimea, at Teshik Tash in Uzbekistan, and at the Levantine sites of Amud and Kebara.

Neanderthal burials often show a body flexed and lying on its side in an attitude recalling sleep (or the foetal position), but we should be careful not to see too much spiritual meaning in that, since the posture requires a smaller grave with less digging. The le Moustier youth was lying on his right side, with his knees slightly drawn up and his head resting on his forearm. It is how we interpret the rest of the apparent 'contents' of his 'grave' that heralds the problem of assessing the ideological import of Neanderthal burials beyond the bare fact of deliberate interment. In short, were some Neanderthal corpses buried with grave goods or other deckings in a way that suggests some sort of belief in a continuity of life after death? Bold claims were made in the past of just such ritual furnishing of Neanderthal burials. The young man of le Moustier was said to have a 'pillow' of flints under his head and a fine stone axe to hand, with all around him the bones of wild cattle charred in some cases (including an ox skull) like the remains of a funeral feast or provision for the afterlife. The excavation of the le Moustier Neanderthal was done in the early days of archaeology and left much to be desired in terms of careful recording, but even the best of archaeological technique cannot always decide on the nature of associations of material from such a remote epoch. Mousterian sites are full of stones, tools and animal bone fragments and, certainly in the case of le Moustier, it is easy to see how, quite adventitiously, an axe might lie near a hand and stones might lie under a head, with a general scatter of animal bones all around (and easily mixed in with poor excavation technique, if not as a result of animal or human disturbance at some time in the past). The bison leg bone on the chest of the old man of la Chapelle must be regarded with scepticism on the same basis.

At Regourdou near le Moustier the bones of an adult Neanderthaler are reported to have been found lying on a flat bed of stones and covered over by a cairn of rocks, with sand and ash on top, in which flint tools and animal bones (mostly of bear and deer) were mixed. Clearly, some doubts as to the significance of the animal bones, tools and stones must remain, but the bear bones are very interesting in the light of further evidence (at Regourdou and elsewhere) of some attachment on the part of the Neanderthal people to the bear, which we will explore shortly. Evidence of fire over the burial at Spy was also noted in the nineteenth century, prompting ideas about Neanderthal provision of warmth for the dead or funeral fires and feasts, but evidence like this is always open to other interpretations, in this case that living occupants had subsequently lit a fire unheedingly over the grave of a quite possibly forgotten forebear.

At the other end of the Neanderthal range, 3000 km from the Mousterian sites of Western Europe, at Teshik Tash in Uzbekistan, a Neanderthal boy of perhaps nine years of age was buried among an array of horns of mountain goat that suggested to his excavators that his grave had been furnished with a ring of six pairs of upstanding goat horns driven point first into the ground in some sort of ritual spirit (see p. 41). Others have pointed out that, without a precise plot of the entire situation of strewn goat horns that litter the site, it is not possible to conclude that a distinct ring was ever in place, and the site had evidently been disturbed by animals in view of teeth marks on some of the limb bones and the incompleteness of the skeleton. The mountain goat was evidently the staple of the Neanderthalers' subsistence in this high-altitude region and so might have figured in some cultic fashion in their thinking, but the case for the ring of horns is not proven. Perhaps some of the horns were used to dig the grave, which was back at the cave wall, with the boy's feet pointing towards the entrance. As with some other Middle Palaeolithic sites in Russia, the stone tools of Teshik Tash's five occupation layers included some rather blade-like forms along with more ordinary flakes and cores, and there were five concentrations of ash with signs of a small fire near the body.

Some 1600 km from Teshik Tash, at Shanidar in the Zagros Mountains of northern Iraq, a number of Neanderthal skeletons were discovered in what, in some instances at least, look like deliberate interments (though one at least of the Shanidar Neanderthalers was evidently killed by a slab of rock falling from the cave roof). One of the graves was interpreted in a very suggestive way as we saw in Chapter 3: a concentration of pollen traces in association with the body in question was speculatively attributed to the casting of flowers on to the grave at the time of burial since the pollen was found in clusters that might have come from flower heads. If not necessarily decked with wreaths, it was possible to conjecture that the body had been laid out on a bed of boughs and flowers. But more sceptical commentators have suggested the activity of burrowing rodents or even the wind as agencies for the introduction of the pollen. The flowers from which the pollen came, by one means or another, were evidently brightly coloured ones: grape hyacinth and hollyhock types.

The Crimean site of Kiik-Koba produced evidence of burials of both an adult male and an infant and the site of Amud in Israel also showed an infant Neanderthal burial

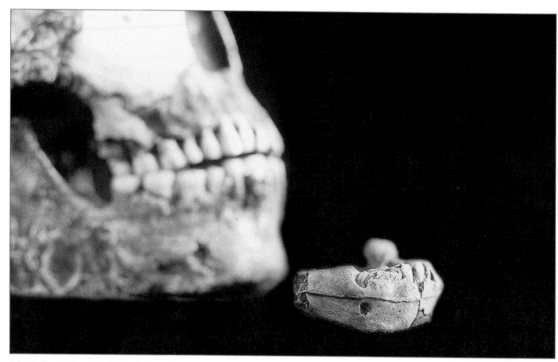

The infant Neanderthaler's jaw from Amud, with the later adult male's skull behind.

(only about ten months old, but already displaying some distinctly Neanderthal features) in a lower and older stratum than the striking adult male Neanderthaler of great height (for a Neanderthaler) and great cranial capacity (for any sort of human being ever). A red deer upper jawbone was found 'leaning against' the infant's pelvis but, again, it is impossible to say whether this really represents any sort of provision of grave goods or is merely an accident of contiguity in the deposit. Fairly complete skeletons were found in the neighbouring sites of Tabun (a rather small-brained Neanderthal female) and Kebara (a male buried in a shallow pit on his back, headless, though possessing the hyoid bone that shows there was really nothing wrong with the Neanderthal voice-box); both were almost certainly deliberate burials, without anything one could fix on for evidence of grave goods. Lumps of red ochre have been reported in close association with some Middle Eastern Neanderthal bones, but not with Neanderthal burials in Europe – the Upper Palaeolithic people do appear, as with the so-called 'Red Lady of Paviland', to have ochred the bodies of the dead on occasion, presumably with something of the same intention as the cosmetic morticians of today, as well as using ochre in their artistic productions. But this practice is not evidenced among the Neanderthal folk. It is in the clear-cut occurrence of grave goods and funerary ritual that the Upper Palaeolithic people are signally to be distinguished from the Neanderthalers. Very interestingly, there are Mousterian graves in Israel that do clearly show the presence of grave goods but they are not the graves of Neanderthalers and they are apparently older than some of the Neanderthal burials like Amud and Kebara, by tens of thousands of years. One of the early moderns from Skhul had the lower jaw of a wild boar in his arms and the Qafzeh child held the antlered skull of a fallow deer in its hands. The stone technology of the levels in which bodies of early moderns like these were found is pure Mousterian, indistinguishable from the Mousterian of the Neanderthalers found in different levels in the same region. The complex implications of this situation are vital to the problem of modern human origins – for the moment, suffice it to note that the clear association of moderns with grave goods and failure of Neanderthal burials to evince the same clear evidence must be important to any discussion of Neanderthal mentality and capacity for symbolic thought and belief.

The nearest the evidence of Neanderthal burials comes to suggesting ritual and belief is reached at the French site of la Ferrassie. Here we have a veritable cemetery of the Neanderthal folk, in a situation without much sign of Mousterian domestic habitation. La Ferrassie is not a deep cave but a rock shelter with only a slight overhang of rock. Most of the graves were found in a position that, nowadays at least, lies out from under the overhanging rock. These may not be the oldest certain graves in the world (which distinction probably goes to the older Levantine burials) but la

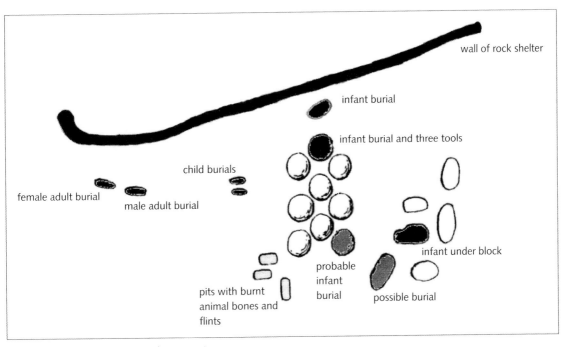

The Neanderthal cemetery at la Ferrassie.

Ferrassie likely constitutes the oldest cemetery, with the remains of at least seven Neanderthal individuals (only two of them adults) and the powerful implication that more children were once buried there. The age and sex distribution of the human remains is strongly suggestive of a family plot, but in the absence of discovery of comparable situations elsewhere caution is to be recommended about any such speculation. Suggestive, too, is the orientation of five of the graves (with two more less obviously so) on an east–west axis – a state of affairs seen at other Neanderthal burial sites like Spy in Belgium and Kebara in Israel. The daily round of the Sun, with its metaphorical linkage in our minds with birth and death and resurrection, suggests itself as a possible factor in motivating such burial orientations, but it is very debatable whether the Neanderthalers were capable of metaphor along those lines. Still, it must be scraps of evidence like this that we go on when we speculate about the prehistoric evolution of the human mind.

The shelter wall at la Ferrassie itself runs east to west, with the burials and associated features to its south. At the westernmost end were the adult burials, lying head to head. The male skeleton was discovered almost complete, but for both hands and the right foot. It is possible that disturbance by animals accounts for these missing parts, as for other absences of remains in other parts of the site. It was the la Ferrassie male that Boule used to supplement his reconstruction of his typical Neanderthaler – and it is the skeleton in which evidence of the effects of lung cancer has recently been identified. The male was buried in a shallow subrectangular pit, in a flexed posture, with three flattish stones at his head, which have been interpreted as some sort of protective covering, or more fancifully as a means of making sure that his dead body would continue to lie in the earth and not walk again among the living. There are parallels for such thinking in the ethnography of modern or recent foraging peoples, as there are for the flexing which might – with bonds – have served the same purpose. On the other hand, the stones may have fallen from the cave roof and flexed burial makes for less effort in digging the grave. Flint tools and pieces of animal bone were recorded with the body, but the usual strictures about accidental association apply.

The female skeleton of la Ferrassie was much more tightly flexed than the male, and must have been bound to achieve the foetal position – an interesting piece of indirect evidence for the Neanderthalers' use of plant fibre or rawhide for rope. The extreme foetal position is commonly encountered in much later human burials (such as the Andean mummies) and is ethnographically attested to be sometimes a means of immobilizing the dead, but certainly in the case of the Neanderthal Woman from la Ferrassie it allowed the provision of a very small grave.

To the east of the adults two smaller children's graves were discovered with the same east–west orientation, and further to the east of them nine low round mounds in

rows of three (staggered like cinema seats) running north–south came to light. The
northernmost of them, nearest the cave wall, contained the remains of a very small
infant with two Mousterian scrapers and a point. (An infant with flint tools under
three blocks of stone was found at le Moustier, too.) To the north of that infant burial,
another was more recently discovered of about two years of age, this time under the
shelter of the rock overhang and very close to the cave wall. One of the other mounds
of this group contained suggestions of a further infant burial, but the other seven
mounds were empty of human remains as excavated. Probably they too once held
children's bones, which were later disturbed by animals or destroyed by erosion
without the benefit of the overhang, or they were just possibly the places where
funerary goods like joints of meat were buried to supply the dead of the cemetery.

At the eastern extremity of la Ferrassie, six more pits were located in a more
irregular pattern with a possible burial in one of them and a certain one in another, of
unique character. Here a child's skeleton was found at one end of the pit, separated
from its skull by about one metre. The skull was under a triangular slab of rock with
a shallow concavity on its underside surrounded by further cup-like hollows in
groups of two and four. If these markings on the slab were indeed of human origin,
then their significance is quite unguessable now – all we can say is that they would
definitely point to some mental symbolism on the part of the Neanderthalers who
made this infant's grave in the cemetery of la Ferrassie. The remaining feature of the
site to be noted is the spread of limestone pieces, about 5 × 3 m in extent, that has

The marked slab that covered a Neanderthal child's grave at la Ferrassie.

been interpreted as the floor of some (tent-like?) shelter. Until we apply the brakes of caution, the whole scene at la Ferrassie can look like some family burial place, with poignant reminders of the toll of disease and deaths of children, complete with chapel of rest or shrine. Touching illustrations have been made to show a Neanderthal father (himself doomed) dropping a goodbye flint into the grave of one of his children, while mother and another child (also destined soon for the same cemetery) mourn beside him; it is not impossible that something like that happened at la Ferrassie some 70,000 years ago, but the nature of Neanderthal family life is not clear to us now (indeed it is not clear, as we have seen, that family life as we know it existed among the Neanderthalers) and any beliefs about life after death that these people may have entertained can only be a matter of conjecture for us. (The possibility must also be noted that the la Ferrassie burials are really the work of very late Neanderthalers of the proto-Upper Palaeolithic Chatelperronian culture, who dug the shallow graves into the Mousterian levels below their feet after 40,000 BP. There is no compelling reason to think that this was the case, but the possibility is there; it would not alter the fact that the la Ferrassie cemetery belonged to Neanderthalers but they would be late Neanderthalers possibly under Upper Palaeolithic influence.) La Ferrassie confirms that Neanderthal burial practice could on occasion go beyond mere disposal of the dead and that by itself is sufficient to establish the human likeness of the Neanderthalers in a manner not evidenced for any other sorts of fossil men before *Homo sapiens sapiens* of the Upper Palaeolithic with the exception of the also Mousterian early moderns of the Levant. If, as seems likely, the Neanderthal folk had not fully made the breakthrough into the modern sort of sentience that characterizes the complex mentality of the human race as we know it, then at least their awareness of death as evidenced by their many burials, seemingly much sharper than that of their evolutionary forebears, indicates a growing consciousness of the problematic status of humanity in the natural world that it tries to control. It has been suggested that their very success in exploiting the harsh world about them with better technology and better hunting methods than their predecessors', however inferior to those of their successors, raised questions never asked before about the limits of human power, especially the ultimate limitation of death.

There are besides deliberate burial, with or without symbolic features, some other areas of the archaeology of the Neanderthalers that might throw light on their possible mental habits. With shades of cannibalism, there are three instances where Neanderthal skulls seem not only to have been opened up to get at the brains but also to have been set up like cult items or trophies. Of course, the usual ambiguities in the evidence dog these cases just as they do in the question of grave goods. The most colourful of the finds, as far as interpretations go if not the hard facts, was made at Monte Circeo south of Rome in Italy, at a cave reputed to have been the very spot where Apollo's daughter

Circe turned the sailors of Odysseus into swine. At the back of the cave, a skull was found lying face down, as it seemed to its discoverers, in a circle of stones as though it had fallen off a long ago decayed stick. The skull proved to have received a blow to the temple sufficiently close in time to the death of its owner for healing not to have occurred to the bone; moreover the hole in the base of the skull – the foramen magnum – where the spine attaches and the nerves run out from the brain in the spinal cord was enlarged as though to get at the brain. Conjecture ran to the idea of ritual cannibalism followed by some sort of trophy cult with the skull set up on a pole in the centre of the ring of stones. There were bones of deer and aurochs around to suggest a ritual feast at the shrine. Sadly, it has to be recorded that the skull was found by workmen operating in near total darkness and subsequent investigation revealed no circle but only a wide scatter of stones with, at best, a hole where the skull had been lifted from among them. The blow to the temple might be real enough, but the enlargement of the foramen magnum could have been the work of animals like wolf or fox, as could the collection of animal bones. In the Far East, in Java, skulls broadly similar in type and age to those of the Neanderthalers (but not distinctively Neanderthal in type) were found in a condition that really does look like ritual treatment: not only are the foramina enlarged

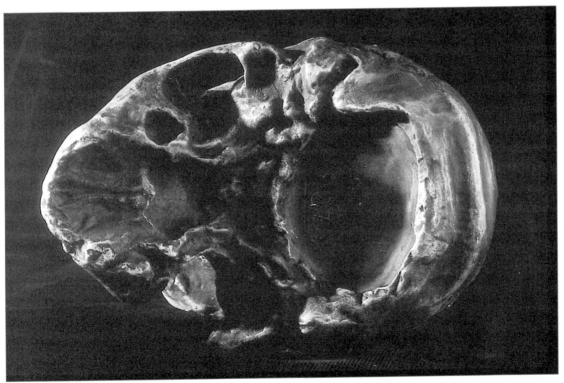

The underside of the skull from Monte Circeo, with enlarged opening to the neck.

but the faces have been deliberately smashed off too. Nothing so clearly indicative of cultic practice exists in the Neanderthal evidence.

But the case for cultic handling of certain animal bones by the Neanderthalers is perhaps stronger than that for their ritual treatment of human remains. And the animal in the case is the cave-bear, the extinct *Ursus spelaeus*, a creature more fearsome (at up to 2.75 m from nose to tail) in its time than the grizzly bear in ours. We recall that the bones of Neanderthal Man himself, in the Feldhof cave, were at first taken for those of a bear – for bear bones are rather commoner on the German, Swiss, Central European and Russian Mousterian sites than in the French (or Levantine) ones and can look surprisingly human (skulls apart) at first glance. The general up-rearing physical configuration of bears resembles the human frame and this, together with the unmatched ferocity of the threat they posed to human beings as contenders for cave habitation in wintertime, no doubt endowed them with a vivid impact on the minds of the Neanderthal folk. It may be that the comparative lack of carnivore rivals to humanity, especially of bears, in the caves of France and Israel accounts for the higher frequency with which fairly complete Neanderthal skeletons are found in these regions in contrast with Central European sites where human remains are sometimes more fragmentary, perhaps as much as a result of disturbance by bears (and wolves and hyenas) as of putative cannibalism. Bears, especially when digging winter dens for hibernation, were very likely to disturb human remains in caves. And living Neanderthalers must frequently have disputed the caves of Central Europe in particular, but of France too on occasions, with dangerous cave-bear foes. It would be small wonder if, like more recent hunting peoples from Lapland through Siberia to the Americas, the Neanderthalers were led to a cult of these potent beasts. The evidence that they were is not always as compelling as it has been made out to be, needless to say, but some of it is quite suggestive.

The place for which the most elaborate claims have been made is high in the Swiss Alps, at 2,400 m: Drachenloch, not the erstwhile lair of dragons but most certainly of cave-bears. The bear bones were found just after the First World War in the innermost part of a cave system reported to show signs of Mousterian occupation just at the entrance. Between the second and third caves of the system (near the remains of a fire) a box-like arrangement of stones, about 1 m square, was found with a single slab over it like a cover. Inside the box, if that is what it was, were seven bear skulls with their muzzles reportedly facing the entrance of the cave. Two of the skulls had a few neck vertebrae in place, suggesting that they had gone into the box with their flesh in place, possibly having had their heads cut off soon after death. At the back of the third cave, between the cave wall and a line of stone blocks, six more bear skulls were discovered as though deliberately placed there and, in one case, a bear femur was thrust through the arch of the cheekbone of a bear skull on top of two bear shin bones. These bones did not all belong to the same bear. A regular shrine to some Neanderthal bear cult could easily be pictured on the basis of these reported finds. But it might equally be the case that bears themselves, in the course of hollowing out new nests for hibernation, disturbed the remains of their own predecessors who had died in the Drachenloch and pushed them up to the cave wall and among the scatter of blocks fallen from the roof that overenthusiastic archaeologists interpreted as human constructions. No Mousterian artefacts have been found in direct association with such bear bone dispositions in Alpine caves, nor are the bones known to carry any cut marks indicative of human interference.

Similar scepticism can be brought to bear, as it were, on other finds, like the one at Petershöhle in Bavaria, where bear skulls were found on a natural rock shelf in the cave, or the Slovenian site with four bear skulls apparently arranged in a circle with their snouts together. Selective collections of bear remains do look rather like deliberate human agency: at Wildenmannlisloch in Germany 310 bear canine teeth had been accumulated, while at les Furtins in France six bear skulls on limestone slabs were accompanied by a collection of long bones on another slab, but all such instances are open to explanations without human intervention and Mousterian associations are not always at all clear. It was inevitable that bear bones and human remains, tools or bones, would sometimes come to rest in the same caves, with or without any real relationship as a result of shared or disputed occupation let alone cultic practices.

There were cave-bears in the French ice age too, if perhaps in smaller numbers than in Switzerland and Germany. Rouffignac, for example, shows the hollowed-out nests of hibernating bears and claw scratches on the walls. At Isturitz in the Pyrenees bear bones were found in alleged alignments. And one cave, quite close to the famous Upper Palaeolithic painted cave of Lascaux, affords the best evidence we have for Neanderthal cultic practice to do with bears. We have seen that this site, Regourdou, features a Neanderthal burial on a bed of stones covered over with a cairn containing an in-mixing of tools and animal bones, mostly of deer and brown bear, including a bear humerus. (All this in evidently warmish times.) Apparently dug earlier than the human grave was a stone-lined rectangular pit found to contain on excavation the remains of more than twenty bears (one complete save for its skull), under a slab weighing about a tonne. Bear bones, sometimes in heaps, were found elsewhere at the Regourdou site; if all these bones were not the natural remains of bears living at the site during periods without human occupation, then it is reasonable to imagine that the Neanderthalers were able to surprise some of them during hibernation and kill them if they were lucky – perhaps as a source of food in hard times but, in view of the grave-like stone-lined cist that seems indisputable at Regourdou, perhaps equally in connection with some real cult of the bear that may even have been widespread among Neanderthalers from France through Germany, Switzerland and Central Europe to

Russia. Certainly the evidence of Regourdou serves to extend some benefit of the doubt to sites like Drachenloch. And if the Neanderthalers really were according some sort of ritual treatment to the bones or even dead bodies of bears, as they seemingly did on occasion with their own dead, then we are faced with some evidence of a symbolic capacity on their part, though we cannot know what precisely they meant by it. With the exception of la Ferrassie, it is difficult to make a case for their burials as much more than disposal of their dead; why they might have collected and arranged bear bones, even perhaps fleshed bear body parts, remains obscure.

The establishment of the Upper Palaeolithic peoples who succeeded the Neanderthalers in Europe saw the flowering among them of the universal human inclination towards artistic creation. Lascaux, very close to Regourdou in location, is separated from it by perhaps 70,000 years in time and a vast gulf in the creative expression of human mental capacity. Virtually nothing at all that could be called art exists in Mousterian and Neanderthal contexts. Rather like the collection of bear teeth from Wildenmannlisloch, collections of quartz crystals and fossil shells have been reported at, for example, El Castillo in Spain, but collecting diverting or puzzling items is not art. Pieces of manganese dioxide and iron oxide (ochre when naturally mixed with clay), with their colouring possibilities, have been noted in a number of sites, sometimes showing signs of rounding or rubbing as a result of use, and possible grindstones for ochre have been identified at le Moustier and Pech de l'Azé. But ochre pieces do not seem to have been burned to increase their colour range. The colouring of bits of stone and even animal bone is just about attested, but there are no designs or patterns let alone drawings and no evidence is available, of course, that hides of animals (as clothes or shelters) or skins of human beings were coloured, though both cases are possible. The evidence for any sort of Neanderthal artistic production, however rudimentary, is pitifully thin when compared with the creations of the Upper Palaeolithic people and really no advance on anything from older contexts than that of the Neanderthalers.

The closest approach to some sort of symbolic design would appear to be the cup marks on the underside of the slab over the infant's grave of la Ferrassie, though their meaning is impossible to guess. One of the other graves on the same site yielded an animal bone with fine parallel lines engraved on it, and other examples of a similar sort come from sites in the Crimea, the Spanish Basque Country and other sites in France. The trouble with finds of this sort is that any notion of pattern-making is hard to distinguish from random marks left by sharp stone tools in the course of butchery or cutting up some other material resting on the bone. Perhaps the zigzag line on a late Mousterian bone piece (after 50,000 BP) from Bacho Kiro in Bulgaria looks a little more intentional and the long parallel lines on a bovid shoulder blade from la Quina are pretty convincing, too, as far as they go – but may have come from Upper Palaeolithic levels of the site. Some cases of perforations in bones are recorded, but carnivore canines

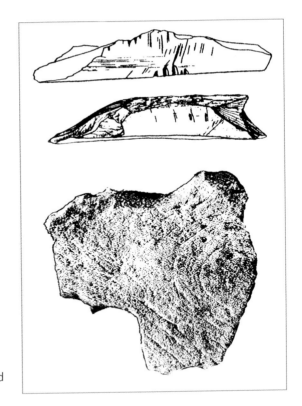

Possibly non-utilitarian markings on
pieces from Mousterian sites: Abri Souard
above, Quneitra below.

may have been responsible for some of these, or chemical action on the bone. There is a
Mousterian bone fragment from Pech de l'Azé with a hole in it, and a reindeer phalange
(toe bone) and fox canine from la Quina were perforated in some way (though the hole
in the fox canine looks as though it was rather given up on before completion). And
even if the swan vertebra and wolf metapodial (foot bone) from Bocksteinschmiede in
Germany, of about 110,000 BP, are genuine Mousterian items with man-made holes in
them, they might be seen as utilitarian toggles (interesting in themselves for that
reason) rather than decorative objects. What do look like truly decorative pieces, in the
shape of grooved wolf and fox canine pendants plus a holed bone fragment and holed
and grooved shells, found in association with a Neanderthal burial at Arcy-sur-Cure in
France, turn out in fact to belong to that enigmatic Chatelperronian phase of the Upper
Palaeolithic, in which a blade tool tradition with part origin in the late Mousterian of
Acheulian Tradition was being employed by the last of the Neanderthalers at a time
after 40,000 BP when the truly Upper Palaeolithic culture of the Aurignacians (made
by modern *Homo sapiens*) had already entered the region. So, just as the tools of the
Chatelperronians were quite likely influenced by the Aurignacians, so we are entitled to
believe that the decorative items on the Arcy site were also derived from Aurignacian
example (as perhaps also were the two huts evidenced there).

Among the remaining candidates for artistic status among the products found on Mousterian sites are: a circular sandstone pebble from Axlor in the Basque Country with a central groove and two cupule hollows; some grooved bear teeth from Belgium; lined bone fragments from Molodova in the Ukraine; a number of perforated bones, a horse canine with parallel lines and a saiga antelope phalange with a fan of lines from the Crimea; pebbles and flakes of flint from RiparoTagliente in Italy with engraved lines, including a double arc; a similar piece from Quneitra in Israel with straight lines and concentric semicircles; and a nummulite fossil from Tata in Hungary on which a natural crack has been augmented with a straight incision at right angles to form a cross. Even if we allow for neglect by archaeologists who have not expected to find any sort of art in Mousterian contexts and have not looked hard for it, and if we credit the available evidence beyond its deserts, all this constitutes a meagre haul of potentially symbolic creation on the part of the Neanderthalers – a situation that has a bearing on discussion of Neanderthal mental capacities.

It has been said of the Neanderthalers in the light of what they left behind them (and what they did not leave) that it looks as though they lived every day like the first day of their lives, with everything on a short-term basis. Their own bones are thick from heavy labour, as if they lacked the wit to make life easy on themselves; their home sites show a low level of organization; their tools are limited in range of types and found without much cultural variation over huge areas like those of their predecessors (and quite unlike those of their successors); they got their food, like their raw materials, opportunistically and stored none of it against a snowy day; they buried their dead on occasions, but without the clear ritual element of later people; they followed no religion that we can see except perhaps for some awe of bears; they produced, to all intents and purposes, no art whatsoever and wore no personal decoration (unless it was colouring of clothes and skin) to mark any complexity in their social relations; a cloud hangs over the very humanity, as we apprehend it, of their sexual and family arrangements. Despite their large brains, they were in some respects more like all their primitive forebears and indeed the ape-like ancestors of the human line than they were like us. But then, the same could be said of the early modern representatives of *Homo sapiens* that were their contemporaries in Africa and the Levant. They were even more like us than the Neanderthalers were in skull shape and postcranial physique, but they made the same Mousterian tools and left nothing behind them for a long time to prefigure the achievement of their Upper Palaeolithic descendants and ourselves. In the latter part of this book we will discuss the factors that have been proposed to propel humanity into the veritable explosion of technological innovation, art and religion that characterizes the Upper Palaeolithic and most of subsequent human history. Language must play some part, whether more as effect than cause or cause than effect, on the evolution of modern human behaviour; suffice it for the moment to note that Neanderthal language

Dardé's imaginative statue of Neanderthal Man at the museum of les Eyzies in France.

A modern reconstruction of a Neanderthaler in the new Neanderthal Museum at Mettman in Germany.

Neanderthal home-life at the Mettman museum.

The bellowing, drinking mammoth of le Thot near Lascaux in the Dordogne.

The woolly rhino at Préhisto-Parc, near les Eyzies in the Dordogne.

Reindeer and wolves at Préhisto-Parc.

European bison at le Thot.

Przewalski's horse — the ice age type with distinctive mane — at le Thot.

Préhisto-Parc's fearsome cave-bear.

A cave lion menaces a Neanderthaler at Préhisto-Parc.

Neanderthal Man looks out at dusk from the museum terrace of les Eyzies in France.

The Vézère river near le Moustier, with limestone cliffs and caves.

Caves at Mount Carmel in Israel.

Coming home from the hunt through the woods of Préhisto-Parc.

Neanderthalers in at the kill at Préhisto-Parc.

Neanderthalers at home in Préhisto-Parc.

A Neanderthal hunting band trap a mammoth at Préhisto-Parc.

Neanderthalers take on a giant elk in a glade of Préhisto-Parc.

The site of the burials at Regourdou.

Brown bears are still in residence at Regourdou.

A Neanderthal family faces up to a cave-bear in a reconstruction at Roque Saint-Christophe in the Dordogne.

Horses were frequently painted and carved in the Upper Palaeolithic art.

Neanderthal man gazes from the terrace of the les Eyzies museum at gathering autumn mists across the Vézère Valley.

(on the current assumption that they were physically capable of it) may well have been limited in vocabulary and grammar, very likely without tenses to remember the past and conjecture the future in keeping with an immediacy of all sensations and lack of introspection about abstract notions. Like children and pidgin speakers, the Neanderthalers probably used language only for the here and now. The near total lack of symbolism seen in all the products of the Neanderthalers and the fixity and limitedness of their stone technology argue against the possibility that they were wielding a complex language with high symbolic content and variety of expression. It is possible, as we shall have reason to discuss later on, that Neanderthal language was restricted to social exchanges with little scope for objective handling of the details of the world at large, let alone for abstract thought and expression. Again, this was probably the state of affairs with the early moderns too: many researchers assume that, all the same, there was something about them that could lead on to enhanced humanity – something which the Neanderthalers lacked. The case of the Chatelperronian, on this view, is seen as a groping acculturation of some late Neanderthal folk towards some elements of the Upper Palaeolithic package: a few new tools, a bit of personal decoration, enough to hold their own for a while, perhaps, but in the end not up to scratch, leaving the Neanderthalers if not to extermination at the hands of the Aurignacians then to the fate of being simply out-competed and terminally marginalized. Some workers believe that the Neanderthal people, or some of them at least, never came to such a sorry pass and were as able as their contemporaries to evolve both culturally and even physically into modern types, or to interbreed with incoming moderns till most of their distinctive traits were lost. (Some people think the Neanderthalers might have invented the Chatelperronian all by themselves, without influence from the Aurignacians.) It is these interpretations of the Neanderthal career that have suffered a setback with the progress of genetic studies on human evolution in general and the study of Neanderthal mtDNA in particular. Perhaps more interesting in the long run is the problem set by the discovery of big-brained human beings, whether Neanderthal or early modern, who went for so long (perhaps forever in the Neanderthal case) without improving themselves one whit that we can see in the archaeological record, without developing complex language, symbolism, personal decoration, art, religion, ever-advancing technology with cultural and stylistic variety. And then, all of a sudden as it looks with hindsight, some of them did achieve all these things, without appearing to undergo any further physical evolution. We will return to this problem at the end of the book. For now, in order to build up a picture of human evolution as a whole, to see the trends that eventually issued in modern *Homo sapiens* and all his wily ways, we need to push back beyond Neanderthal Man into the common evolution of all mankind, starting for the sake of our central subject with the immediate background to the Neanderthalers and their Mousterian culture.

CHAPTER 8

Before Neanderthal Man

The classic Neanderthalers of Western Europe mostly belong to the cold phase of the Last Glaciation that began about 75,000 years ago, though some of them like the le Moustier youth and perhaps the la Ferrassie burials may well belong to a late stage in the Neanderthal career and some of them certainly, as at Saint-Césaire, are very late indeed (after 40,000 BP) and contemporary with the appearance of modern types. Probably some of the classic Neanderthalers go back to the earlier phase of the Last Glaciation, after about 120,000 BP, and somewhat more generalized (i.e. less distinctively classic Neanderthal) types flourished in the preceding Last Interglacial, seen at sites in Central Europe, Italy and France. Against the hundreds of later Neanderthalers from the Last Glaciation (though some of them are represented only by fragments of bone and a few teeth), we have the remains of only some seventy earlier Neanderthal individuals in all and none of them is a remotely complete skeleton, which suggests that deliberate burial was only practised after the onset of the last ice age when death's impact on the Neanderthal folk perhaps assumed weightier significance. The Last Interglacial roll-call of Neanderthalers includes finds from the Saccopastore and Abri Bourgeois-Delaunay sites in Italy and France respectively, and probably some of the Krapina people (the rest of whom belonging to the early and not so severely cold phase of the Last Glaciation). These earlier Neanderthal folk are not so very different from the later classics, as we saw, and plainly belong to the same evolutionary lineage even if they do not display quite the same degree of what we might call 'total Neanderthalization'. The earlier individuals may be smaller-brained on average than their successors. The Saccopastore female skull looks very Neanderthal from the front – low vaulted and with a projecting face – but though the Neanderthal suprainiac fossa is present at the back, there is no sign of the typical Neanderthal bun; the male is very robust and harks back in some ways to much older types like the skull from Petralona in Greece, as we shall shortly see. The Krapina folk were slightly more lightly built than the classic Neanderthalers of the later ice age, as was the female (of possibly about the same age as the bulk of Krapina specimens) from Tabun in Israel – and she was small-brained for a Neanderthaler at about 1250 ml, though equipped with the usual heavy brow arches.

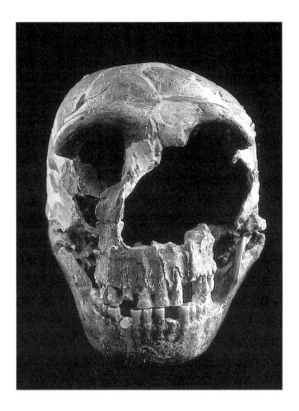

The Tabun Neanderthal woman's skull.

The fragments from the Abri Bourgeois-Delaunay reach further back in time than Saccopastore and Krapina and demonstrate, where they afford enough evidence to identify their characteristics, that Neanderthal traits like, for example, the gap between the molars and the vertical part of the jawbone can be traced back through the Last Interglacial to the preceding glacial period. The site of Biache-Saint-Vaast in northern France confirms the presence of proto-Neanderthal people in Western Europe during that penultimate glaciation, with dates determined by the thermoluminescence method on burnt flints to lie between about 200,000 and 160,000 BP. Biache-Saint-Vaast shows an individual with the characteristically low oval skull shape seen from the rear of the Neanderthalers, with the equally characteristic bun at the back, but the cranial capacity is very low by later Neanderthal standards at only about 1200 ml. The dated burnt flakes of flint belonged at Biache-Saint-Vaast to a stone tool industry, without any axes, of the sort associated with pre-Mousterian toolmaking traditions.

The thick-boned skull fragments from Fontéchevade in the Charente are probably of about the same age in the last ice age but one, and are similarly deemed to hint at the development of Neanderthal traits. They were found in association with stone tools of the Tayacian culture which is clearly the European prototype of the

Neanderthalers' Mousterian. The Mousterian is one version of the Middle Palaeolithic sort of toolmaking that evolved out of the Lower Palaeolithic in Africa and Europe after about 250,000 BP. In Africa these Lower and Middle Palaeolithic phases are traditionally called the Early Stone Age (ESA) and Middle Stone Age (MSA) by archaeologists, but the same broad features characterize Lower Palaeolithic/Old Stone Age and Middle Palaeolithic/Middle Stone Age phases everywhere. Whereas the all-purpose hand-axe tool, arrived at by striking flakes off a core of stone, is the prominent type of the Lower Palaeolithic, the Middle Palaeolithic toolmakers put the emphasis on the use that could be made of the struck flakes, either raw as they came off the carefully prepared cores or retouched into points, scrapers and so on. The Levallois technique was an elegant way of achieving the sort of flake tool desired, by elaborate shaping of the core prior to striking off the flake, and some Mousterian assemblages from particular sites and periods make more of this technique than others. It was pioneered in East Africa perhaps as long ago as 250,000 BP and, whether or not intentionally to begin with, it produces rather readily haftable flakes to tip wooden spears. Where the Levallois technique was not employed by Middle Palaeolithic toolmakers, cores were more simply rotated during knapping to get off roughly consistent flakes without the highly controlled pre-shaping of the Levallois style, which required abundant supplies of good flint. Middle Palaeolithic (or MSA) toolmaking traditions do show variety through time and in different places, but they are basically the same all over their range in Africa, Europe and Western Asia. Not surprisingly, there were places where Lower Palaeolithic traditions lived on into Middle Palaeolithic times; indeed, the flake component can really be very similar between Lower and Middle Palaeolithic assemblages and contemporary manifestations might be assigned to one or the other on the grounds of the absence or presence of axes and the type of those axes – small heart-shaped axes, or none at all means Middle Palaeolithic while typically Acheulian axes mean Lower Palaeolithic. At this point, the formality of the distinction is obvious as a classification convenience, without chronological implications. It is appropriate to note, also, that not all Lower Palaeolithic assemblages included hand-axes in any case – we will be reviewing the worldwide technological progress of evolving humanity later on.

In Europe it was the Tayacian industrial tradition that led on to the Mousterian of the Neanderthal folk. The Tayacian, named after the locality in the Dordogne around which so many spectacular and important palaeolithic finds have been made since the middle of the last century, shows large numbers of small and often rather roughly shaped flakes, sometimes made with the Levallois technique. There are scrapers, denticulate pieces and points, sometimes even leaf-shaped bifacial points that look forward to much later phases of the Mousterian in Central Europe. There are axes of a Lower Palaeolithic sort, too, on occasions and chopper-like cores that hark back to earlier non-hand-axe industries: the Tayacian may be derived from either the Acheulian hand-axe tradition or a Lower Palaeolithic axeless tradition with flakes, or both. Tayacian tools, or something to all intents and purposes the same, are found widely in European sites of the penultimate glacial period. Taubach and Weimar in Germany have Tayacian type tools with points and side-scrapers, and even Tabun in Israel, in its lower levels, shows something essentially Tayacian to antedate the Mousterian of the Levant (after an intervening episode with Acheulian axes). At the Grotte de Rigabe in Provence, a Tayacian with many scrapers and Levallois flakes looks like a good precursor of the Mousterian back in the times of the penultimate glaciation.

Pre-Mousterian flake tools, Tayacian above, Clactonian below.

The Tayacian itself has possible antecedents at earlier dates beyond the penultimate glacial period. From Bilzingsleben in North Germany comes an industry with flakes not unlike the Tayacian and diminutive chopper-like cores. Bilzingsleben belongs to another interglacial period that came before the penultimate glaciation, lasting from about 420,000 to 300,000 BP, with a sharp but short (only 12,000 years) glacial episode within it. To that same interglacial or the end of the preceding glacial phase dates the chopper-core and flake material from Clacton in Essex in association with which was found the oldest pointed wooden spear fragment yet discovered anywhere in the world, perhaps as much as 450,000 years old. Doubts sometimes cast on the Clacton spear as being really a digging stick or snow probe (both would be sophisticated enough to impress us) are rather dissipated by the recent discovery in Germany of three spears of spruce (the longest 2.3 m in length) long enough to qualify as throwing rather than thrusting spears and dated to some 400,000 BP. These spears, from Schöningen about 90 km west of Berlin, were even accompanied by grooved fir branches that look like holders for sophisticated composite tools – not otherwise evidenced at such an early date and not thought to constitute a part of the Mousterian tool kit, let alone anything earlier. The Schöningen site yielded up many flint flakes including points and scrapers and animal bones, mainly of horses, bearing marks of butchery. In the light of all this evidence, quibbles about the hunting abilities of the Neanderthalers of more than 300,000 years later seem misplaced. At the same time, the very slow progress of all technological innovation, if that word is at all appropriate, in the pre-Upper Palaeolithic world is well brought home to us.

Human remains to go with the finds of stone tools from before the last ice age but one are few and far between in Europe, as in the rest of the world. Ehringsdorf in Germany yielded the very partial remains of four individuals including a child, with

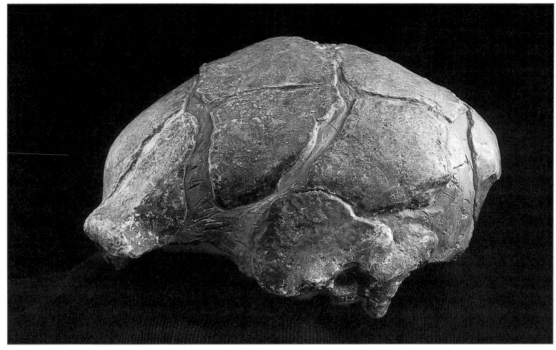

One of the Ehringsdorf skulls.

excellent preservation in the limestone deposits of a warm spring of both faunal and floral evidence. Dating by two methods based on radioactivity produced an age estimate of around 225,000 years, but the faunal remains suggest a perhaps later date, within the Last Interglacial after 130,000 BP. The human remains resemble those of the generalized Neanderthalers (the adult mandible, however, also resembles the jaw from Mauer, near Heidelberg, which is much older than any Neanderthalers) and the tools look like the run of pre-Mousterian flake products, so the later date still recommends itself to some workers. But Ehringsdorf could belong to a warmer interstadial within the penultimate glaciation, in which case the human remains represent a pre-Neanderthal type and the tools a pre-Mousterian like the Tayacian and so forth. The jaw from Montmaurin near Toulouse, dated by physical means to between 130,000 and 190,000 years ago, also displays a mixture of Neanderthal and older features: in particular there are indications of the retromolar gap of the Neanderthalers and their taurodont tooth pattern, while the massive build of the jaw harks back to older jaws like that from Mauer. The very fragmentary remains from Pontnewydd in Wales also display the taurodont teeth tendency, typically seen later in the Neanderthalers, at about 225,000 BP. The stone tools of Pontnewydd are very rough-and-ready hand-axes, probably owing their crudity to the poverty of the available raw material. The very oldest tools that can be seen to belong to the Mousterian or pre-Mousterian tradition date from just a little earlier than this time: at an age of about 238,000 BP at the Cotte de St Brelade on Jersey, at about 250,000 BP in the Grotte Vaufrey in France, and at the same date at Mesvin in Belgium. Before this sort of date, no distinctively pre-Mousterian foreshadowings can be positively identified and what flake tools are found constitute the flake component of the Acheulian hand-axe tradition or belong to the early non-hand-axe manifestations of the Lower Palaeolithic. But if the beginnings of the Neanderthalers' Mousterian tool tradition cannot be traced back earlier than about 250,000 BP, some of the physical traits of the Neanderthal people can be glimpsed at and beyond this date – Neanderthalers as such are not found in these early times but some of their physical characteristics were evidently in process of evolution. From Steinheim in Germany comes a skull, dated to about 250,000 BP, with several Neanderthal traits on view alongside others that the Neanderthalers did not display. The taurodont tooth formation is present, as is the suprainiac fossa at the back of the skull, where a distinctly Neanderthal look obtains. But the face, though brow-arched, is flatter than Neanderthal faces and shows the canine fossa at the cheeks that Neanderthalers lacked. The skull suffered some post-mortem distortion, but it seems clear that its sides were flatter and more vertical in the tin-loaf form of modern *Homo sapiens*, although cranial capacity was low at about 1100 ml even for a modern woman let alone a Neanderthal female. Skull fragments from Swanscombe in England show the suprainiac fossa of the later Neanderthalers, too, though the area of the likely brow

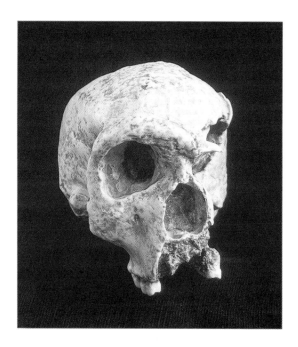

The Steinheim skull.

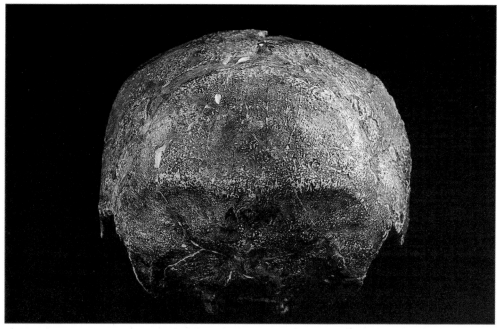

The back of the assembled Swanscombe fragments.

arches is missing. The Swanscombe fragments are noticeably thick in section like rather earlier human skulls, but the cranial capacity has been estimated at the quite high figure of 1325 ml. The associated faunal remains and Acheulian axes suggest a date between 400,000 and 250,000 BP for the Swanscombe skull, putting it potentially in the same age range (maybe a little older) as the Steinheim skull, with which it is quite well matched in character. (The faunas of the two sites are similar, too, and they both probably belong to the long interglacial period before the penultimate ice age.) The fine Acheulian hand-axes of solidly Lower Palaeolithic character found with the Swanscombe skull, with its very incipient Neanderthal features, point to the likelihood that the Neanderthalers' Mousterian tool kit itself evolved, at least in part, from the hand-axe tradition.

Deep in a cave complex in the Sierra de Atapuerca in northern Spain, a cache of bones of many individuals was recently discovered and is still under study. Dating indications suggest that this material belongs to a period before 200,000 BP, and perhaps as far back as 300,000 years ago. There are over a thousand bones and teeth from at least thirty individuals: men, women and children. It may emerge that whole skeletons are included among the remains since even the little bones of fingertips have been found and one of those hyoid bones that have a bearing on speech capacity. Whether the Sima de los Huesos ('pit of bones') was the scene of human disposal of the dead or the dumping ground of predatory and scavenging animals is not clear. Again, some signs of incipient 'Neanderthalization' are to be seen on these remains. The cranial bones are thick and of the two main skull finds noted to date one is of small capacity at about 1125 ml but the other is certainly large for its date at an estimated 1390 ml of cranial capacity. The double-arched brow-ridge formation of the Neanderthalers is evidenced in these skulls, as is the projection of the mid face. In one of the chinless mandibles, which in their massive build resemble those of earlier forms of humanity, there is a suggestion of the Neanderthalers' retromolar gap (which goes with the forward projection of the mid facial area). One of the skulls exhibits the typically Neanderthal lack of a canine fossa, which partly accounts for the inflated cheek appearance of the Neanderthal folk – though another does possess the canine fossa. Preliminary assemblings of skeletal material indicate that the Atapuerca people were shorter than their ancestors (in the shape of *Homo erectus*, who achieved an impressive stature in Africa hundreds of thousands of years earlier) and were on their way to the development of Neanderthal traits of arm and leg proportions and even finger shape. Of the many teeth from the site (which are smaller than *erectus* teeth) some incisors show signs of scratching with stone tools, in the way that some Neanderthal teeth also do; the practice of cutting off meat held in the front teeth is strongly suggested here and the directionality of the scratch marks indicates that the Atapuerca people were right-handed. All in all, the Atapuerca remains constitute a variable population already displaying the early development of certain Neanderthal traits, at a period probably between 250,000 and 200,000 BP. It is interesting to note that no tools were found in association with these human remains but among the animal bones of the site there were found the remains of an ancestral form of the cave-bear, with which beast Neanderthal Man was to have his enigmatic dealings later on.

The skull from Petralona in Greece is hard to date precisely. It is certainly older than 200,000 BP, to go by physical dates on material found over it, and younger than 730,000 BP, on the grounds of the magnetic polarity of rock beneath it. Something in the range 500,000 to 300,000 BP is indicated. The Petralona brain-case is more expanded than those of *erectus* and comes in at about 1220 ml, though its shape at the back resembles *erectus* skulls. It lacks the mid-face projection of the Neanderthalers (its face is bigger altogether) but it shows their double brow arch configuration, broad nasal opening and inflated cheeks. It rather resembles the Broken Hill skull from Kabwe in East Africa (also called Rhodesian Man) and we may broadly conclude that both Petralona and Broken Hill represent a similar stage of human evolution after *Homo erectus*, with Petralona in Europe on its way to *Homo sapiens neanderthalensis* and Broken Hill in Africa perhaps on its way to *Homo sapiens sapiens*. We shall be looking at Broken Hill again later on and must also, in the meantime, recall that some scholars believe that Neanderthal Man too has contributed to the final

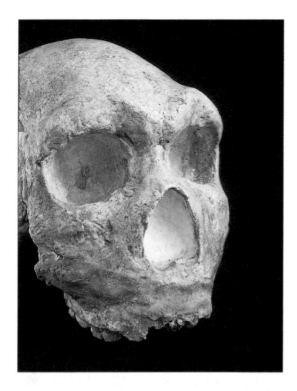

The skull from Petralona.

evolution of modern *Homo sapiens*. No tools were found with the Petralona skull or close faunal association, but if it belongs with the sort of faunal remains found elsewhere in the cave, it might just be as old as 500,000 BP.

To about 400,000 BP dates the fossil human material from the Caune de l'Arago at Tautavel in the Pyrenees. A similar situation prevails here as with the finds discussed above: an incipience of Neanderthal traits against a background of *erectus*-like characteristics. The site has yielded fragments of some sixty individuals, including hip bones, two jaws and the front, right side and face of a skull. The hip is robustly made, like the same bones of an *erectus* skeleton; the larger jaw is *erectus*-like, the smaller one is more like a Neanderthaler's; the skull is brow-ridged and without a canine fossa, and rather Neanderthal in general shape, though more straight-sided than real Neanderthalers' are and showing no mid-face prognathism. At about 1160 ml, the Arago skull was bigger-brained than *erectus*, though well short of Neanderthal capacity, with less of the constricted look behind the eye sockets than *erectus* skulls show. The Swanscombe fragments could fit fairly well into the Arago skull. Tools found in association with the human remains were mostly flakes, with a few hand-axes. Large stones among the tools have been interpreted as pointing to some sort of built structure in the cave, perhaps a wood and hide shelter anchored by the stones. The cave deposits are mostly of a cold climate character, indicating that at Arago we

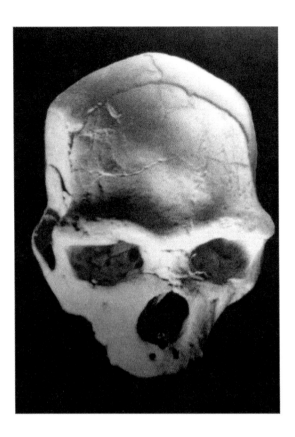

The skull from the Caune de l'Arago, Tautavel.

have pushed back dim Neanderthal and Mousterian foreshadowings into a period three ice ages ago. The massive shin-bone from Boxgrove, near Chichester in England, probably belongs to an interstadial of that same ice age, along with the fine ovate hand-axes found in association with it, as do the retouched scrapers and flakes found without any accompanying hand-axes at High Lodge in East Anglia and the irregular flakes and chopping tools found at Swanscombe (below the level of the skull) and Clacton in England. The absence of hand-axes at High Lodge and presence of refined ones at Boxgrove, which look too good for their early date, only goes to show that no hard and fast characterization of the Lower Palaeolithic (or Middle or Upper for that matter) should be made: availability of raw material, functional requirements and a degree of some sort of cultural variety were apparently in force.

No tools at all were found in association with the jaw from a gravel pit at Grafenrein, near Mauer, not far from Heidelberg in Germany. The jaw today goes by both the names of Mauer and Heidelberg and, by virtue of primacy of scientific naming, *Homo heidelbergensis* is the name that many scholars give to the whole stage of human evolution that comes between *Homo erectus* and the various representatives of early *Homo sapiens* (whether on the way to fully modern or Neanderthal forms) that have been found in Europe, Africa and Asia. But others are content to call Mauer itself (and its contemporaries in Africa) and what came after them by the name of 'archaic' *Homo sapiens*. (It is worth noting that there can be nothing hard and fast about any of these classifications, either, in view of the paucity, fragmentariness and evident variability of the specimens to hand.) The Mauer jaw is a massive fossil, with a very receding chin area (where there is no chin in our terms) and very broad rami ascending to the points where the jaw articulated with the skull: a sign of heavy musculature for hard chewing. For such a massive jaw, the teeth are rather small, and Neanderthal-like in their taurodontism, though no other Neanderthal features could be said to be present. The date of the Mauer jaw is not known for certain, but it appears to belong to an interglacial period predating the ice age time of the Arago find – in other words, to three interglacials ago. Something like 500,000 BP is indicated. With the Mauer jaw, we have followed back in time, as far as we can, even the faintest hints of the Neanderthal type; as much as 350,000 years may separate Mauer from the earliest true Neanderthalers. The researchers who have recently identified some of the Neanderthal mtDNA profile reckon that something like that length of time is required to explain the divergence of this part of the Neanderthal genetic make-up from our own. On this interpretation, Mauer at 500,000 BP would represent the last sort of common human

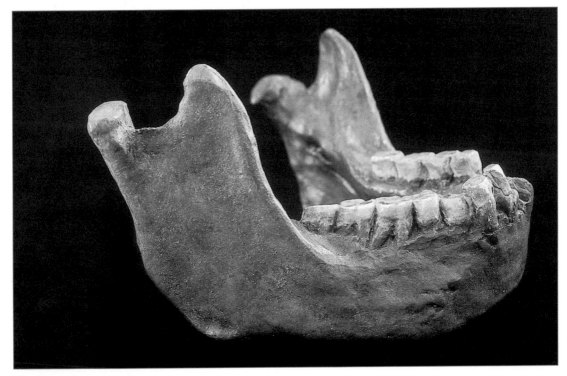

The Mauer jaw.

ancestor between ourselves and the Neanderthalers. *Homo heidelbergensis* would have started on the way to *Homo sapiens sapiens* via the non-Neanderthal sorts of early *Homo sapiens* seen outside Europe. For it is a fact that the distinctively Neanderthal turn of human evolution seen in Europe, Western Asia and the Levant has no antecedents outside Europe; in Africa and Asia (east and west) there are no foreshadowings of the Neanderthal package of physical traits. The Neanderthalers evidently evolved in Europe; their presence in Western Asia and their appearances in the Levant are the results of spread and movement rather than in situ evolution. People of broadly the same stage of human evolution as the Neanderthalers did evolve in Africa and Asia, but none of them could be called Neanderthal as such. Whether the Neanderthalers could breed with their non-Neanderthal contemporaries is a matter of controversy (though the mtDNA evidence as far as it goes suggests they did not), as is the question of their capacity to evolve into fully modern *Homo sapiens sapiens* (where, again, the genetic evidence suggests they could not).

Homo heidelbergensis belongs to that previous broad stage of human evolution from which both Neanderthalers and fully moderns emerged, with or without interbreeding. Back beyond Mauer, we shall find no distinctly Neanderthal traits, however faintly expressed. Beyond Mauer stretches back the era of *Homo erectus* or, if one thinks that this name should be reserved for the typical specimens mostly discovered in the Far East, then of *Homo ergaster* – a separate species that some researchers think evolved in Africa, and spread to Europe after *Homo erectus* as such had developed in the Far East. Beyond the time of the Mauer jaw, no faint prototype of the Mousterian culture can be traced among the Lower Palaeolithic tools that are found in considerable quantities in Western Europe, often along the old courses of rivers where flint was exposed in the banks for the making of tools and the waterways offered routes through the interglacial woods and drinking places for men and beasts. The Lower Palaeolithic period was dominated by the presence of hand-axes, though there were times and circumstances when flakes without axes were made and used – perhaps for shortage of good raw material, or for some limited function, or even as a result of incursions into Europe of different people from the Far East, where the hand-axe never caught on as a cultural product. Hand-axes also gradually diminished in importance through time as the Lower Palaeolithic gave way to the Middle Palaeolithic of traditions like the Mousterian, as though more flake varieties with possibilities for hafting in wooden spears or handles reduced the attraction of the weighty all-purpose hand-axe tool. For all that, it was the hand-axe in its various forms that characterized the Lower Palaeolithic era in Africa and Europe, after its development in Africa more than 1.3 mya. Hand-axe toolmaking traditions are called after the name of the French site at St Acheul where these tools were found in abundance in the nineteenth century: Acheulian.

The Acheulian flourished in Europe into the period of the penultimate glaciation, by which time intimations of the Mousterian were well in evidence: it had first appeared in Europe some time after about 700,000 BP. There were thus some half a million years of the European Acheulian during which hand-axes of various forms (but with little evidence of progressive change) were made in the hands of *Homo erectus* (or *egaster*) physical types and their descendants like *Homo heidelbergensis* or early *Homo sapiens*. The fossilized bones of human types predating *Homo heidelbergensis* in Europe are few and far between. We may assume that the makers of the early hand-axes of Torralba in Spain, of the Somme gravels at Abbeville in France and of Kent's Cavern in Devon were broadly of the *Homo heidelbergensis* type. In Africa the Acheulian developed out of a more primitive tradition, named Oldowan after Olduvai Gorge in East Africa, which centred upon knapped pebbles that archaeologists call chopper-cores and chopping tools. That development from Oldowan to Acheulian took place in Africa at the early date of about 1.4 mya but it seems that the Acheulian with its axes did not reach Europe until about 700,000 BP. Before that, Europe was going on with a sort of latter-day Oldowan of choppers and associated flakes, itself of ultimately African origin. Such an industry has been discovered at Isernia near Rome, dating to at least 730,000 BP, to go by the magnetic polarity of the volcanic rock that overlies the level of the tools. The sort of

A fine Acheulian hand-axe.

human beings who made these tools probably belonged to a transitional form between *Homo erectus* (*ergaster*) and *Homo heidelbergensis*; at Gran Dolina in Spain some teeth, jaw and skull pieces and hand and foot bones from four individuals represent this type of fossil man, in a fragmentary form, at about 780,000 BP. (Some of the fragments carry cut marks similar to others on animal bones from the site and unlike the marks made by carnivore teeth, which raises again at this early date the possibility of cannibalism of some sort.) The German site of Kärlich has yielded choppers and flakes that may go back to about 900,000 BP, and a similar situation is evidenced at le Vallonet and Soleihac in France, the latter site showing among its choppers and scraper flakes a single prototypical hand-axe. Chopper and flake assemblages are in fact quite widespread in Europe, if not always of certain early date. It looks as though all these early pebble tool assemblages represent a first wave of human spread out of Africa; in Africa the late Oldowan culture with its development towards Acheulian with axes was associated with early *Homo erectus* (*ergaster*) and we can reasonably assume that it was the same sort of early human beings who brought the Oldowan and then the Acheulian to Europe. The Acheulian (firmly associated with *erectus/ergaster* in Africa) could have come across the Mediterranean (with low sea levels and much extra dry ground during glacial periods) via Gibraltar and Sicily and Italy, but the earlier Oldowan probably came through the Levantine region. The site of 'Ubeidiya in Israel already shows a sort of crude Acheulian axe development against a background of chopper tools at between 1.4 and 1.2 mya. A few very fragmentary human remains accompany these finds. It is worth noting that the Jordan Valley is in fact an extension north of the Great Rift Valley of East Africa and enjoyed, at the time in question, a similar ecology to that heartland of human evolution which includes the important area of Olduvai Gorge. At Dmanisi in Georgia an *erectus/ergaster* jaw, associated with animal bones and pebble tools, has been dated by three physical methods to 1.8 mya.

At about 1 mya we have taken the human story in Europe back as far as it goes, far beyond any evidence of physical types that could usefully be called incipiently Neanderthal or of tool types that could be called proto-Mousterian. All of that lay in the distant future when Europe was first occupied by man. At this point, we have linked the career of Neanderthal Man back into the big story of human evolution out of Africa – the story in which we all, *Homo sapiens sapiens*, *Homo sapiens neanderthalensis*, archaic *Homo sapiens*, *Homo heidelbergensis*, *Homo ergaster*, *Homo erectus* and *Homo habilis* before them, play our parts. In the next chapter we will review the long evolution of mankind from the ground up, as it were – from the ancestry we share with the apes. Before that, the general pattern of life of the pre-Neanderthal people we have discussed in this chapter needs to be explored.

Fire was certainly wielded by them in at least the later phases of our pre-Neanderthal period and it is very doubtful whether Europe could have been infiltrated at all in the basically cold times that came on after about 800,000 BP without fire, which gives warmth and light and defence against animal enemies as well as offering the possibility of cooked food. But cooking was perhaps a low priority for a long time and fires do not seem to have been often built in any very structured way with proper hearths. Evidence for the use of fire at about 200,000 BP has been found at the Hungarian site of Verteszöllös, at a somewhat earlier date at Bilzingsleben in Germany, and at up to 400,000 BP at Menez-Dragan on the south coast of Brittany and at Terra Amata, near Nice, where a hearth-like floor (with burnt mussel shells) has been identified among stones that possibly anchored some sort of shelter of poles and skins. From such remote times, as far back as about 1 mya, it is not likely that all occupied caves have survived as caves but were lost to erosion and collapse in some cases, though it seems clear that in coldish Europe caves would have been occupation sites of choice. If the evidence of Terra Amata and a few other sites like Ariendorf in Germany and Latamne in Syria is correctly interpreted as signs of structure, then people were already building additional shelter for themselves. But it has to be said that most sites, including ones with good preservation of evidence, show no real organizational patterns at all – no regular hearths, no storage pits, no intentional arrangements of stones. There are just scatters of ash and the debris of flint knapping and butchery. These people were living, of course, like their Neanderthal and Crô-Magnon successors, as foragers, gathering plants and scavenging or hunting animal food. We have seen that finds of wooden spears do go some way to vindicating the hunting prowess of these pre-Neanderthal people and the decline of hand-axes throughout this period in favour of flake tools that could be hafted and mounted on wood probably charts the slow improvement of hunting techniques and technology in general. Microwear traces on hand-axes from Hoxne in Suffolk suggest that on occasion at least these all-purpose tools were used to cut meat (as well as work hides, bone and wood, and chop up vegetable matter). In addition to wooden spears and perhaps holders for flake tools, small wooden containers might well have been in use and even, just conceivably, wooden rafts of some kind; low sea levels may have facilitated Mediterranean crossings of Acheulian folk into Europe from North Africa, but Gibraltar might have been reached by boat – there is one Indonesian island colonized by *Homo erectus* that geologists believe was never connected to any mainland and so European *erectus/ergaster* people too may have been able to boat or raft over short sea crossings.

We have seen that hints of cannibalism, which always carry the possibility of some sort of ritual behaviour, have been discerned at Gran Dolina as early as about 780,000 BP; the Tautavel skull of a pre-Neanderthaler of about 350,000 BP was smashed at the back in a suggestive manner, too. But indications of any ideologically motivated cannibalism have to be said to be vanishingly sparse, as do signs of any artistic endeavour on the part of the Acheulian and proto-Mousterian people. You might say that the symmetry of the hand-axes, which are sometimes painstakingly refined in execution, points to a developing aesthetic sense but any further manifestations of such feeling are few and far between. Several of the French sites have yielded up bone pieces of Acheulian times with straight lines, arcs and parallels that do not look like the results of cutting into joints for meat or using bones as cutting boards. The site of Becov in the Czech Republic offers a red striated piece of stone which may have been collected about 250,000 years ago for its visual appeal. Hand-axe makers seem sometimes to have worked around fossils encountered in flint in the course of knapping, as though these features had somehow taken their fancy. The Terra Amata site produced seventy-five bits of natural pigment, not evidently of local origin, in yellow, brown, red and purple, abraded by use – to colour hides or people's skins? African Acheulian sites, and others outside Europe, have produced similar evidence. From an Acheulian site at Bhimbetka in India there has come a stone bearing a meandering line of peck markings with a shallow cupule depression, and from Berekhat Ram in Israel a 4 cm high fragment of tuff whose naturally human shape (faintly human, at least) has apparently been improved artificially around the 'neck' and along the 'arms'. Finds like these are too meagre to form the basis for any speculation about the state of mind of their makers, indeed too utterly uncommon to build anything on at all. The unstructured nature of the dwelling sites of these people without anything to suggest any possible divisions of labour or specialized activities, the extraordinarily slow pace and limitedness of technological change over hundreds of thousands of years, the absence as far as we can tell of graves, the lack to all intents and purposes of any ritual or artistic tendencies, all these things paint a picture of a long-persisting way of life even more culturally restricted than that of the Neanderthalers of the last ice age. If we may doubt the humanity (in our terms) of the Neanderthalers' sexual and social relations, then we must be even more doubtful about the same sides of life as far as the pre-Neanderthalers are concerned. Anything like monogamous mating and kinship relations seems very unlikely indeed. The minds that piloted these people through their short and exigent lifetimes must have been significantly less adept than those of the Neanderthalers, as the much smaller cranial capacities of the skulls that have come to light would anyway imply. Whether they wielded speech and language we cannot tell, though the development of areas of their brains associated in us with speech would seem to allow the possibility that they could speak up to a point, but even if they did it must have been speech of a very limited kind, restricted to a narrow range of mental expression that was probably more to do with social relations within the group than anything else. The reasons for this speculation will be discussed in the following chapters, as we chart the evolution of humanity out of our remote ape ancestry.

CHAPTER 9

From Apes to Hominids

We have seen that the European evidence for early man peters out at somewhere around 1 mya. The trail leads back beyond that time to Africa as the cradle of humanity. There were non-human primates in Europe back from some 3 mya but they neither evolved into early forms of man nor persisted as part of the European fauna.

Homo sapiens sapiens is the only extant subspecies of the species *Homo sapiens* which in its time has embraced (as far, at least, as many anthropologists have believed) another subspecies we call *neanderthalensis* and another rather varied and loosely defined one that people are in the habit of calling 'archaic' or early *Homo sapiens*, without gracing it with a proper piece of Linnaean nomenclature (because, frankly, it is too loosely defined). The genus *Homo* has seen a number of species before *sapiens*: *heidelbergensis*, *erectus*, *ergaster*, *habilis*. Within a given species, individuals look more or less alike (though with a wide range of superficially different appearances, on occasions) and can all interbreed. The different species within a genus will have significantly diverged in appearance and interbreeding between species will be very rare, though sometimes possible. Speciation occurs when small populations become relatively isolated from their erstwhile fellow species members and are subject to pressures of natural selection (or to genetic drift sometimes) which can bring about very rapid evolutionary change. Because speciation is an affair of initially small numbers and rapid change, fossils that record periods of transition between species are almost impossible to find. The paucity (and inevitably somewhat random nature) of the fossil record of human evolution is the result of this state of affairs, exacerbated by vagaries of vastly differing chances of survival and discovery in different locations today.

The genus *Homo* belongs to the family Hominidae, which it is convenient to know more colloquially as the hominids. The Australopithecines of Africa were hominids, too. The hominid family belongs to the superfamily Hominoidea, which groups the hominids with the pongids (great apes and their ancestors) and hylobatids (gibbons and theirs). The Hominoidea belong to the Primate order of mammals, which also includes both the monkeys and such unmonkey-like animals as the bushbaby and the tree shrew (and included some even more unlikely relatives of ours in the distant past). It is interesting to note that all the living non-human primates are tropical or subtropical animals. Old World monkeys, apes and humans (on grounds of teeth, ear and eye bone structures and nasal form) belong more together than even Old World monkeys do with New World monkeys. Apes and humans, in turn, are more alike than apes are to Old World monkeys, in terms of trunk shape, shoulder structure (permitting rotation of arms around the shoulder joint) and absence of tails. The pongid apes are closer to humanity than are the gibbons, and the chimpanzees and gorillas are closer still than the orang-utans. Gorillas, in fact, share nearly 98 per cent of their genetic material with humans, and chimps share over 98 per cent, though the two apes have it distributed over 48 chromosomes and humans have 46. This situation is a pointer to the fact that it is in areas of control gene structures that human beings most crucially differ from the apes (the control genes orchestrate the sequence and duration of genetically guided developments as each new individual grows up from the fertilized egg). It is the control gene function that makes a chimp so different from a human being despite the near totally shared genetic material in common. And it is evolution by natural selection that has brought about the divergent evolutionary courses of apes and men since the time, reckoned to be only some six or seven million years ago, when the hominid and pongid lines separated. The differences that distinguish human beings from the apes and all the other primates have evolved because they are useful to survival in certain ecological circumstances; the walking posture of bipedalism, regular toolmaking, the unique features of human social arrangements, the progressive enlargement of the brain, the use of language, the quality of mind that produces art and even irrational belief, all these specifically human traits and more have been evolved because they have so far benefited the survival and reproduction of the human line.

When we review the trends and processes of human evolution and try to reconstruct not just the physical remains of our remote ancestors but also their likely social habits and states of mind, we have in the world today just the two opposite ends of the scale to look at for glimmers of enlightenment. At our own end, as it were, we can consider the ways of life still existing or only recently vanished foraging folk (non-farming hunter-gatherers) like the inhabitants of Tierra del Fuego who might be said to have taken the simple life to extremes or the coastal Indians of north-west America who lived very well without any technology that went beyond that of Crô-Magnon Man. Much can be learned about the common human patterns of life that go with foraging from people like these but, like us descendants of the first farmers and city-dwellers, they too have long histories and have had plenty of time to sophisticate themselves in all sorts of ways that were not open to, say, *Homo heidelbergensis*. What we can, minimally, conclude to be the core traits of life for *Homo sapiens sapiens* were set out when we asked, in Chapter 7, whether the Neanderthalers truly shared any significant number of behavioural ways in common with modern foraging peoples. Those traits include home life with provisioning of wives and children by males, meat sharing with family and relatives, more or less monogamous but decidedly regular mating (with marriages outside the immediate group), kinship systems and alliances in a wider social network. One of the most interesting questions of human evolution asks when these traits were assembled into the fully human pattern. Teasing some hints of an answer (or answers) to that question out of the exiguous archaeological remains that have come down to us is one of the chief pleasures of the study.

At the other end of the scale of evidence available to us today when we want to think about the evolution of the human way of life is the world of the apes, in particular the chimpanzees who most resemble us not only genetically but also behaviourally, though the resemblance could not be called close. The chimpanzees, too, have enjoyed as many years of evolution as we have since their ancestors diverged from ours and they have, necessarily, adapted to a particular survival niche in the world, which is quite unlike our own; thus what they can tell us about the likely lifestyle of our own remote ape-like ancestors must be limited, but it is suggestive, if only for the contrast it offers to humanity as we know it.

Before we explore the life of the chimpanzees, it is worth looking into the general character of the primates, to see what inheritance we and the chimps already share from tens of millions of years ago. The primates in general retain some primitive mammalian features like clavicles (collar-bones) and a five-fold pattern of digits at the ends of the limbs. Their digits are highly mobile and prehensile, with opposable big toes as well as thumbs (though this feature has been lost in human beings). Mostly primates have flat nails on their digits instead of claws, and tactile pads on their fingers and toes, whose sensitivity chimes in with the dexterity of their feet or hands. Locomotion is largely powered by the hind limbs. The sense of smell is relatively well developed but not dedicated to any specialized extent; colour vision on the other hand is exceptionally good with the blessing, thanks to the forward positioning of the eyes in the skull, of stereoscopic imaging in depth, probably evolved to facilitate the negotiation of a world of tangled branches in dimly lit forests on the look-out for insects and fruit to eat. The all-important eyes of the primates are protected by bone around and (in the higher primates) behind them. Primate brains are often larger in relation to total body size than those of other animals (strikingly so in human beings) and it may well be that the processing of complex visual information from the two convergent eyes played an important part in forcing brain expansion in the course of primate evolution. Primate brains also exhibit a unique pattern of folds on the surface under the skull. To go with their sound but unspectacular olfactory performance, primates usually have short muzzles with reduction of the numbers of incisor and premolar teeth *vis-à-vis* their mammalian ancestry and unspecialized molars of relatively simple and primitive cusp pattern. The lower primates, like the lemurs, show less development of the distinctively primate traits and put more emphasis on the sense of smell and on night vision, which probably witnesses to the nocturnal nature of our remote primate ancestry of about 65 mya.

The very earliest primates (or potential primates) we can discern in the fossil record of the world were mouse-sized creatures like *Purgatorius* that lived on insects and the somewhat larger *Plesiadapis* that probably ate leaves and fruit. By about 55 mya the first recognizably primate forms, resembling today's lemurs and tarsiers, were flourishing in North America – *Notharctus* being the best-known fossil of this sort. These were the first of the primate line to possess brains larger in relation to body size than the general run of animals of their time; they must have had a use for those enlarged brains and that use most likely related to their cleverness in spotting and securing high quality food in the shape of ripe fruits and new leaves against the visual background of a noisy clutter of branches and foliage. High quality food could sustain the energetic nervous activity of their clever brains without requiring the elaborate and sizeable gut needed to extract nutrition from poorer food. Thus was initiated a promising evolutionary feedback involving good food, braininess and reduction of gut that has played an important part in human evolution.

Primate 'society' (the grouping of primates in relationships between themselves) shows considerable variety, but most monkeys and apes live in social groups in a way that is unusual, if not of course unknown, among mammals. Society brings liabilities in the shape of greater chances of disagreement and competition and greater risk of disease spread, but also benefits in the form of mutual support through cooperation and shared defence against enemies. Because primate females, like the mammals they are, carry, give birth to, suckle, nurse and feed their young, society among the primates is based on the females who perform these steady duties – male primate roles range from mere impregnation without further responsibilities to constant attendance, care and protection. Physical differences between the sexes among the primates are emphasized or downplayed in relation to the social arrangements of particular creatures. Gorilla males, for example, are large beasts in relation to their females because they live in social circumstances where there is heavy competition between males to secure harems; the monogamous gibbons who live largely as couples outside a wider society do not show much sexual dimorphism. Social relationships, whether between sexual partners and rivals or relatives and allies within the group, are an important part of primate life; monkeys, let alone apes, show a keen awareness of close kinship, for example. The demands of social life probably played as big a part in the evolution of quick-wittedness and cleverness among the higher primates as did stereoscopic vision and the rewards for securing a high quality diet. Though we must use anthropomorphizing words when we talk about it, it is clear that monkeys and apes in social groups prosper by their mental capacity for buttering one another up and deceiving each other, for cooperation and selfishness as it suits, for forming alliances and breaking them in season, for second-guessing the intentions of their fellows and dissembling where their own are concerned. All this requires great brain power to run experimental models of behaviour and consequences in the 'mind', with a good back-up of memory; indeed, all this is very likely the reason for the evolution of the mind and that elusive entity we call consciousness. In many sorts of animals, it is the social species that are the brightest and biggest-brained – parrots, dolphins, wolves, and apes all exemplify this – but the application of their cleverness can be very restricted to their social world. Vervet monkeys, for example, are finely focused on their social interactions, but relatively dense about everything else including dangers from their enemies that look obvious to us. It is the great trick of modern humanity to have extended our social acuity to so many other areas of experience: a topic to which we shall return in due course.

The lineage that runs from the first primates to the common ancestor of the great apes and humanity includes, at about 35 mya, the oldest known monkey-like creature called *Aegyptopithecus*, from the Faiyum lake deposits of Egypt. Between 35 and 31 mya many genera of related monkey-like forms flourished in the Faiyum region. Their small eye sockets indicate that these were no longer nocturnal primates and their teeth suggest that some of them, at least, were in fact closer to apes and men than to monkeys. Though they had larger brains per body size than the lower primates before them, their eyes were not so perfectly forward facing as those of later higher primates and their muzzles were longer. They were about the size of a modern gibbon, but they lacked the very long arms of tree-swinging apes of today.

It is during a gap in the fossil record of about ten million years after the last known Faiyum specimens that genetic studies suggest the split between monkeys and apes was consolidated. By 23 mya East Africa was home to many genera of hominoids in its environment of tropical forests and woodlands. There were few lower primates left in this region and very few monkeys, who were probably thriving in some less forested area like North Africa. *Proconsul* is the best known of the early apes of East Africa, representing a definite progress over *Aegyptopithecus* towards the apes of today: muzzles were shorter, brains large both relative to body size and absolutely, with shoulders and elbows suggesting the development of the suspensory, tree-swinging habits seen in modern apes. Some at least of the earlier monkey-like forms appear to have had tails – these later hominoids of East Africa probably did not. They enjoyed a long run of evolutionary success, down till at least 14 mya and possibly millions of years later. Some of them show dental traits that point towards the living apes and men (with indications that the diet could include hard nuts and tubers as well as soft fruit) but the long arms of today's apes (and of our earliest ancestors, too) were not yet in evidence.

After about 15 mya, to go with the onset of colder conditions in the northern latitudes, the tropical and subtropical world grew drier and the increasing aridity of the East African environment put selective pressure on its primate inhabitants which saw a

Aegyptopithecus.

decline in the fortunes of the apes in that part of the world (except for one aberrationally specialized sort of ape) and a corresponding rise in those of the monkeys. The apes of Africa began their retreat into the tropical forests where they hang on today, though relatives of theirs were able, thanks to Africa's final closure through continental drift with Europe and Asia, to spread out into the woodlands of southern Europe and Asia as far as south-west China. The orang-utans are thought to have differentiated from this generalized ape line at about 12 mya. Some relative or descendant of *Proconsul* gave rise to

Proconsul.

the line of the African pongids and the hominids between about 10 and 7 mya – remains from the Samburu Hills in Kenya show a creature with rather gorilla-like molars (though very thickly enamelled) that belongs roughly to this evolutionary phase. Genetic studies suggest a date of something like 6 mya for the divergence between the chimpanzees and the hominid line, though other lines of evidence might add a million years or so to that estimate. Unfortunately, direct fossil evidence for the period when the ancestors of chimpanzees, gorillas and men parted company is lacking. In terms of genetics and way of life, the chimpanzees (and, perhaps, the pygmy chimps called bonobos, in particular) are our closest living non-human relatives and can, provided that we always remember that they and ourselves have enjoyed six million years or more of separate evolution in very different circumstances, shed some light on the likely constitution of our very remotest ancestors, who lurk just behind the veil, as it were, of hominid fossil availability at about 4.5 mya.

The differences between chimps and men, both in appearance and behaviour, are great. Human beings, unlike all other primates, can walk bipedally, on two legs, with pelvis and spine adapted in shape to this form of locomotion, whereas chimpanzees can at best walk for only short distances in an awkward fashion on their legs alone and usually go about on all fours, knuckle-walking with their long arms. Humans have tiny canine teeth in comparison to those of the chimps, and flat faces with protruding noses in place of the prognathous muzzles of our nearest animal relatives. Human teeth are arranged in a curved arcade instead of the parallel-sided and rather box-like arrangement of ape jaws. Humans are relatively hairless except for their heads, armpits, and pubic areas, and they sweat all over. Human males' penises are large and pendulous by comparison with chimps' while, uniquely among primates, signs of ovulation are suppressed in human females. Human beings eat (and share) meat on a much more regular basis than chimpanzees do and, among foraging peoples, hunt cooperatively to acquire it (which chimps do not do on anything like the same scale). Even the most 'Stone Age' of human groups make tools in large numbers to a regular and culturally coloured pattern and communicate with complex languages which chimps lack altogether, as they do every sort of symbolic expression. Humans are culturally adapted to survive in almost every environment this world affords, however hot or cold, dry or wet; they will eat just about anything that can safely be eaten, with cooking to render edible even certain foodstuffs that could not otherwise be eaten. Victorian explorers occasionally reported seeing apes warming themselves in the heat of dying embers of natural fires, but chimpanzees cannot make fire or control it when it occurs in nature. Human beings have much bigger brains in relation to their body size than chimps do and are manifestly cleverer in every way, with powerful hands capable of a fine dexterity to carry out the clever purposes of their brains. Human beings, moreover, are markedly 'handed', right or sometimes left, which is a situation not seen in any other creatures. They are long-lived and their children mature postnatally much more slowly than ape infants, with an extended period of learning that includes an adolescent boost to growth and sexual maturity.

The way of life of the chimpanzees does show some faint resemblance to that of foraging *Homo sapiens sapiens*. They do eat meat on occasion (young monkeys, for example) and acquire it sometimes by means of cooperative hunting operations, involving driving prey towards their fellows or blocking escape routes. This is a clear advance on any monkey performance; though baboons (whose life in troops brings them, too, some resemblance to the human hunter-gatherers' situation) will now and then catch hares or small antelopes, they do not organize themselves cooperatively to do it and they do not share their pickings. Chimpanzees will hunt socially from time to time but they are essentially opportunistic, without perseverance and often ignoring easily caught prey under their noses. They are not, unlike modern and Upper Palaeolithic hunters, good stalkers or chasers. Plant food is the main component of their diet and they get it individually and eat it on the spot. They use no weapons in the hunt and no tools to cut up their meat (biting, bashing and twisting off heads is their style). In play chimpanzee youngsters will occasionally throw sticks and stones, but adults in real fights resort to no weapons but their own teeth. Chimpanzees do use and even make tools sometimes, but in the wilds this is only a matter of stripping leaves off a twig to make a stick to poke into a termite nest or crumpling up a handful of leaves to use as a sponge; stones are sometimes used to help break up food. This level of toolmaking and use is really only an extension of the cleverness of food acquisition seen in the big-brained and stereoscopically sighted primates from way back. Tools at the chimp level are made without any specialized techniques: pulling leaves off a twig is just like pulling off leaves to eat. Young chimps, moreover, are slow to learn from their elders in tool-using groups. Even after tediously repeated demonstrations, experimenters have been unable to teach chimpanzees to use an Acheulian hand-axe to make their twig tools. The concept of using a tool to make a tool, with all its connotations of foresight and prefiguring in the mind's eye, is evidently beyond the chimpanzees. They cannot be induced to make even the simplest sort of Oldowan pebble tool, though they have been interested in smashing off flakes that resemble the very earliest pre-Oldowan 'tools' that have ever been identified in the archaeological record. (Gorillas, incidentally, do not use tools at all, nor do the pygmy chimpanzees.)

Attempts have been made to teach chimpanzees the use of language by signing according to systems employed by the deaf and dumb, and more recently with special computer keyboards. They are not physically capable of the vocal production of language, any more presumably than our common ancestor with them of six or so million years ago can have been. But they can learn to interpret and use for themselves some of the signs taught to them by their human teachers. These are mostly, if not exclusively, signs for concrete things or actions and everyone recognizes their quite impressive feats with these signs. Contention arises where some workers have claimed a degree of concept-building on the part of chimps using signs; a famous example involved the signing for 'water' plus 'bird' when a particular chimpanzee encountered a duck, but most researchers have concluded that even this extent of conceptualization is not proven by the evidence and that syntax, the complex arrangement of words into abstract relationships in the mind, is beyond the chimpanzees. Their use of language is really restricted to demands with very little in the way of comment on the world about them, vastly inferior to the language skills of a human three-year-old. And no ape infant has ever learned signing from a parent capable of it. In the wild chimpanzees merely produce sounds (growls, screams, barks) to communicate a very limited range of moods and wants and warnings, in association with grimaces and posturings. It is even suggested that a different part of the brain is employed to control these sounds from the parts employed by humans to generate vocalization.

Chimpanzee society is based on the females' relationship with their infants. Females tend to forage for themselves and their young offspring, taking plant food and insects. Males roam between the females of their group, looking for sexual opportunities as they arise and warding off rivals as far as they can. On the whole they undertake the hunting of animal prey, though females do sometimes join in that activity, which certainly shows a degree of cooperation at times, with some meat sharing as a result. Chimps do not scavenge dead animals or take over the kills of other predators.

It is in the area of social relations (and strategies) within the group that chimpanzees perhaps reveal their most human-like traits, however unflattering these traits may be at first glance to our time-honoured picture of ourselves at our best. Quite simply, chimpanzees deceive one another and this gift for deception, and being on the look-out for it, represents a colossal advance on the achievements of the lower primates and all the rest of creation, save for mankind where the practice has been brought to new heights. The advance is in the sphere of mental capacity, the imaginative ability to run through behavioural stratagems 'in the mind's eye' and conjecture about their consequences for one's advantage. Chimpanzees feign intentions that they do not intend to carry through, they pretend not to be about to do things that they mean to do. In these ways they cheat each other out of food and sex – if they can get away with it, for their alertness to possibilities of cheating matches their penchant for doing it. Chimpanzee society is a field of shifting alliances for power, sex and food, facilitated by deception and guile. The chimpanzee mind seems better equipped to deal with this aspect of their lives than any other, though by the standards of most animals they are no mean performers all round. But it is into navigating their way through their social relations that the bigger part of their cleverness is invested. It is as though they make their rudimentary tools and acquire their food in the natural world about them on automatic pilot while their best mental efforts are put into dealing with one another. To get advantage for oneself in the social context calls for a certain self-consciousness about one's own desires and possibilities together with an imaginative insight into the potential wants and talents of one's fellows. Consciousness and imagination (and bigger brains to operate them) look like the products of natural selection in circumstances favouring their development among competing apes in a particular ecological adaptation. Of course, all this begs the question as to what life actually feels like to the chimpanzees, and what quantity and quality of consciousness they experience, but then not one of us has any real idea of what life feels like to our fellow human beings, even those nearest to us. Some researchers believe that consciousness is doomed to remain forever incomprehensible to itself; all we can do (though it is quite a lot, in fact) is to track its adaptive benefits, as it emerged, to our close relatives like the chimps and our evolving ancestors. Chimpanzee 'consciousness' (we put it into inverted commas to mark recognition of its inevitable difference from our own) would appear to be largely restricted to the world of social relations, without much application to the natural world or to food acquisition or tool use or sex and reproduction as such. With the chimps, no imagination has been brought to bear on a deeper knowledge of nature, to exploit it more fully, or on tool production to increase hunting and food processing skills – no imaginative powers seem to be available to chimps to focus on these matters even when they are repeatedly nudged by example to develop them. It is as though their mental capacity is severely compartmentalized with many departments flying on autopilot and only their social dealings open to introspection and experimentation. All the same, their minds clearly exceed those of monkeys, even the social baboons, in their complexity and flexibility; chimps (and gorillas) can recognize themselves in a mirror in a way that monkeys cannot and monkeys plainly lack any sense of themselves or of other monkey selves. Chimps do 'know' quite a lot about their world and are even able to make tools to work on it (a trait once thought to be the hallmark only of humanity) but they are unable to handle their

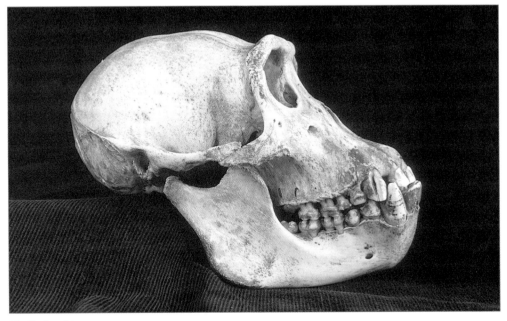

Skull of a chimpanzee.

The Lothagam mandible fragment.

knowledge creatively; they do not appear to know that they know and they have not tumbled to what can be made of knowledge. Still, they have come far enough along a parallel road with ours to deceive each other to the manner born and even to make war on their own kind in other groups, killing males and taking over females and territory – something in chimpanzee life which shocked human researchers when they first encountered it. And they have done this in an environment rather different from that of our ancestors, whose success can now be seen to have ultimately depended on the extension to all departments of the mind of the sort of mental capacities that are seen in only rudimentary and restricted form among the chimpanzees. It is interesting to learn from psychological tests on human subjects that we ourselves maintain an enhanced mental acuity where problems with a dimension of social cheating and cheat-detection are concerned – conundrums that require alertness to social advantage and disadvantage are solved more frequently and quickly than neutral puzzles. And, of course, cheating and social jockeying have not to be seen as the finest achievements of human mental evolution; it is simply, but very importantly, that increased awareness and inventiveness in these directions appear to have been the motors of all-round mental development. Altruism, impulses like mother love for example, go back a long way in ape and human evolution (chimpanzee mothers have been known to carry around dead infants for days) but such behaviour comes rather easily to creatures evolved to have such impulses, while it requires real agility of mind to fool your fellows. Increased mental agility brings evolutionary advantages to its owners, and in the right circumstances natural selection favours the development of more and more of it, and its ultimate extension beyond the purely social realm into all aspects of survival. When the only moderately clever apes retreated under the impact of aridification after about 10 mya, the cleverer hominids prospered.

Some seven million years ago our ancestors must have resembled a sort of unspecialized chimpanzee, quadrupedal but without the very long arms and knuckle-walking that the chimps and gorillas would go on to evolve, still mainly arboreal but not too evolved in the direction of the living apes to be incapable of adaptation to bipedal locomotion on more open ground: a big-brained, probably black-coated, fruit and insect eating (and maybe already tool-using if not toolmaking) forest dweller that soon diverged into the chimpanzee line and the line of early hominids.

The very earliest hint of what could at least be a genuine hominid comes from Kenya at a date between 6 and 5 mya. The Lothagam mandible is too fragmentary to say for sure that it belonged to an early hominid, but it is at just the time range of this specimen that we can expect to find the first signs of hominid existence (and, indeed, a

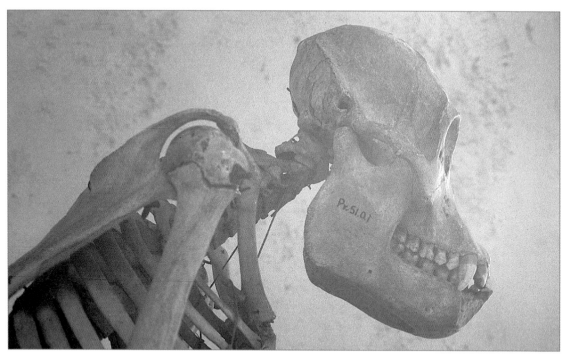

An ape's skull needs strong musculature to support it on its inclined spine.

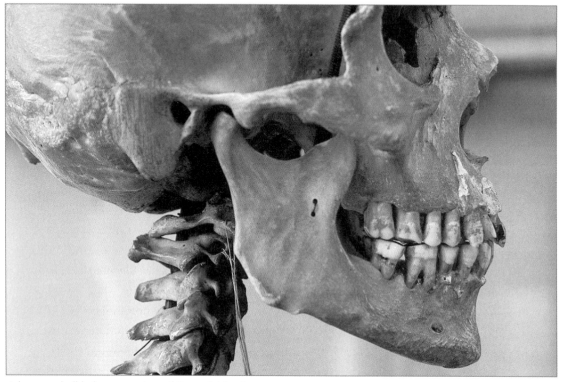

A human skull balances on top of its upright spine.

new find from this age range has recently been reported from the Awash Valley region of Ethiopia). From a time about a million years later comes something more suggestively hominid in the shape of the remains of *Ardipithecus ramidus* from Ethiopia. The finds, from several individuals (and new ones continue to be made), include teeth and jaw pieces, some arm parts and part of a skull which shows the hole, the foramen magnum, through which the nerves pass to the spinal column on which the skull sits. Unlike the conformation seen in the apes, the hole is well forward under the skull in a manner which suggests the evolution of upright walking: bipedalism. Apes carry their heads thrust forward, with strong musculature to hold them from hanging on their chests, in keeping with their quadrupedal locomotion; human beings have their heads balanced on top of their spines, thanks to their upright bipedalism, with less need of musculature to keep them up. *Ardipithecus* at about 4.4 mya thus offers a muted indication of the development of bipedal posture and may tentatively be seen as a just incipiently hominid creature living only a short time after the divergence of chimp and human lines. The area where the jaw articulates with the skull is very ape-like in *Ardipithecus* and the molars and premolars are small but the canine teeth are more hominid in form. Associated floral and faunal remains indicate that *Ardipithecus* lived in a more wooded environment than was to come in East Africa as the drying associated with the cooling climate of the ice ages progressed.

Australopithecus anamensis from Kenya takes on the hominid line in a period between 4.2 and 3.9 mya. Finds include teeth as well as jaw, tibia and humerus pieces from nine individuals. The jaw arcade is more like those of apes than of men but the leg parts display evidence for bipedalism. The world of *A. anamensis* was still one of woodland, with some bush, and the teeth indicate a vegetarian form of subsistence. But climatic changes, with the general aridification of the times perhaps exacerbated by mountain building in Kenya and Ethiopia, began to see a growing isolation of the early hominids of East Africa in a drier and less wooded world that was not suited to the lifestyle of their still close relatives the ancestors of the chimps and gorillas, who carried on their lives in the slowly shrinking humid forests further west. In East Africa the grasslands spread at the expense of the wooded areas and we know from the fossil record that faunal evolution produced elephants and rhinos, for example, with teeth better suited to chewing and grazing than before. *A. anamensis* appears to have given way to *A. afarensis* after 4 mya, a species whose most famous representative is known to the world as Lucy, dating to about 3.2 mya.

Australopithecus afarensis is known from enough individuals of both sexes, with some fairly complete specimens like Lucy, to make feasible, for the first time in hominid evolution, a rather full account of the physical attributes and lifestyle of the type. There was clear dimorphism between the sexes (and Lucy may yet prove to have been a male). At Hadar in Ethiopia the remains of at least thirteen individuals were found having

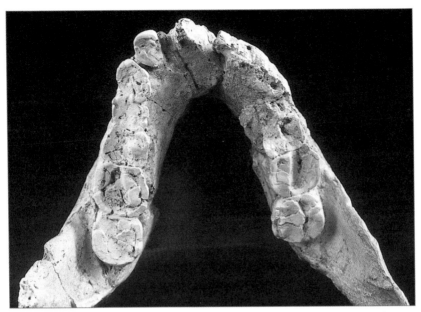

An Australopithecine dental arcade, not as parabolically open as humans' are, with large molars but reduced canines.

evidently perished all together, perhaps in a flash flood; there were nine adults and four juveniles, allowing identification of sexual differences. Males were much taller than females, at about 1.5 m vs. 1 m, and very much heavier at an estimated 65 kg vs. 30 kg. This degree of dimorphism outdoes that seen among the chimps today and resembles the situation of the harem-keeping gorillas, though it may point more to a protective and defensive role in the open grasslands for the males than to a situation of sexual rivalry between the males. Brain size, at between 350 and 500 ml, was in the ape range (but big for body size), in skulls with sloping foreheads and projecting muzzles. But the canine teeth were smaller than those of apes and now the molars were bigger, presumably for chewing harder foods than fruit, like nuts and seeds. Lucy's short legs and long arms, with rather curving hands, hark back to the generalized ape ancestry of the hominid line, pointing to a way of life not just recently but still in some part arboreal (for example, as far as sleeping arrangements were concerned), but the shorter and broader blades of the pelvis are much more human in their bipedal implications, as are details of femurs, knees and feet, though the walking gait was probably somewhat different from that of subsequent hominids of the genus *Homo*. The mixed ape-like and human-like traits of *afarensis* leave no room for doubt that these early hominids were descended from some common ancestor of the apes and men. But it was the hominid branch that was to thrive while the pongid line went into slow retreat.

CHAPTER 10

The Human Line

Australopithecus afarensis enjoyed a long career in East Africa, down to about 3 mya, but left behind no tools that we can identify. It seems very likely that *afarensis* was at least as handy in the tool-using and toolmaking line as are chimps today; indeed the bipedal posture in freeing the hands from locomotion (except during sojourns in the trees) must have facilitated tool use, so probably the tools in question (such as they were) were made of perishable materials. Be that as it may, it is certain that bipedalism constituted a great step towards the evolution of humanity. Many suggestions have been made to try to explain the coming about of bipedal posture and locomotion. People have pointed out that it reduces the amount of skin area presented to the heating and potentially damaging direct rays of the sun (on the assumption that the presumed thicker pelts of our ape ancestors were shed to promote sweating as an aid to heat loss on the savanna); at the same time, it brings the head up away from the heat-radiating earth and into the cool breezes above ground level. Bipedalism may initially have recommended itself as a means to scamper from one patch of woodland to another as quickly as possible as these familiar places of shelter shrank on the encroaching savanna (and it may have come rather naturally to a creature used to hanging upright from branches). It was an advantage, too, for the Australopithecines to be able to stand up and look over the grasses of their aridifying world for enemies and prey. All these explanations very plausibly relate bipedalism to the ecological changes which saw woodland giving way to grassland during the several millions of years of hominid evolution away from the apes. It was hotter out in the open in the direct light of the sun, with less in the way of shelter and protection not only from the sun's rays but from enemies in the animal world; and life in the open needed more heat-generating activity at times, to escape enemies and, maybe, run down prey of one's own as diet turned from the purely vegetarian to elements of meat eating. Standing up and walking freed the hands to carry stones and throw them when danger or opportunity arose. The hands were free, moreover, to evolve into ever better manipulative agents under the pressure of natural selection and thus to work in with ever improving mental performance by bigger brains. Bipedalism may also be seen to have altered the visual appearance that

Australopithecine footprints from Laetoli.

evolving hominids regularly presented to each other, especially perhaps where sexual relations were concerned. The big penises and full breasts of the human line may have evolved in concert with bipedalism, helping ultimately to promote more monogamous relationships between food-sharing males and females with concealed ovulation, with less of the indiscriminate mating of most other primates (including the chimpanzees) who can never track paternity and develop family units. With more in the way of full frontal encounters of every kind, bipedalism must in general have enhanced the subtlety of all social encounters, calling for even more agility of mind to negotiate the social scene and perhaps thereby extending the range of facial and vocal signals that underlie the development of language. At all events bipedalism marks the turning point at which hominids and pongids decisively parted company.

The very footprints of *afarensis* have wonderfully come down to us at an East African site called Laetoli (where *afarensis* remains have been found), from 3.6 mya. Among many animal tracks and even raindrop marks preserved in volcanic ash that, after wetting, hardened in the sun and was subsequently buried under more

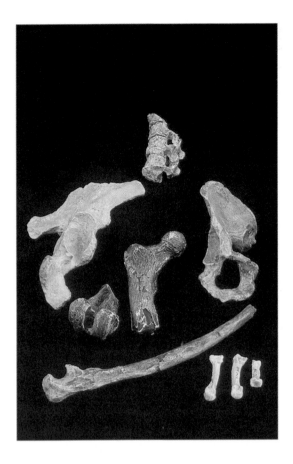

Australopithecine spinal, pelvic and limb bones.

protective layers of ash, there runs a 27 m line of hominid footprints, seventy or so in all. Here two Australopithecine individuals, perhaps a male and female or an adult and child, walked from south to north one day some 1.3 billion days ago, turning halfway along for a moment to look to the west. (A third individual seems to have walked in the steps of the larger of the original pair!) The impressions reveal that their big toes were in line like ours, and not opposable like apes', and that their feet came down with a good heel strike in the way we would expect of accomplished walkers. We recall that the bipedalism of the Australopithecines had already been established just after the Second World War – at the South African site of Sterkfontein, where pelvis, femur and vertebrae revealed it in 1947.

Australopithecines of various related sorts were possibly quite widespread in the unforested parts of Africa of their time (a find has been reported from Chad), but they have overwhelmingly been dug up as fossils in East and South Africa. A very early form of Australopithecine has recently been discovered in South Africa, dating to between 3.6 and 3.2 mya. This new find represents the most skeletally complete Australopithecine discovered to date and its foot bones confirm its bipedal status,

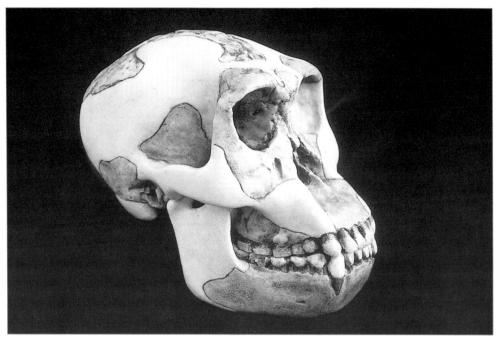

Reconstructed skull of a gracile Australopithecine.

though some features have been interpreted as indicating a certain extent of tree-living too, and it may be that South Africa was not at this time as unwooded as East Africa. The slightly later species called *Australopithecus africanus* is already well known from South Africa and looks in some ways like an evolutionary advance on *afarensis* (in the direction of humanity, at least). *Africanus* shows less sexual dimorphism, has still smaller canines and bigger molars with a slightly flatter face and higher, less heavily browed forehead. Australopithecines like *africanus* were probably living more in the open, with fewer arboreal episodes, than their predecessors, perhaps rather like baboon troops today. The diminished sexual dimorphism may well point to the beginnings of a more human sort of society with many males and many females in the group, organized into hierarchies rather more like baboons' than chimps'.

In both East and South Africa the relatively lightly skulled Australopithecines of the *afarensis* and *africanus* types and their descendants were joined after about 2.5 mya, when things were getting drier still in keeping with the glaciation of northern climes, by other forms with much more robustly turned out skulls. These robust Australopithecines had thick jaws with big back teeth that it is very tempting to link with a diet of chewing hardy vegetable matter in the increasingly arid world they inhabited. Their brains and bodies were not much bigger than those of the gracile forms, however. They were a long-lasting line of specialized hominids, so distinct in

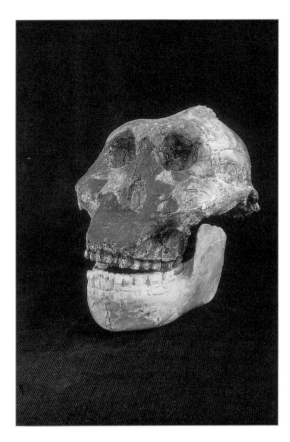

A robust Australopithecine with keeled skull top and massive jaw.

character in both South and East Africa (though showing different species in the two regions) that some anthropologists want to revive the old genus name *Paranthropus* for some of them to mark their particular evolution into something well off the general line of hominid descent from *Australopithecus* to *Homo*. But the evolutionary relationships of the various sorts of gracile and robust Australopithecines of Africa make a tangled web, with the distinct possibility that evolutionary convergence brought about the robust forms quite independently in different places out of different gracile species. We may note at this point the suggestion that has recently been made that a robust Australopithecine might be the ancestor of the gorillas of today, even that a gracile one might have evolved into the chimpanzees; intriguing as this idea might be, it seems unlikely if only because the modern chimps and gorillas are so anatomically non-bipedal when more in the way of bipedalism would be of quite frequent use to them, and it is hard to see them as creatures evolved from previously well and truly bipedal ancestors. At all events, chimps, gorillas and men are alike descended from some pongid, that is to say ape, ancestry. No Australopithecine remains of any sort have ever been discovered out of Africa.

It was to be the gracile sort of Australopithecines that gave rise to the genus *Homo*; despite their unmistakably ape ancestry (including their long arms), none the less their enlarged brains relative to their body size (particularly in the cortical parts of the brain) and their bipedalism point equally unmistakably towards humanity. Sometime after 2.5 mya the gracile Australopithecines disappear from the fossil record, while the robusts continue on, down in fact to about 1 mya or even later. There is something of a fossil gap between the gracile Australopithecines (especially the East African ones) and the first representatives of the genus *Homo* at before 2 mya, but when that genus first appears in the shape of *Homo habilis*, the fossils in question so thoroughly hark back to *Australopithecus afarensis* in some respects that it is clear that evolution had been going on smoothly in the interval and it might be quite hard to assign definitively some fossil material to, say, *Australopithecus afarensis* or early *Homo habilis*. Some *habilis* specimens exhibit, for example, the rather long-armed character of *afarensis*. But the brain size of *habilis* was significantly greater than that of any Australopithecines: absolutely top size for them was about 600 ml whereas *habilis* ranges from about 650 ml to 750 ml or so. Teeth were more human in form than Australopithecine teeth, faces were flatter, skull bones thinner, foreheads higher. The oldest of the fossils of early *Homo* comes from Hadar in Ethiopia: a maxilla showing a more parabolic dental arcade than that of the Australopithecines (i.e. further away from the squarish shape of ape jaws), with less of their prognathism of the muzzle. The *Homo* maxilla from Hadar has been dated to about 2.3 mya. Significantly the geological horizon in which it was found also contains, in the same fresh condition, Oldowan tools; this is the oldest known association of hominid fossil material with tools, though a new find of a rather long-legged Australopithecine from Ethiopia, at about 2.5 mya, is reported to be associated with evidence of animal butchery.

Toolmaking to some recognizable pattern in stone certainly goes back beyond 2.3 mya. We recall that tools have never been found in association with the gracile Australopithecines – there is a little more to say about tools and robust Australopithecines – and it seems likely that the innovation of stone toolmaking belongs to early *Homo* in the form of something like *H. habilis*. The oldest tools, flakes smashed off pebbles found in the region of the Omo river in Ethiopia, date back to about 3 mya, which is the likely date for the beginning of the evolution of *Homo* out of *Australopithecus* (though representatives of both gracile and, later, robust Australopithecine species continued on in parts of Africa). The ongoing process of aridification through the millennia would have contributed to the development of toolmaking. Bipedalism, which perhaps first arose to get back from the savanna to the woods as quickly as possible, became the established posture of *Australopithecus* and even more so of *Homo* as the grasslands spread, releasing the hands from all arboreal preoccupations and promoting their use for throwing, carrying and tool-wielding

An Oldowan pebble tool.

purposes. In the dry savanna landscape it was by ponds and lakes and along the beds of streams that the hominids lingered, where pebbles for toolmaking purposes were easily to be found – and potential game came to water alongside the early humans. Ground-living, toolmaking and meat eating are the trinity of habits that made humanity.

By the time of the Hadar *Homo* maxilla, the simple pebble-smashing of the Omo tool types had evolved into the Oldowan, the first toolmaking tradition of any recognizable distinction. This was the work of creatures with a socially shared habit of making stone tools to a definite pattern. The Oldowan, too, was based on pebbles, to manufacture both knapped flakes and their remanent cores, which served as some kind of general-purpose chopping tool. Finds of broken animal bones in association with these early tools suggest their use on meat-bearing animal parts, whether scavenged or even hunted on a limited scale. Raw material for tools was evidently acquired close to the sites of toolmaking and tool use, but not necessarily immediately to hand, for materials were transported some distances from their sources. The Oldowan tools are crude items and it took a million years for them to turn into anything better but they mark, for all that, another great progression in human evolution. We have seen that chimpanzees, the toolmaking non-human primates, make only the most minimally modified of tools, by means like chewing and tearing of twigs that barely exceed the natural procedures of fruit peeling and eating. Their only use for stone is as unshaped hammers and anvils for opening up difficult foods. They can scarcely be induced to produce anything like the knapped stone tools that we see even in the Omo material, let alone the Oldowan. The making of such tools is a concept beyond them.

Indeed, toolmaking in stone can fairly be called the first concept ever entertained by evolving humanity. To take a pebble and permanently modify it according to some pattern 'in the mind's eye' is to first isolate it out of the general run of the world's phenomena, and then transform it, in a way that preserves the evidence of the human agency of that transformation, into a long-lasting product with prospects of future use built into it. Present action results in a product with a past and a future; there is a sort of grammar in the hierarchy of operations and uses that go into making, through various steps of flaking to a socially shared pattern, and then employing the finished tool. Only the clever brain of a primate, whose line stretched back through millions of years of stereoscopically sighted and socially honed ancestry, could be in a position to undertake the revolutionary step of stone toolmaking. It may be that life in the grasslands enhanced the brain's capacity to process the stereoscopically derived information in fine detail that came into it in abundance; it may be that social life in the open in multi-male/multi-female hierarchical groups further quickened the wits of the evolving *Homo*. It is certainly true that brain development, leaving the apes far behind, got under way with the Australopithecines and greatly accelerated with *Homo habilis*. It is in the neocortex of the brain that the spectacular developments of human cranial capacity have occurred: the neocortex where processing of sensory data is conducted without necessary reference back into the older, limbic and purely instinctive regions of the brain.

The 'grammar' that we can see in the processes of toolmaking and tool use, with their insinuations of tense and mood (making a tool now, according to a necessary sequence of steps to a standardized pattern derived from the past, for potential use in the future) raises the question of language development among the earliest species of *Homo*. The chimps, as we have seen, cannot produce the necessary sounds for language and can only learn the most rudimentary use of human sign language, with no proven grammar to it at all beyond the imperative ('Gimme!'). The distribution of the various parts of the vocal tract needed to assume a far more human character than the chimps display before the physiological capacity for language sounds could arise. Bipedalism with its balancing of the head on the top of the spinal column and allowance for the pulling-in, under the skull, of the jaw initiated the required alteration to the vocal tract and later representatives of the genus *Homo* do start to show a more human configuration of the vocal tract, which suggests the use of language at some level – unfortunately no *habilis* remains include the parts that would throw light on the positioning of the larynx in this species. But *habilis* brains (and even those of the Australopithecines) display the markedly lopsided character that is associated in us with handedness and most of the Oldowan tools appear to be the work of right-handed makers – handedness is present to a much less marked degree in the apes and the cortical areas associated with it are also identified with speech production and reception in modern human beings. Handedness may be a brain development associated with toolmaking that played in with the evolution of language use. Going by the crudity and extreme slowness of evolution of the toolmaking of the early species of *Homo*, we can safely conclude that language, too, though probably primitively present among these remote ancestors of ours, was correspondingly crude in its utterance and in its range of expression and very, very slow to evolve. The probability of its presence is buttressed by its likely conceptual relationship to toolmaking and by its adaptive usefulness to tool-using, socially organized creatures like *Homo habilis*. Just as human babies before they learn to talk are given to a stream of burbling that resembles speech in rhythm without having any words, so it is possible that language use evolved in our ancestors out of a stream of mood-communicating vocalization (of which they had become physiologically capable) that first supplemented, then stood in for and finally superseded the mutual grooming habits that are seen today to ease social relations among chimpanzees. Much of what passes between ourselves by way of chatting is scarcely more than mutual grooming to this day. Such vocalization would have evolved into a primitive language for use in social exchanges. Language may have been pregnant with possibilities for mind expansion into abstract thought in directions that we shall discuss later on, but in its initial manifestations it is likely to have been very limited in scope and chiefly employed in the social sphere, in line with the special character of primate, hominid and human cleverness which excels in social awareness and manoeuvring. Any use in more objective contexts, as with toolmaking, may well have been a rather unconscious affair; tools would have been made, and remarks about the natural world passed, in automatic mode, as it were, without being brought into the sphere of social consciousness. (Of course, all the caveats as to what we mean by consciousness continue to apply.) Early language can have had little or no symbolic content, one of its chief glories among its best practitioners today; indeed, symbolism of every sort is conspicuously lacking in the archaeological record until the arrival of the modern form of humanity. From an Australopithecine site in South Africa there has come a small water-worn ironstone pebble whose natural face-like appearance seems to have been appreciated enough to cause it to be carried at least 30 km home from its source as long as 3 mya. But it is an utterly stray find on which nothing can be built against a desert of signally lacking evidence of any sort of art or symbol over millions of years. Incipient language is likely to have been a very concrete, as well as socially orientated, affair.

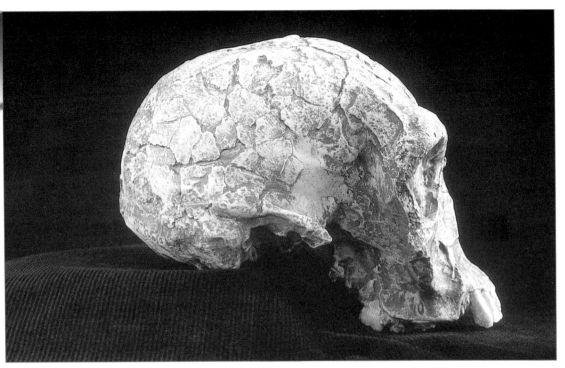

Homo habilis.

Stereoscopic vision had already equipped the brains of our remote primate ancestors with a capacity for highly detailed analysis of the material (non-social) world about them, allowing them to isolate parts of it (like food) that concerned them with great precision and thus laying the basis for a mental categorization of experience into related but discrete parts that simpler creatures just cannot achieve. Toolmaking, in taking hold of such discrete components of the world as pebbles and endowing them as tools with new features related to the habits and intentions of their makers, extended the categorization of the world into a new mental area; in place of the lower animals' instinctive interaction with the world outside itself, with little or no awareness of self *vis-à-vis* the wide world, there was now an intermediary zone of things that were neither mere natural details of the external realm nor parts of oneself, but rather features of the wide world given human significance through human action upon them. With the progress of language, words of standardized meaning arranged in complex sentences were to fulfil a similar role, but inside the mind, as intermediaries between the self and the world outside the self, making it possible to construct and experiment with whole microcosms in our imaginations that model the world in which we live, first perhaps the all-important social world in particular and eventually everything that we can know.

The life of *Homo habilis* was still a simple one, with no unambiguous evidence of home bases with any sort of built structures or the use of fire. Much food no doubt came as ever in the form of vegetable matter but it seems clear that *habilis* was extending the business of procuring and processing meat beyond anything seen among today's chimps or the Australopithecines. In the nature of things, it is difficult to know whether just scavenging or some resort to hunting accounts for the collection of meat-bearing animal bones (of pigs, antelope, horses, even elephant, hippo and rhino, and some carnivores) found in association with Oldowan tools. It certainly looks as though cuts of meat on the bone were being brought away from kill-sites to be cut up and consumed by *habilis* groups, but whether *habilis* or predatory animals were doing the initial killing is not so clear; the occurrence of lower limb bones and skulls, typically left over by carnivores, suggests that *habilis* scavenging was more to the fore than hunting, especially where larger prey was concerned. Cut marks on the bones do establish that the Oldowan tool kit was being used to process the meat, but the marks of carnivore teeth indicate that at some stage, either before or after *habilis* got at them, the bones also received the attentions of predatory animals. If *habilis* was scavenging after carnivore kills, he was at least a top scavenger on the strength of the animal bones he left among his tool debris and the marks he made on those bones. The situation was probably very like the savanna scene today, with clusters of bones building up in the shade of trees where various carnivores from time to time consume meat they acquire by hunting or scavenging – only in those remote times, *habilis* was one of the hunters or scavengers (on rather a grand scale, it seems at Olduvai) and he perhaps kept his tools handy on the spot to help deal with any meat that came his way. Sharp-edged flakes would have served to cut up meat and the heavier core tools would have facilitated the breaking of bones for marrow. Meat eating provided more energy more readily and economically than a vegetarian diet could ever do and it has been ingeniously proposed that it went hand in hand with brain enlargement; to preserve the metabolic balance overall, as the energy-demanding brain expanded with evolution, the gut could be usefully reduced in size through the eating of energy-rich meat. On this proposal, meat eating was the *sine qua non* of brain development, upon which natural selection set such a premium for the sake of cleverness in social behaviour and resourcefulness in survival and reproduction.

The complex interaction of brain development, ground-living, bipedalism, toolmaking, meat eating, social and sexual relationships, all at the mercy of natural selection, cannot be underestimated as the motor of anthropogenesis, the process of becoming human. Once a formerly arboreal and largely vegetarian line of ex-apes embarked on a bipedal, open living, group structured, toolmaking and meat eating way of life, there was no going back on cleverness unless it be to extinction. Even scavenging from carnivore rivals, to say nothing of hunting, required organization and social skills to a high degree and reliance on animal food, however acquired, called for cleverness well beyond that required for a steady diet of vegetation; meat could only be had from mobile, changeable, tricky and frequently dangerous sources, in competition with creatures fiercer and in some ways more cunning than early *Homo* himself. (Predator animals tend in general to be bigger-brained than prey animals.) Getting meat demanded powers of observation and interpretation, together with memory and communication of information, and socially coordinated action, that had not been seen in the hominid world before. *Habilis* and his descendants simply had to be clever to survive and prosper, and enlargement of the neocortical part of the brain was the mechanism to afford that cleverness, extending mental acuity forged in the social context to more and more aspects of life. The ratio of neocortex to total brain size among the primates goes roughly hand in hand with group size; cleverer primates can successfully associate in larger social groupings and it has been estimated that a *habilis* individual might have had social knowledge of up to about eighty other individuals in his band. Larger bands meant greater security in numbers and greater scope for organized food procurement. It may be that the beginnings of a sort of family life were made during the *habilis* era, with males cooperating in the search for meat, some at least of which they shared with females and offspring back at whatever in the way of 'home' they could be said to have had. Bipedalism would have made it easier for the hunters or scavengers to forage quite widely in their environment and raw meat makes a package of food energy that is easy to transport back 'home' at the end of the foraging day, along with tools or the raw material for making them.

Among modern foraging (hunter/gatherer) peoples, meat is eaten in as great a quantity as it can be got and is the very stuff of food sharing, both with fellows in the foraging group and with wives and children back at base. It has to be shared by presently successful hunters with the less successful for the moment, against the day when fortunes are reversed. At home, meat succours the women and children whose plant foraging is necessarily limited by the rest of the demands of life upon them; meat sharing promotes more or less monogamous relations and family life. If such distinctively human arrangements as these were beginning to evolve in *habilis* groups, then it may equally well be that the human phenomenon of long postnatal maturation of the young was initiated, if only faintly at first, at about the same time, with its drawn-out period of maternal care and its slow but extensive growth of the brain after birth. Postnatal brain growth is closely related to human infants' capacity to learn so much and go on learning. We have seen that, even as late on as Neanderthal times (one-and-a-half million years later than the last of *habilis*), the evidence of infants' fossils indicates a rapider maturation than is seen with the children of *Homo sapiens sapiens*, but for all that the big-brained Neanderthalers were born with large heads like ourselves through birth canals big enough to accommodate them. Australopithecine

Homo habilis (right) with '1470', which may represent another related but more evolved species.

pelvic arrangements, on the other hand, though adapted for bipedalism, were more ape-like in respect of birth canal dimensions and Australopithecine infants were not big-brained at birth, nor destined to go on to be very much bigger-brained than chimpanzees when they grew up. The small Australopithecine child from Taung in South Africa was only, according to details of the teeth, about three years old but already displayed features suggesting to its discoverers that it was, in modern human terms, some six years old. Somewhere between the Australopithecines and *Homo erectus/ergaster*, presumably in the times of *Homo habilis*, modern patterns of gestation and brain development before and after birth were begun.

The remains assigned to *Homo habilis* exhibit a range of variability that leads some anthropologists to question their being lumped together into one species. There are marked size differences that may be attributable to more than sexual dimorphism. Some exhibit features that foreshadow, more than those of the others, the physical characteristics of the next stage of human evolution, that of *Homo erectus* and *Homo ergaster*, with marked brow-ridges and a more angular shape to the back of the skull, a new prominence to the nose (away from the ape-like flattened formation of earlier hominids), and a face more tucked in under the vault of the skull. The postcranial skeletons of various representatives of *Homo habilis* also vary considerably, with some individuals still displaying the short-legged, long-armed configuration that goes back to the Australopithecines, while others have the longer-legged anatomy of *erectus* and *ergaster*.

Homo habilis fades out of the fossil record at around 1.8 mya, at which time the next stage of human descent is in evidence in Africa, and – according to some evidence – in other parts of the world, too. The robust Australopithecines of Africa did not quit the scene with the departure of *habilis* and the appearance of his successor, but we can practically say 'goodbye' to them too at this point, though they may have persisted in places until as late as 1 mya or even later. They had evolved into an adaptation to a specialized ecological niche on the savanna which saw their ultimate extinction after a long (and therefore successful) career. Whether they ever made stone tools cannot be yet answered with certainty; their remains are sometimes found in association with Oldowan artefacts, as are those of *habilis*, the reliably presumed maker of those tools. The conclusion that the robusts in these circumstances were accidental intruders on the scene or victims of *habilis* is strengthened by the fact that, after the disappearance of *habilis* and, for the most part, the Oldowan culture, the robusts who remained at later dates are not found in further association with Oldowan-type tools.

The later stages of the Oldowan tool tradition show features that prefigure the Acheulian hand-axe cultures of Africa and the wider world. Hand-axes are bifacially worked tools, rather than crudely shaped pebbles with only a few flakes removed from them. The later Oldowan includes bifacially worked pieces on their way to Acheulian axes. Properly bifacial artefacts begin to appear in the African archaeological record at about 1.5 mya. The development of the standardized all-purpose hand-axe tool surely points to the related development of enhanced mental powers among the *habilis* populations transitional to *Homo erectus* or *Homo ergaster*, who appeared at much the same time as the toolmaking changes occurred. We can reasonably infer that the slow progress of language saw significant developments along with the tool improvements and the anatomical changes associated with the evolution of the *erectus/ergaster* species. The more highly patterned nature of hand-axe production, involving more steps in the making and better previsioning of the finished product for general-purpose use, is likely to have been mirrored in a more structured, standardized and extended use of language.

Some anthropologists see among the various representatives around the world of the stage of *Homo* evolution after *habilis* only a single if variable species called, after the species name conceived so long ago by Haeckel and taken up by Dubois in Java after him, *Homo erectus*. Others believe that an African expression of this post-*habilis* stage of human evolution was so significantly different from *erectus* as discovered in Java and China as to merit a species name in its own right – *ergaster*. ('*Erectus*' was meant to draw attention to the full achievement of un-ape-like posture, '*habilis*' to handiness with tools and '*ergaster*' to the capacity for useful labour.) In recognition of the possibility of a real distinction between the African and Asian species, at the same time as noting their essential similarity at a stage of human evolution, we shall sometimes use the slightly awkward formula *erectus/ergaster* (or vice versa) to refer to the fossils that take on the story of human descent from *H. habilis* to *H. sapiens*. (It has to be said that on the same principle, we might as well refer to a very much later stage of human evolution by way of *neanderthalensis/sapiens*.)

It used to be assumed that the transition from *habilis* to *erectus* was effected solely in Africa, to the accompaniment of the development of the Acheulian out of the Oldowan, with a subsequent spread out of Africa by way of the Jordan Valley, which is an extension of the East African Rift Valley. This view retains much force, especially in the light of the continued absence of anything like *habilis* fossils outside of Africa. But with tools, it might be a different story. There are claims for Oldowan type tools (if they are tools at all) in Pakistan back to 2 mya and in China to perhaps 1.8 mya; and early appearances of pebble tools in the Middle East and Europe are not unknown, though none in Europe is proved to reach back as far in time as the last of the Oldowan in Africa. If any Oldowan assemblages outside Africa really do date back as far as the Pakistan material is claimed to do, then the possibility arises that despite the absence of fossils, *habilis* or *habilis*-like creatures (though probably already evolving towards *erectus*) were at large in Asia, for example, at a time predating the evolution of *ergaster/erectus* in Africa as we know it from the fossil record there. On this view, the case for a real distinction between Asian *erectus* and African *ergaster* is strengthened, with separate but convergent evolution in the two areas leading, perhaps with some long-distance genetic interchange via neighbouring groups strung out along the way, to the evolution of *erectus* and *ergaster* as convergently similar but specifically different versions of *Homo* at much the same stage of human physical evolution. Controversial dates for new *Homo erectus* finds in Java at 1.8–1.6 mya and for an *erectus* tooth in China at 1.9 mya certainly seem at odds with the idea of *ergaster/erectus* origins solely in Africa, unless those origins extend somewhat further back into the past than presently available fossils indicate. Some anthropologists think that *ergaster* must have evolved in Africa (out of one of the *habilis* types) at an earlier date than the fossil record so far demonstrates, and that East Asian *erectus* is descended from this early African *ergaster*. At Dmanisi in Georgia, in association with a tool assemblage described as Oldowan, a jaw fragment was discovered dating to about 1.8 mya that is claimed to resemble African *ergaster* more than East Asian *erectus*. If the characterization of this fragment is correct and its date holds up, then a very early representative of *Homo ergaster* has been identified well out of Africa. The route taken by evolving humanity out of the continent of its origins is likely to have been through the Jordan Valley continuation of East Africa's Great Rift Valley; both valleys enjoyed similar ecological conditions before the era of the ice ages began. At 'Ubeidiya in Israel a succession of Oldowan levels is topped by a Developed Oldowan that features some crude hand-axes at about 1.4 to 1.2 mya with some very fragmentary skull and teeth remains. Evolving humans, incidentally, were not the only creatures to make the journey out of Africa at this time – lions, leopards and hyenas took the same course.

It is interesting at this point to recall that no Acheulian tradition ever existed in many parts of the Far East, where altogether simpler and less patterned stone tools persist until late palaeolithic times; it is likely that the best part of the tool kit of these easterners was always based on long-term perishable materials like bamboo that have vanished from the archaeological record. Possibly the Acheulian idea never reached the Far East because its inventors and their descendants never went there either. The oldest archaeological material from China, in the form of stone tools, dates to some 1–0.75 mya, well after the African development of the Acheulian, but none of it is Acheulian in China, though finds of hand-axes have been claimed in Mongolia and Korea.

In the absence of any *habilis* and late *habilis* material in the region, there are really no fossils whereby to trace any in situ evolution to *erectus* in Asia, which – while it does not

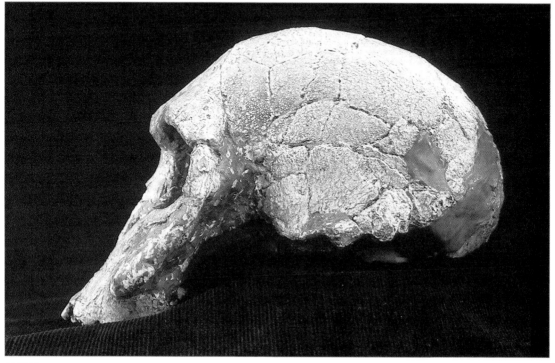

'1470'.

prove that no such evolution took place there – has traditionally strengthened the impression that Asian *erectus* origins are ultimately to be traced back to Africa. It can be argued that some among the African *habilis* specimens we have, like the individual from Koobi Fora known as 1470 and dating to about 1.9 mya, were already on their way to an *ergaster/erectus* character well before the oldest clear-cut *ergaster* specimens we know. In particular, it has been said that brain casts of the large-brained (for the time) 1470 – at about 775 ml, way out of the range of any Australopithecine – show signs of the development of brain areas associated in ourselves with the generation and comprehension of speech. If the projection of these associations back into such representatives of our remote ancestry as 1470 is justified, then speech development is just what we might expect as one of the accomplishments of *habilis* on the way to *ergaster/erectus*. The high neocortical ratio of evolving *habilis* suggests enlarging group size and ever more complicated and demanding social relations, to be negotiated ('groomed') with ever subtler chatter. With speech, you can groom whole gaggles of people at a time, as politicians know so well, and be doing something else at the same time.

We have seen that some of the *habilis* specimens to hand have rather long arms in the tradition of *Australopithecus afarensis* (like Lucy) and smallish brain capacities, but the large-brained 1470 remains lack arm bones to tell us whether this primitive feature persisted among the larger *habilis* types (who may be so different from the others that they should really be assigned to a new species, as some anthropologists now propose). The true *ergaster/erectus* remains from a couple of hundred thousand years or so later on do not display, where the relevant bones are available, the long-armed character of some of the *habilis* specimens. Several skull and jaw fragments of *ergaster/erectus* are known in Africa from about 1.75 mya but the most spectacular remains are those of the Nariokotome Boy of about 1.6 mya, much of whose postcranial skeleton is available for study and whose cranial capacity can, thanks to the state of preservation of his skull, be precisely determined: more than can be said for any other human fossil over 100,000 years old. Though a juvenile whose age is estimated at about eleven years (on the strength of his teeth characteristics), the Nariokotome Boy was already some 1.6 m tall, with a cranial capacity of about 880 ml – assuming a somewhat earlier age of maturation than is seen among modern people (and his skeleton as a whole suggests a fifteen-year-old, though his teeth tell a different tale), we may guess that he would have reached about 1.75 m in height and perhaps 900 ml of brain capacity at full adulthood. The modern human brain is about three times larger than we would expect for primates of our body size, so that – at 900 ml – *Homo erectus* at Nariokotome can be seen as well on the way to the modern ratio of brain to body size, and in fact brain size doubled between about 2.5 mya and 1 mya from something scarcely outside the ape range to a capacity only about one-third less than the brains of people today (and Neanderthalers). This

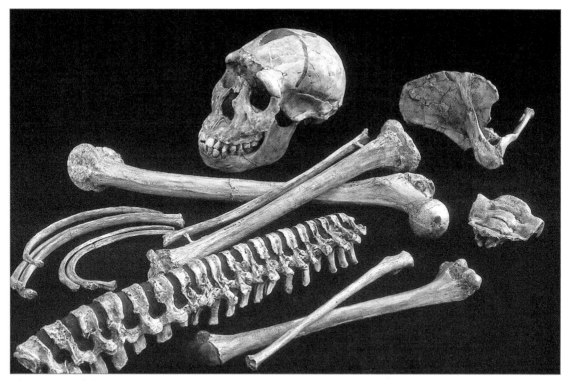

The remains of the 'Nariokotome Boy'.

increase in brain size can be seen as indicative of growing group sizes among the bands of our *ergaster/erectus* ancestors. It is the prefrontal cortex of the brain that has seen the greatest expansion in the course of human evolution, with some relative loss of capacity in brain areas associated with smell, sight and motor control in our monkey relations (who had to be able to leap about in the trees, after all). The areas of gain in evolving brain capacity are those plausibly thought to be associated with speech and conceptual thought. Interestingly, the larynx of *ergaster/erectus* appears to have fallen about midway between the positions seen in the Australopithecines and in modern humans, bolstering the supposition that speech and language were developing, however slowly, along with physical evolution. And another telling respect in which *ergaster/erectus* resembles modern people more than his predecessors resides in the details of the inner ear that have been preserved in some specimens. The modern sort of nasal opening is fully realized with *ergaster/erectus*, too, perhaps to help cool the burgeoning brain.

All of the teeth of *ergaster/erectus* are smaller than those of his ancestors, with the molars particularly reduced in proportion to the incisors and canines. It is likely that much more in the way of meat eating lies behind this development, with a premium on biting and tearing at the front of the mouth rather than (vegetable) chewing at the back. The whole skull architecture of *ergaster/erectus*, and of many of his successors until the appearance of fully modern *Homo sapiens sapiens*, points to the need for hefty and securely anchored musculature to work the front teeth; the heavy brow-ridges, pronounced occipital tori and sagittal crests along the top mid-lines of some skulls attest to the presence in life of this powerful musculature. Teeth were doing a meat-handling job that only the eventual development of much better tools could finally render redundant in wholly modern people.

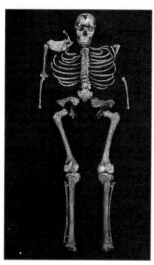

The skeleton from Nariokotome.

Postcranially, the *ergaster/erectus* skeleton as seen at Nariokotome is basically very like that of a modern human being, with a fully evolved bipedal status and limb proportions like our own. (It may be that full bipedalism in itself, with its high requirements for nervous control of balance and motion on two legs, benefited from brain enlargement.) Where he differs from modern youths, it is in details like the longer spines on some of his vertebrae and the constricted aperture of the spinal canal through them, together with the elongated 'neck' leading to the ball of the femur and the narrowness of the pelvis. The constriction of the spinal canal has been held as of some significance for the speech-producing powers of the Nariokotome Boy, limiting as it might the nerve provision for control of the thoracic region in subtle breath production for utterance. At worst, this might only point to an inferior capacity for speech relative to ourselves, not an absence of it. Certainly, the Nariokotome specimen exhibits for the first time in human evolution the barrel-chested configuration in marked contrast to the tapered chest shapes of apes, Australopithecines and *habilis* specimens. All in all, we can say that – provided that the Nariokotome Boy was not some freak of his time who has perversely come down to us as the best preserved of his kind – then *Homo ergaster/erectus* had more or less acquired by 1.6 mya the modern sort of postcranial skeleton and stature that would serve our ancestors from his time to ours.

The *ergaster/erectus* skulls of Africa are really very like those of the *erectus* specimens from Asia in their strong brow-ridges and reduced faces *vis-à-vis Homo habilis*, their low vaults, keeling along their mid-line tops, rounded occipital areas and cranial bases wider than what comes above (in keeping with their small cranial capacities by comparison with ourselves). Like all *erectus* specimens (and all human fossils until the first intimations of really modern types) the jaws are chinless, though the African *ergaster/erectus* examples tend to be smaller than those of Asian *erectus* and the cheek

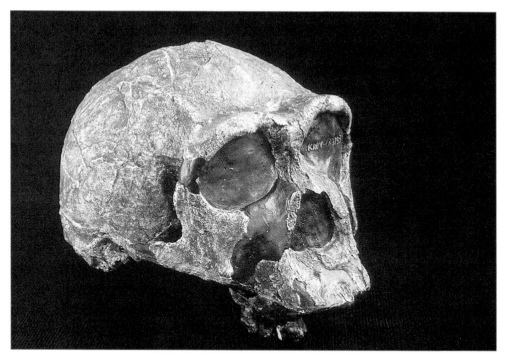

A specimen of *Homo ergaster*.

teeth in particular are small by comparison with those of their Asian counterparts. It is details like these that incline some anthropologists to place them in the species *ergaster* rather than lumping them in with *erectus*, and to discern in them a more direct line to later human types like *Homo heidelbergensis* that we saw in an earlier chapter were likely candidates for the ancestry of the Neanderthalers (and, as we shall also see in due course, of ourselves, too). Some African fossils, be it said, are even more like Asian *erectus* than those dubbed *ergaster* are, and it suffices for our purposes to see in the worldwide phenomenon of *Homo ergaster/erectus* a definite stage of human evolution in which brain size was significantly enlarged over everything that had gone before and the postcranial skeleton achieved more or less its modern form, whatever variability may be identified in detail in different parts of the world.

It was *H. erectus*, or just possibly his immediate ancestors in the form of a version of *H. habilis* with strong *erectus* foreshadowings, that spread over much of the Old World after millions of years of Australopithecine and hominid evolution that had been confined to Africa. The stone tools that *erectus* carried out of Africa into Europe and the Middle East were initially of the simple Oldowan variety but in due course Developed Oldowan and more particularly Acheulian tool kits were largely adopted over most of the inhabited world, with the clear-cut exception of those parts of the Far East like China and Java that never went Acheulian. The Acheulian centred upon

An Acheulian hand-axe.

the making of hand-axes, though the flakes produced in their manufacture were also much used and, in some circumstances, favoured to the exclusion of hand-axes – a process that accelerated into the Tayacian and Mousterian traditions later on. Wood was no doubt in regular use too, and perhaps it furnished the digging sticks of foraging mothers in search of plant food that did as much to keep *erectus* populations alive as the stone axes of hunting and scavenging males did. Even bone, though not recovered to any significant extent in the archaeological record, may have been employed to some degree. Sites like Olduvai in East Africa and Swartkrans in South Africa have yielded bone pieces polished by use to cut meat and perhaps to dig up plants, but bone tools as known from the archaeological record go on to show no distinct typography through hundreds of thousands of years. (Until, that is, a spectacular and, to date, rather isolated instance in Equatorial Africa at going on for 100,000 BP, if the date holds up, long after the career of *erectus* was over, but also long before the appearance of the Upper Palaeolithic worked bone pieces; we shall return to this intriguing evidence in a later chapter.)

Microwear studies of Acheulian material reveal marks consistent with meat cutting, woodworking and the cutting of stemmed plants. As with the ancestors of *Homo erectus*, the gathering of plant food must have remained an important element in subsistence, but *erectus* no doubt ate more meat than his predecessors and animal bones bearing the cut marks of his tools attest to this. Meat eating remained the means by which brain enlargement could be maintained alongside gut reduction in an active and energetic creature, fully bipedal in posture and locomotion. Acheulian tools are found in Africa among the bones of pig, zebra, hippo and elephant; when it came to spreading out of Africa into potentially cooler climes, meat eating very likely became even more important as a convenient way to acquire and transport a much needed source of energy. The relatively large size of the incisors and canines of *erectus* jaws point to their use in biting and tearing meat just as surely as the stone tools indicate butchery.

To what extent *Homo erectus* hunted rather than scavenged and established any sort of home bases rather than simply wandered through his world remain contentious questions. Sites in Africa and in Spain do show instances of Acheulian tools in association with animal bones that carry no signs of carnivore gnawing; in warm environments scavenging holds little appeal for modern foraging peoples, not only because of the high risk of confrontation with the jealous killers of the prey and with other scavenging carnivores, but also because the micro-organisms that feed on carrion have equipped themselves with toxins to deter their bigger competitors. It may be that scavenging, of the sort that many anthropologists believe the Neanderthalers to have practised, was a development suited to more northerly and cooler regions as mankind spread out of Africa and the world's climate took a turn for the colder and more antiseptic.

As the *erectus* type of humanity began to people the globe, travelling out of warm Africa at the same time as the cooler epoch of the ice ages set in, fire became a crucial component of the technological armoury of evolving mankind. There are indications of the first use of fire in East Africa at a very early date in the career of *ergaster/erectus*. At Koobi Fora tools of the Developed Oldowan type (on their way to Acheulian) have been found in association with deposits of baked earth to which a date of about 1.6 mya is assigned; the form of the baking, as soil oxidized in a bowl formation, and the evident high temperatures involved indicate that the fires that baked the earth were more intense than those that result from accidental grassland conflagrations and so were probably deliberately tended by human agency. In another East African instance lumps of burnt clay were found in association with stone tools and animal bones at a date of about 1.5 mya, the largest lumps – in a reportedly hearth-like arrangement of stones – having been heated to an estimated 400–600 °C, beyond the expected range of natural fires. At Swartkrans in South Africa burnt bones (including those of robust Australopithecines) of about 1 mya have been deemed to have suffered temperatures associated with camp fires rather than wild fires. (The robusts' bones would represent the victims of *ergaster/erectus* in this case, while the *ergaster* fragments from the site, with heavy brow-ridges, would represent the fire-users who perhaps ate them.) Whether any means of starting fires were available to these presumed pioneers of the use of fire is not known – it is likely that materials kept alight from grassland fires as a result of lightning strikes were carefully conserved for continued use. And whether the camps that went with the 'camp fires' were worthy of the name of 'home bases' is similarly hard to determine. Evidence for home bases, in the shape of patterns of large stones with empty areas where perhaps wind-breaks or protective walls of thorn bush were piled up, has been proposed even for sites of human occupation predating the appearance of *ergaster/erectus*, but scholarly opinion has been divided about such instances, for natural causes and animal activity could have generated the evidence. Regular use of fire, especially perhaps out of Africa in colder zones where cave shelter became more desirable, increases the likelihood that home bases were a feature of the *erectus* way of life. The fireside provided not only a source of warmth and a deterrence against foes, along with heat to thaw, cook and smoke food, but also light to prolong some of the activities of life (like toolmaking, for example) beyond the time allotted by the natural cycles of the days and seasons; and above all perhaps it promoted social life after the day's labours and social grooming in the form of 'conversation', as we might a bit prematurely call it. 'Home' was also potentially the scene of food sharing, of proto-familial relationships, of care and provision for the young. The long process of maturation seen in human beings today from infancy through adolescence to adulthood was probably not entirely in operation in *erectus* populations (as it probably was not, either, among Neanderthalers), but the pelvis of the Nariokotome Boy strongly argues that *erectus* babies were born in a similar state of development to that of our own, even if the age indications of his teeth versus his general skeletal status point to a noticeably more rapid postnatal development than we know today. *Erectus* firesides may have been centrepieces of home bases in which children matured more slowly, played their educative games and generally went on learning more extensively, both about their social world and the wide world about them, than any non-human animal ever does. It is very interesting to note that, with the arrival of *ergaster/erectus*, there is for the first time in human evolution no question but that sexual dimorphism was markedly reduced, a situation indicating a relative absence of competition between males for females, which further suggests that more or less monogamous pair-bonding may possibly have been a feature of *ergaster/erectus* society, with greater likelihood of investment on the part of both parents in the upbringing of their offspring.

With their sophisticated tools (by comparison with what had gone before), their use of fire, their greater reliance on meat eating in competition with rival predators and scavengers in the animal world, the people of the *erectus* stage of evolution needed not just the intelligence and awareness of their ancestors in the social field, but also a growing technical and environmental application of intelligence to handle the business of toolmaking and tool use, of identifying and going after their food, of outwitting their competitors. From the Australopithecines to *Homo ergaster/erectus*, the size of the brain doubled to some 900 ml and then, in keeping with the slow progress of toolmaking innovation that we see in the archaeological record, brain enlargement rather stalled; evidently the *erectus* brain was good enough to facilitate the spread of its carriers over much of the temperate world beyond Africa. The really cold areas that were to be found in the world as the era of the ice ages came on remained beyond the scope of *Homo erectus*, who probably sallied out of Africa into Europe and Asia via the region of the Levant and its hinterland. The spread to the Far East probably followed the coastal areas adjacent to the Arabian Sea and the Bay of Bengal and then north into China and south to Sumatra and Java. As we saw, if the very early dates for archaeological material and human remains in Java stand the test of time, then it is just possible that a sort of late *Homo habilis* evolving into early *Homo erectus* reached the Far East by 1.8 mya, without its carriers' and their ancestors' participation in the development of the Acheulian, which is not found in China and Java. *Homo erectus* was to enjoy a very long career in the East, lasting until perhaps some 300,000 BP, and among his accomplishments in those parts is apparently to be counted the crossing of seas on at least one occasion by means of rafts, for there is an island in the Java Sea with *erectus* remains which was never connected to the mainland (unlike Java itself) during any fluctuation of sea level during *erectus* times. Some 19 km of open sea needed to be crossed to reach Flores, apparently in about 800,000 BP!

In China *Homo erectus* remains have been found in contexts dated back to about 1 mya (and even half as much again according to some determinations), but the best known of the Chinese *erectus* finds came from the cave site near Beijing (one of the few caves to have lasted from so long ago) that is now called Zhoukoudian. The climatic indicators at the site, taken together with evidence of ancient patterns of the Earth's magnetic polarity, suggest a date going back to some 450,000 BP for *erectus* at Zhoukoudian, which puts Pekin Man into one of the interglacial periods of the ice age era, at a time when the climate was about as cool in northern China as it is nowadays. There is evidence of the use of fire on the site (in the form of thin lenses of ash with concentrations of charred bones and seeds) and stone tools in coarse quartz and quartzite are found in some abundance, but they are of the sort that would be called 'Oldowan' in Africa, where the Acheulian was a million years old by the time of Zhoukoudian. The remains of about forty *erectus* individuals have been discovered at Zhoukoudian, including fragments whose damage hints at cannibalism, but, of course, the original finds from before the Second World War vanished in the 1940s

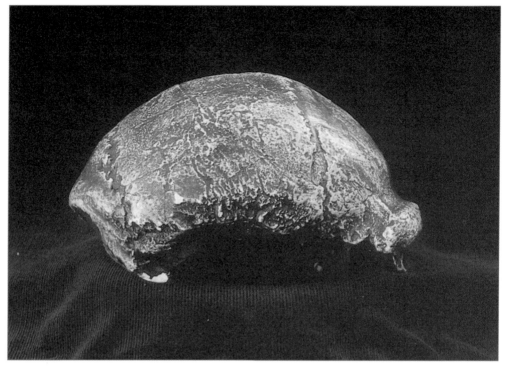

Skullcap from Zhoukoudian.

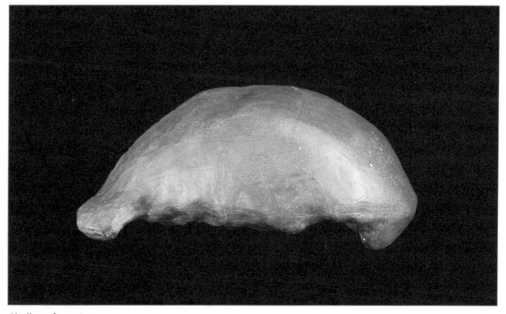

Skullcap from Java.

and are known today only by the excellent casts made by Franz Weidenreich in the years after their discovery. (Weidenreich believed, it is interesting to recall, that Pekin Man already displayed certain proto-Mongoloid traits – among other things in details of cheeks and teeth – that persuaded him that some broad racial differentiations appeared early in the human story and were maintained through the successive stages of evolution driven by gene flow between population borders over long distances and by convergent evolution under the same pressures of natural selection in different parts of the world.) The Zhoukoudian people were big-faced with heavy jaws, but their brow-ridges were a little smaller than those of other *erectus* types. At just over 1000 ml, their average brain sizes are large for an *erectus* population. Their Java contemporaries (later than the fragmentary pieces claimed to date from as far back as 1.8 mya) were more ruggedly made in their skulls and of slightly lower average brain size. In both Java and China the massive build of the skulls with many indications of strong muscle attachments to work the bulky jaws points to a diet dependent on heavy tearing and chewing capacities. No tools are known from the Java sites.

All the East Asian *erectus* skulls are thicker, more brow-ridged and more sloping from brow to skull top than those of their African counterparts, with pronounced keeling along their tops and incidence of occipital torus at the back. Their cheek teeth are larger. Many of them, moreover, are younger than the African examples and the tools associated with them are quite different. If we are justified in making two distinct species out of all these remains, then the East Asian people must retain their long assigned species name *erectus* and the African (and other) finds must own another one – *ergaster*, on the precedent of the name already applied by some anthropologists to the Nariokotome Boy and others. Where *erectus* and *ergaster* differ, it is *ergaster* that foreshadows *Homo sapiens* rather more than *erectus* does, and so it is tempting to see a line of descent from the African *ergaster* populations that leads on to archaic *Homo sapiens* (with *Homo sapiens neanderthalensis* and *Homo sapiens sapiens*) without the *erectus* populations of the East. The situation in which *erectus* went on thriving in the East until about 300,000 BP (in Java certainly and perhaps also in China) while archaic *Homo sapiens* arose and flourished in Africa and Europe is deemed by some anthropologists to mirror the similar situation they believe to have obtained when Neanderthalers enjoyed their heyday in Europe at the same time as fully modern forms of *Homo sapiens* were evolving elsewhere.

Remains, often very fragmentary, of *ergaster/erectus* types have been found in parts of Africa other than the East African homeland of the species where dates run from about 1.8 mya to 560,000 BP; in South Africa *ergaster/erectus* dates from about 1.6 mya down to perhaps 700,000 BP, while in North Africa finds made so far seem to cover a range between about 750,000 and 500,000 BP. By this time, the

Acheulian tradition had appeared in Europe and the story of human evolution we have been telling in this chapter links up here with the ancestry of the Neanderthalers that we reviewed in Chapter 8. Whether the feat of ocean crossing seemingly achieved by *erectus* in the Java Sea was emulated by *ergaster/erectus* across the Mediterranean is not presently known. It has not generally been thought that a crossing was made into Europe via Gibraltar (any more than a passage to Madagascar was ever accomplished); the early dates of Developed Oldowan or early Acheulian in the Jordan Valley (to say nothing of the finds in Georgia) have tended to suggest that humanity and technology spread into Europe at the eastern end of the Mediterranean rather than crossing the Mediterranean in the west, though affinities between the tool types of the North African Acheulian and the Acheulian of Spain have been noted. At all events, with the appearance of the Acheulian tradition in Europe and of the fragmentary human remains, which may be classified as *Homo heidelbergensis* or late *Homo ergaster* (or late *Homo erectus*, for that matter), discovered as we have seen at places like Gran Dolina in the Atapuerca Mountains of Spain, our story has brought evolving humanity to the point at which the very distant ancestry of Neanderthal Man and his Mousterian culture can be discerned in Europe – at about 700,000 BP where the Acheulian tools are concerned and perhaps as far back as 800,000 BP with the skull and skeleton fragments. Arrived in Europe, evolving *Homo ergaster* (on his way to *Homo heidelbergensis*) faced in short order by the standards of geological time a climatic deterioration that would set the huge challenge of much colder times (if interspersed with milder ones) to which the Neanderthalers rose so doggedly, even heroically, in the end.

CHAPTER 11

The Emergence of
Homo sapiens sapiens

By about half a million years ago human evolution had put on earth, in places as far apart as South Africa and northern China, a form of human being with – whatever regional and even perhaps species variations – a postcranial skeleton to all intents and purposes like our own and a brain about twice the size of the first hominids of two million years or so before. Brain size remained rather stable among *ergaster* and *erectus* populations for many hundreds of thousands of years, and with it there went a long conservatism in toolmaking habits and, we may presume, in any use of language too, which was probably still almost entirely restricted to social relations and unable to admit much 'discussion' of other topics, even potentially vital ones that related to observation of the natural world and to technical matters like toolmaking and food procuring and processing. In so far as these creatures could be thought to have possessed consciousness at all, it must have been a consciousness dedicated to the social realm, to awareness of oneself as a social agent, to guessing of others' 'intentions' and prediction of their likely actions, to dissembling and deceiving for advantage, to forging and dissolving of alliances, to wriggling out of trouble and smoothing one's path through social life. For the rest, the same old tools were to be made in the same old ways, without 'thought' of innovation, and nature's rewards were to be gathered (and threats avoided) in the same old instinctive ways, without much in the way of reflection and conjecture as to how to do it better. Perhaps there was a trickle of other considerations into social consciousness, with some slight improvements in tools, language and hunting skills, but not very much. Of symbolic imagination there appears to have been nothing at all.

After a million years of *Homo erectus/ergaster*, the fossil record starts to show some clear-cut novelties at around 500,000 years ago, with further brain enlargement and skull changes to go with it. Because much of the fossil evidence is fragmentary, it is not possible to say exactly when the changes first appeared, and no doubt they happened at different times in different places among the small populations that were strung out across the inhabited world. In Europe, for example, the Atapuerca

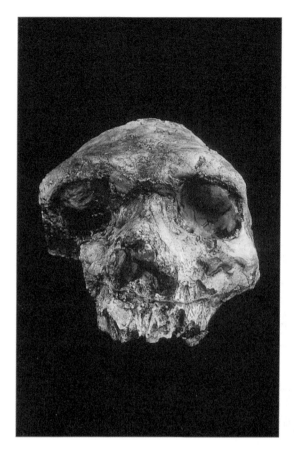

The face from Bodo.

fragments (about 800,000 BP), the Mauer jaw (perhaps 500,000 BP) and the Boxgrove leg bone (also about 500,000 BP) have all been classified as *Homo heidelbergensis* to mark their sufficient evolution out of *Homo ergaster/erectus*. In the Far East *Homo erectus* was flourishing without any detectable evolution towards later forms at the same dates. In Africa the scientific classification *Homo heidelbergensis* has been given to a massive skull found at a place called Bodo (Ethiopia) which convincingly combines *ergaster/erectus* features with others foreshadowing *Homo sapiens* in just the way that we would expect the skulls, if we had them, of Mauer and Boxgrove to do: all this at an estimated date of 600,000 BP. Bodo has the biggest face of all known human fossils, with a very prominent ridge over the eyes (which extends as a single bar, though rounded over each eye) and a midline keel on the skull top which hark back most emphatically to *ergaster/erectus*, and cranial capacity is not much larger. But the nasal area of the face and the frontal area rising over the brow-ridge look forward to *Homo sapiens*, as do the places on the skull's underside where the jaw articulated. The skull represents a clear advance over even late *erectus* types with

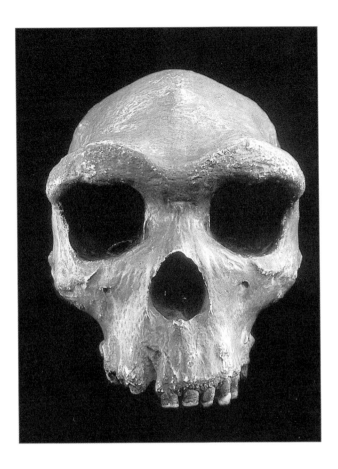

The Kabwe skull.

whom it is, if its early date is correct, contemporaneous. Interestingly, there are cut marks round the eyes, on the cheeks and forehead, at the top and back of the skull that – being never healed – point to defleshing of the Bodo skull at the end of the individual's life; cannibalism or some postmortem ritual treatment suggest themselves, with implications for some glimmering of symbol-driven behaviour to do with the dead. The tools found in association with the Bodo skull show a surprising mixture of Acheulian with Oldowan items, reminding us that simpler tools of the Oldowan style did not altogether disappear with the start of the long career of the Acheulian even in Africa (and Europe), while they went on as the mainstay of stone technology in the Far East to the end.

The jaw fragment and skullcap from Elandsfontein in the Cape Province of South Africa (also known by the names Saldanha and Hopefield), found in apparent association with faunal remains suggesting a date between 500,000 and 200,000 BP, are also very much like *ergaster/erectus* but with a significantly greater cranial capacity at an estimated 1200 ml. Acheulian axes were also found in association. At Broken

Hill in the old Rhodesia, a site now called Kabwe, a skull was unearthed that looks very much like a progression from Bodo in its very massive brow-ridge construction. When it was found, before the Second World War, its superficially Neanderthal features caused it to be called in the state of knowledge at the time an African Neanderthal Man or at least a 'Neanderthaloid', but the skull shape as a whole more closely resembles that of modern *Homo sapiens sapiens* than the distinctive lines of the Neanderthalers' skulls. Faunal associations suggest a date of at least 125,000 BP and very probably older, perhaps as old as 300,000 BP. Brain size is estimated at 1300 ml, with a skull shape considerably evolved beyond *ergaster/erectus* in its loaf-shaped aspect seen from the back and its fullness in the occipital area where there is a steeper rise to the skull top. (The Kabwe skull is essentially rather like the Petralona skull from Greece, and both stand at a similar point in the evolution of *sapiens* out of *heidelbergensis* traits.) The Kabwe skull lacks any distinctively Neanderthal characteristics (like the pulled forward face and the bun at the back) and limb bone fragments found at the same time look rather modern in form, though with very thick outer bone in the manner of *ergaster/erectus*. Their association with the skull may be doubted. The teeth, incidentally, are unique in the fossil record of early man in showing a degree of dental caries with abscesses not seen again till the times of the first farmers after about 10,000 years ago. A hole near the left ear may be the result of affray involving some sharp instrument or of the attentions of some carnivore. The arrangement of the voice-box, as inferred from the basal flexing of the Kabwe skull, has been deemed to suggest a better capacity for forming a wide range of sounds for potential use in speech than is seen in the Eurasian Neanderthalers. A maxillary (upper jaw) fragment from the same site at Broken Hill seems to reveal a less ruggedly built individual who may not belong with the Kabwe specimen in time and indeed resembles the Ngaloba remains mentioned below. Meanwhile, the Ndutu find from Olduvai may represent a more lightly made female of the same general sort as the Kabwe male.

Two skulls from Omo on the banks of the River Kibish in Ethiopia may take the story on from Kabwe, if they truly belong to the levels in which they were found. That they might not is, unfortunately, suggested by the marked differences between them which raises the possibility that one or the other is intrusive, perhaps both. Omo II shows a relatively heavily made skull with a receding forehead but at the same time a loaf-like breadth between the parietals and a cranial capacity of some 1400 ml. At a date

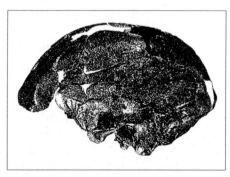

Omo II.

of about 130,000 BP, judging by dating of mollusc shells from the levels in which it was found, Omo II makes a plausible descendant of Kabwe. The fragmentary Omo I, from the same levels on the other side of the river, reconstructs as very modern looking with parietal breadth, high forehead, a short face, brow-ridges not outside the range of rugged individuals today, and a jaw with a chin. Brain capacity was up to modern standards. There were bones from the shoulder, arm, hand, spine, ribcage, leg and foot areas that suggest a tall and lightly built body of a modern sort. It has been hard for some anthropologists to conclude that Omo I could really date to some 130,000 BP or that Omo I and II might together represent some very variable population on its way to *Homo sapiens sapiens*. Omo I might be the remains of a much later individual whose bones have got mixed into the dated levels of his discovery; unfortunately, the same might be true of Omo II, though his features would not perhaps be out of place in 130,000 BP. Kabwe, at over 125,000 BP, and Omo II, at perhaps 130,000 BP, can be seen to represent a stage of evolution out of an *ergaster/erectus* ancestry via *heidelbergensis* (Bodo) that roughly equates with the early Neanderthalers of Europe, similarly derived via European *heidelbergensis* from *ergaster/erectus*, but the African specimens do lack the distinctive traits of the Neanderthalers and their differences from their European cousins impress many anthropologists as looking forward to modern *Homo sapiens sapiens* better than do the characteristics of the Neanderthal folk.

In Africa it is possible to list a few more finds that seem to take on the line of incipient modernity. The remains from Singa in the Sudan (at about 150,000 BP and from Ngaloba in Tanzania (at some 130,000 BP), together with those from Florisbad

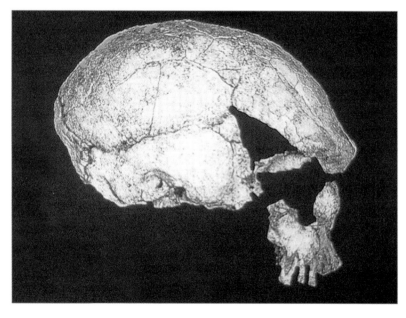

The Ngaloba skull.

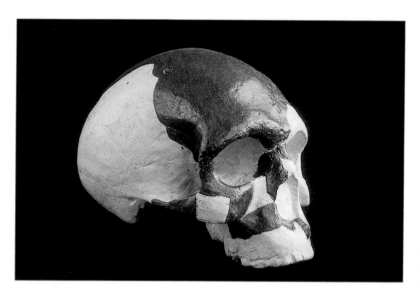

A reconstruction of the Florisbad skull fragments.

in South Africa have a borderline modern look about them but are really too enigmatic to make much of. The fragments of five individuals from Jebel Ihroud in Morocco do, however, show clear signs of evolving modernity at perhaps as early as 150,000 BP. A femur fragment is robust and teeth are large, but a rather delicate jaw has signs of a chin. The skull shape looks 'primitive' at the back but more 'modern' at the front, being broad and flat-faced with hollowed cheeks in marked contrast to the inflated cheek appearance of the Neanderthalers who were to flourish later on the north side of the Mediterranean. All the same, the Jebel Ihroud type shows rugged brow-ridges. The remains from Border Cave in South Africa, including an adult's skull and two broken mandibles along with some postcranial bones and the skeleton of an infant, are very modern in character but cannot be confidently dated since they were found in uncontrolled circumstances (by guano shovellers in the 1940s) and are not in the same condition as some animal bones from the site that might otherwise help to date them to perhaps 100,000 BP. Much more useful are the bones from the site called Klasies River Mouth in South Africa. Five fragmentary mandibles, a maxilla, several small cranial pieces, a few teeth and a few postcranial bones paint a picture of a population in which individuals might have no primitive-looking continuous bar of brow-ridges over their eyes, some real chin development on their jaws, and slender limb bones. Floral and faunal evidence and some date determinations by physics put the Klasies River Mouth remains at between 115,000 and 75,000 BP. For all that, some of the jaws are rather robust with big teeth (and one of them has no chin) in a way we should not expect to find among fully modern populations. Traces of burning on some of the bones and cut marks on the frontal

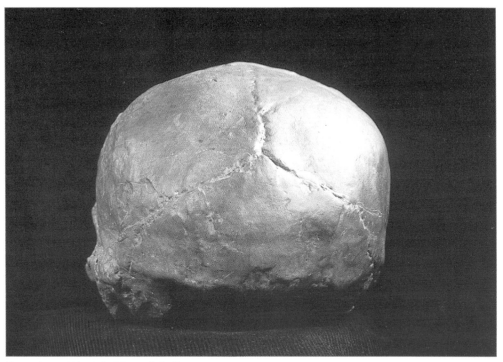

Rear view of the Jebel Ihroud skull.

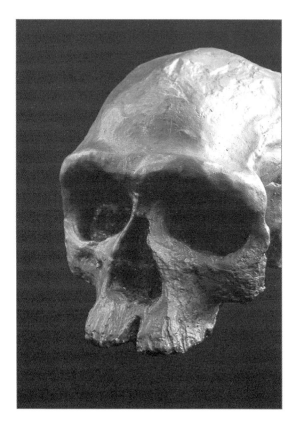

The face of Jebel Ihroud.

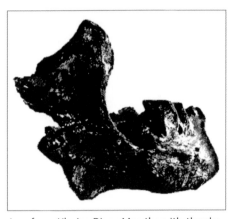

Jaw from Klasies River Mouth; with thanks to University of Chicago Press.

fragment have been seen as suggestive of cannibalism at this site. Fragmentary though the Klasies pieces are, they are consistent with the notion of an emerging constellation of modern *Homo sapiens sapiens* physical traits not seen outside Africa as early as 115,000 BP, and certainly not among the contemporaneous Neanderthalers of Europe. Even so, the rather skimpy array of African evidence, not always well dated, could scarcely support any firm conclusion that fully modern human beings evolved first in Africa around 100,000 years ago without the addition of some other line of argument – and a powerful one at that. After all, we might only be fortuitously picking up in Africa stray hints that modern humanity was evolving in the *sapiens sapiens* direction in more than one part of the inhabited world (excluding Europe).

It was first suggested in the 1970s by geneticists that comparisons of blood groups, enzymes and proteins in modern populations across the world might make it possible to estimate the lengths of time that have ensued since some of the major peoples of the world separated into largely non-interbreeding groups with 'racial' characteristics. Of course, all sorts of human beings all over the world remain completely interfertile, constituting a single species that looks superficially quite variable but, in genetic terms, is tremendously homogenous – more so than are the chimpanzees or gorillas within their own species. This suggests either that no populations in the long history of evolving humanity have ever been so isolated as to lose genetic interchange with other populations however distant, or that all human beings in the world today have only rather recently descended from a common source in a single small population ancestral to every one of us. The first proponents of this latter view, arguing from the evidence of blood group and protein variation, estimated that the Mongoloid peoples of today became effectively separated from the Caucasoids at about 40,000 years ago and their joint common stock split from African peoples at about 110,000 BP. The coincidence of this latter date with the dates arrived at for the early African appearances of fossil men with modern traits in places like Klasies River Mouth is unmissable. Since the 1970s genetic studies of modern human variability have made great strides and, on their basis, schemes of human evolution have been vigorously argued that have all human beings in the world today descended from a small population of *Homo sapiens sapiens* evolved in Africa at some time not so very long before 100,000 years ago. Many anthropologists have welcomed ideas along these lines but some have steadfastly opposed them, standing by the scheme of human evolution expressed by Weidenreich before the Second World War that sees mankind as evolving all over the world through the broad stages represented by such creatures as *Homo erectus*, *Homo heidelbergensis* and *Homo sapiens* (*neanderthalensis* and modern *sapiens*) without large-scale extinctions of local populations in the face of expansionist invaders from Africa (or anywhere else). In this view it is genetic interchange across group borders that has kept evolving humanity genetically homogenous all over the world.

Genetic and related studies have not only been brought to bear on questions like the degree of closeness between modern human populations (taking in, as we have seen, certain Neanderthal specimens, too), but also on the problem of dating the stages of human evolution in terms of real, if approximate, years on the geological time-scale. These genetic dates rest ultimately on agreed dates for genetic events (like, for example, the divergence of the orang-utan line from the rest of ape evolution) that have been determined by dating methods based on physics, but they go on to handle the dating framework of human evolution in a novel way. Before exploring that field, it is worth reviewing the means by which fossils have been sorted and above all dated before the development of the genetic approach. Physical anthropologists have traditionally ordered human fossils by noting their distinctive features, mainly of the skull and jaw, and comparing these with other fossils to build up a scheme of evolutionary relationships on a framework of dates for the fossils in question where such dates may be available and reliable. In the course of the century-and-a-half of anthropological enquiry, dating methods have run from quite speculative estimates of geological dates for events like ice ages to modern tests based on physics for age determination. Dates come in two basic sorts: relative and absolute. Relative datings allow us to judge only on grounds of, say, stratigraphy and faunal associations, that one fossil or hand-axe is older or younger than another, by a bit or a lot, without knowing exactly when any particular fossil man lived or any tool was knapped, or how long a bit or a lot really was. Absolute dating methods aspire to tell us, in terms of real years elapsed, just how old a fossil or an archaeological find might be. Some methods really are absolute, in principle at least, such as counting tree rings or annual varve deposits in northern lake beds. But these methods are of very limited application in general, covering a period back to 8,000 and 12,000 years ago respectively, and of no use at all with fossil man. All the worthwhile methods of absolute chronology are related to radioactive processes in nature and their 'absoluteness' is tempered with more or less wide margins of error in practice. The dates we have been assigning in the past chapters to the fossils of Australopithecines or of *Homo erectus* or the remains from Klasies River Mouth and so on are all ultimately dependent on determinations made by means of physics in connection with radioactive processes. Not all datings by any means have been directly arrived at from the fossils themselves, but many rely on dating of associated materials (like shells and flint) or on faunal associations and climatic indicators known at other sites to date to such and such a time. All the methods result in individual dates quoted with plus-and-minus ranges (sometimes of tens of thousands of years) and all suffer from the complications and uncertainties inherent in the physics on which they depend. The best dating situations are ones in which several different determinations can be made, preferably by different methods, so that statistical clusters emerge with greater likelihood that the date sought after lies within a narrow margin of possibilities. The most famous of the methods uses the decay of radiocarbon in organic materials to measure time elapsed, but C14 dates are unreliable in absolute terms beyond about 30,000 BP (though they can still provide relative chronology) and effectively unobtainable beyond about 40,000 BP, which means that only the latest, for example, of the Neanderthalers fall within the scope of radiocarbon dating. Of application to much remoter epochs are the methods called Potassium/Argon and Argon/Argon which can date materials like lava and volcanic ash by measuring relative quantities of isotopes of these elements in rock samples. The same rocks, volcanically reheated in the past, can also entrap palaeomagnetic patterns that log the changes in the Earth's magnetic polarity over long periods of time – before about 730,000 years ago (within the times of *Homo erectus*) magnetic polarity was reversed by reference to today's and so, even without Potassium/Argon dating, magnetic polarity in volcanic rock can help to assign dates to fossil and archaeological finds. Previously heated materials like volcanic glasses may also contain the tracks of particles emitted by uranium within them since erasure of any former tracks at the time of heating; Fission-Track dating relies on this circumstance to arrive at age determinations, by counting tracks, for geological events reflected in stratigraphies containing fossil remains and artefacts. The gap between the very old dates afforded by such methods and the comparatively recent dates supplied by C14 is closed in part by the dating procedure called Uranium Series, which depends on the precipitation, out of water-soluble uranium, of the decay products thorium and protactinium over time. This method can be used to date shells and coral and carbonate precipitations like stalagmites, stalactites and travertines (spring limestones), covering a very useful range between about 350,000 and 150,000 BP.

A potentially very useful dating technique, called Thermoluminescence (TL), makes further use of the fact that naturally occurring radioactive elements can irradiate substances in which they are contained, in such a way that electrons become cumulatively trapped in the crystalline structures of, for example, flint, loess particles and the clays out of which pottery is made. Heat and light drive out the electrons when, say, flint tools are accidentally heated in a camp fire or newly shaped pots are fired in kilns or particles of loess are exposed to sunlight. After the electrons are driven out and the interiors of flints and pots return to relative cool and darkness, or loess particles are buried under deep deposits, the entrapment of radiated electrons commences anew, so that a further, controlled application of heat in laboratory conditions is able to drive them out again, in the form of a light output that can be measured to equate with time elapsed since the previous heating or exposure to light. A technique applicable to an inorganic component of tooth enamel and called Electron Spin Resonance (ESR), refines the process by directly counting the trapped electrons.

Such methods, derived from physics and applied to the geological record, have enabled us to date the fossils that mark the separation of the (old world) monkey and ape lines at 30–25 mya and the emergence of the orang-utans from more generalized ape and human ancestry at 15–12 mya. With a few (more or less) absolute dates like these it has been possible (by comparison of blood group, enzyme and other protein differences) to estimate the likely date for the separation of the line that leads to ourselves from the line that leads to the chimpanzees at about 5.5 mya – which is indeed close to the age of the very earliest fossils we have to hand that mark the incipience of hominid traits. (Another method, which tests the bonding propensities – i.e. genetic closeness – of actual strands of DNA from different species, shows that chimpanzees are closer to humans than gorillas are to either of them, and puts a date of 7 mya on the chimp-human separation.) Such methods of date estimation for episodes of primate and human evolution rest on the assumption that protein and underlying genetic differences between species and genera (most of them neutral in terms of natural selection) accumulate at fixed rates, on the basis of random misreplications of the genetic code in the DNA of living creatures, occurring and piling up at a steady pace that can be timed by the dating of certain instances of evolutionary change. This assumption appears to be largely justified, but subject to complications. It is on the basis of this approach that the recent tests on the mitochondrial DNA remaining in the original Neanderthal specimen have been interpreted to demonstrate a genetic distance between the Neanderthalers and all modern human populations that puts back their last time of common ancestry to the days of *Homo heidelbergensis* at about 500,000 BP.

Mitochondrial DNA has been favoured as especially useful in tracing the line of human descent – we should more properly say, at the outset, not *the* line but *a* line. MtDNA has the advantage, for these purposes, of having nothing like the part in determining our genetic make-up that is played by nuclear DNA. The chromosomes in the nuclei of cells are made of DNA and are replicated at cell divisions as bodies grow and renovate themselves through life. The genes of the chromosomes direct the production of the proteins out of which bodies are made and determine the pattern of development of each living thing, not as rigid blueprints for some finished product but rather as a developmental scheme that must at every second of an individual's life interact with the environment in which that individual is living. The impact of the environment is, of course, a very complex thing; its effects range from the crudely obvious to the invisibly subtle, and the individual creature is at every stage of its progress from conception to death the result of the ongoing interaction of its genetic developmental pattern and the ever-changing environment in which development takes place. Nuclear DNA is inherited from both parents, and the rearrangement of the chromosomes at conception when egg is fertilized by sperm is the immediate source of human variability in genetically determined developmental patterns. It is upon this variability that natural selection does its ruthless work.

The mitochondria are the energy suppliers of cells, outside the nucleus but also containing DNA. Their DNA is, by comparison with nuclear DNA, only marginally concerned with protein functions and it is thought that its workings are restricted to certain effects on the nervous system which can play a part in, for instance, some forms of eye disease and epilepsy. But, overwhelmingly, the mitochondrial DNA appears to have no bearing on our inheritance of physical characteristics; for this reason, its characteristics are not subject to the pressures of natural selection in the way that some of those of nuclear DNA are and mtDNA mutations occur at a faster rate than they do with nuclear DNA, with far less reconditioning to keep them in line (because it doesn't matter so much). This makes them easier to track through different populations in the world today.

But the main interest of mtDNA is that it is transmitted very largely, if not entirely, by mothers. In every offspring, the mtDNA of the fertilized egg comes from the mother's egg cell and what mtDNA was in the tail of the fertilizing sperm is lost. The nuclear DNA of the fertilized egg comes equally from the father's sperm and the mother's egg, but the mtDNA comes from the mother and, with cell division as the new individual grows, the mtDNA in all the cells of its body is derived from the mother's mtDNA.

If the rate at which mutation of mtDNA occurs in primates, including humans, can be determined with sufficient accuracy, then the real possibility exists to trace lines of female-only descent among human populations around the globe, and to put dates to them. We shall not, by this means, be tracing the lines of descent of the nuclear DNA that shapes the bodies of both men and women; rather we shall be tracing the descent of the mtDNA in the power supply cells of the bodies of men and women. Women pass on their mtDNA to all their offspring, male and female, but only their daughters pass it on again – their sons forfeit their own mother-derived mtDNA with each generation, whether they father sons or daughters. It is easy to see that lines of mtDNA descent can come to an end when only sons are born to their carriers, rather as surnames can be lost in modern families when only daughters are born.

Rates of primate and human mtDNA mutation have been estimated on the basis of the generally agreed date for the separation of chimp and hominid lines at around 5.5 mya (though with some arguments acknowledged to put the time at more like 7 mya), together with the dates assigned by archaeological dating techniques to events like the arrival of human beings in Australasia and America. Armed with their estimates of mtDNA mutation rates, geneticists have been able to judge the degree of mtDNA genetic distance between various populations in the world today in terms of years elapsed since they shared the same mtDNA configurations. There have been many arguments about technical details of sampling and statistical methods employed, but the picture that emerges has one or two striking features, of which the most immediate is that today's populations in sub-Saharan Africa show slightly more mtDNA variation than any other peoples in the world, with the implication that people have been living for longer in Africa than anywhere else with more time to pile up mutations, whereas the rest of the world is populated by more recently arrived people with more similar mtDNA derived from a single (African) source. The geneticists have variously dated the origins of the female lines of mtDNA descent back to between as early as 800,000 and as late as 40,000 BP, though the consensus is that something like 400,000 to 100,000 BP represents the most likely time back to which all lines of mtDNA inheritance through mothers can be traced. Arriving at a reliable date is complicated by the fact that episodes of mutation can be hidden by subsequent mutations and even reversed on occasions, and there are inherent uncertainties about the calibration of the rate from archaeological and evolutionary events. Even the evidence as to the African origin of the mtDNA lines is open to some doubt since the slightly greater diversity in Africa may reflect long-term greater population levels there, in which variations are slower to die out – in the same way that surnames are more likely to survive somewhere among large populations. It seems that it is possible, moreover, to construct family trees of mtDNA descent which do not necessarily point to Africa as the source of the oldest roots. There remains the possibility that a small amount of paternal mtDNA can be inherited in addition to the maternal inheritance, in which case the time-scale of mutation would be extended further into the past.

For all that, mtDNA evidence does appear, as things stand at present, likely to support the idea of an African origin for the inheritance through females of humanity's DNA component in our cells' mitochondria at somewhere between 400,000 and 100,000 BP. Since the bones of the original Neanderthal Man have yielded mtDNA that shows a divergence from modern samples far outside the modern range anywhere in the world (including Europe where Neanderthal traits might be thought most likely to occur), we may tentatively conclude that the classic Neanderthalers, at least, probably shared a common mtDNA ancestry with ourselves no later than the times of *Homo heidelbergensis*, and contributed little or none of their own mtDNA inheritance into the pool of modern mtDNA patterns.

Understandably, people have tended to link the idea of mtDNA descent to the entire question of the origin of modern *Homo sapiens sapiens*, but strictly speaking the mtDNA evidence only argues for a common female ancestry at somewhere between 400,000 and 100,000 BP in Africa. That female ancestry might well not have been *Homo sapiens sapiens* as we know it; we have seen how few and frequently enigmatic are the fossil remains from Africa in that time-frame. Moreover, the means by which that common mtDNA ancestry was spread across the globe need not necessarily involve, without other evidence, the conclusion that females accompanied by their males spread out of Africa in bands who never interbred with people they found along the way, their children and children's children doing likewise. We must remember that with mtDNA genetics, we are only tracking mtDNA inherited in the female line. This mtDNA might have been introduced from one group into another by exogamous mating systems operating between neighbouring bands; we have seen that this is part of the standard pattern of the hunter/gatherer way of life of recent times and it may even be that beginnings of this uniquely human behaviour trait (apes do not show it) go back into *ergaster/erectus* times. By the times of *Homo ergaster* and archaic *Homo sapiens*, it may have been women who always left home to go to another family or band, while men stayed at home and received their mates from neighbouring groups. Indeed, there is evidence to show that Y chromosome variants (a sort of male equivalent in terms of genetic tracking of female-inherited mtDNA) are always much more localized than variants of mtDNA. It is possible that the line of mtDNA descent from the females of some small population in Africa was taken all over the world in this way, eventually displaying in different branch lines the small accumulations of mutations (slightly more of them in Africa where they have been going on longer among larger numbers of people) that we see today. (The idea, incidentally, of an 'African Eve' from whom all our mtDNA derives is more of a notional mathematical inevitability than a prehistorical fact; it is rather a question of a smallish group of females sharing a common mtDNA pattern back to which all our mtDNA is linked. Any idea of a 'Mother of Us All' is even more far-fetched, since as we have been at pains to emphasize, this line of research can only trace the genetic pattern in our cells' power supplies and not the whole story of our nuclear genetic inheritance.)

The possibility that it was exogamous mating systems operating between neighbouring groups that was able, over a long time from group to group to group, to spread such a near uniformity of mtDNA patterns around the world without whole population treks (and without the expulsion or extermination of indigenous people along the way) could be bolstered by two other considerations. Firstly, the chimps and gorillas show much more mtDNA variation than we do; two chimps from the same group are likely to be more different than two human beings from the opposite ends of the earth, and this is not because chimps live in such large numbers by comparison with ourselves that mtDNA lines do not go out of existence easily. One way in which chimps differ from ourselves is that they do not have exogamy. Secondly, there is the possibility that the mtDNA line that eventually 'won out', as it were, over all the others in the world of, say, 100,000 BP was associated with characteristics of the nuclear DNA in the same cells as itself that conferred some crucial survival benefit on its carriers; what if the sons and daughters of exogamously mated mothers were so clever or capable in some valued way that both natural and human selection favoured them highly, making the daughters much sought after as mates by neighbouring groups (where their children outshone, outsurvived their fellows), steadily spreading their mtDNA and their nuclear DNA through many if not most of the human groups in the world? It is thought that it is in just such circumstances, when small and scattered groups keep on exchanging genes across their boundaries, that evolution may proceed at a fast pace for all concerned. In Africa an always greater population density would have allowed for slightly more mtDNA variation to persist down to the present day. Of course, there would still very likely have been places where populations who had become more isolated than most and for longer could be, for some reason, unamenable to mate interchange when its possibility arose – it need not have been speciation to the point of non-interfertility, but simply an overwhelming lack of mutual attraction or some other cultural barrier. The Neanderthalers of Western Europe and some other populations attested by fossil finds around the world may be candidates for such non-participation in the evolution of *Homo sapiens sapiens*, though some anthropologists are prepared to argue for the survival of some Neanderthal traits into later populations in Central and Eastern Europe.

If only the evidence of mtDNA were available, we might still conclude that the scrappy fossils sometimes claimed to establish the incipience of modern *Homo sapiens sapiens* in Africa before 100,000 BP had not received sufficient support to advance the case made out for them as the precursors of a conquering exodus from their homeland that would, in a matter of a few tens of thousands of years, see them supplanting by fair means or foul all pre-existing populations in the way of their global spread. (Fair means include 'outcompeting' their rivals; foul means are all too obvious. One cannot resist noting that many nineteenth-century anthropologists thought *Homo sapiens* had exterminated his 'primitive' forerunners in the manner of European colonists on the loose in Tasmania and the Belgian Congo, while some later twentieth-century anthropologists see him outcompeting them like a successful businessman. Of course, noting these things does not necessarily make the ideas factually wrong, any more than noting that the idea of global human ascent to *Homo sapiens sapiens* by peaceful exogamy owes more than a little to today's progressive, liberal, anti-racist sentiment.)

The study of mtDNA recommends itself as a way of getting into the business of tracing human descent without fossils because its line is clear, though it suffers the vices of its virtues in that its very clarity arises out of the limitation that it does not really track the family trees of evolving humanity but only the thread of mtDNA inheritance through females. It is nuclear DNA that (in interaction with the environment) really makes human beings different, among themselves and through time with evolution from one stage to another. But nuclear DNA is much more complex than mtDNA and inherited in a complicated way from both parents, unlike mtDNA, so its lines are far more difficult to trace, to the point of practical impossibility. Some assistance in tracing at least parts of them is afforded by the strange fact that much of the DNA sequences appears to be quite meaningless, encoding nothing that controls protein manufacture or inheritance of anything at all. Here and there on the sequences are the genes for height, for example, or eye colour or something else about our inherited constitution, but much of the DNA in the nuclei of our cells seems to consist of long lists of various repetitions of chemical bases, differing in detail from individual to individual, whose particular presence or absence has absolutely no bearing on our make-up (or our survival potential in the face of natural selection). The usefulness of such neutral but recognizable patterns is, of course, that they may be trackable through populations. And it happens that, as with mtDNA, it is in Africa that certain combined patterns of nuclear DNA show more variety, while in the rest of the world the same patterns are very limited in expression. Again, this situation suggests that DNA patterns have been exported relatively recently from a particular African group, out into the rest of the world, and that Africa has gone on displaying more variety with these patterns because it contained, at the time of the export, other groups with different variations on the patterns that have persisted to this day, while in the rest of the world insufficient time has elapsed for the patterns to break down into greater variety. It has been possible to estimate the time of the first appearance of some of these patterns in Africa at between 140,000 and 90,000 BP. This dating is not based on any presumed DNA mutation rate but upon rates of recombination of DNA sequences. Because we are dealing here with nuclear DNA, inherited from both parents and subject to recombination at the fertilization of egg by sperm, the evidence can be seen as strongly indicative that certain genetic patterns, probably appearing first in one particular group of people in Africa some one hundred or so thousands of years ago, were spread so vigorously around the world that they have come to be a feature of virtually all non-African human beings (as well as a feature, of course, of some Africans, but alongside many variations on the themes). The proponents of the 'Out of Africa' hypothesis of modern human origins take this judgement to embrace the certainty that these patterns were carried in the bodies of both males and females migrating out of Africa to colonize the world, who went on to have no truck with any pre-existing people they found along the way, to as near as makes no difference the total exclusion of the genetic inheritance of those futureless people. Extensive genetic studies that statistically estimate genetic distances between modern human populations on the basis of frequencies of many different gene types are held to support this view fully. Average genetic distances between populations in modern world times are interpreted to record a separation between Africans and the rest of the world at about 100,000 BP, subsequently between Eurasians and Australasians at about 50,000 BP, and later still between Asians and Europeans at about 30,000 BP, all on the assumption that a single emigration of modern humans took place out of Africa at about 100,000 BP, with further genetic differences becoming apparent among the descendants of those emigrants as time went by as a result of genetic changes within themselves and not as a result of interbreeding with any people they came across in the course of their spread.

But some anthropologists continue to maintain that long-term local continuities of physical traits, seen particularly in fossil skulls, support the hypothesis of 'multiregional evolution' by constant gene flow across group boundaries without population replacements by massive emigration and extermination or outcompeting. They might admit that a worldwide web of exogamous mating habits, never seriously impeded by mountain or desert or any other sort of barrier, can look like a tall order; but it looks to them like an even taller order to be invited to conclude that certain physical characteristics seen in *erectus* populations in some particular part of the world could be accidentally reinvented by evolution in an entirely unrelated *sapiens* population in the same place at a later date. They point to certain traits seen in the *erectus* remains from Zhoukoudian in China that prefigure modern Mongoloid racial characteristics: the relatively small faces with flattened cheeks (notched by the anatomical feature called 'incisura malaris') and unprominent noses, together with a shovel-like shape to the backs of the front teeth. A bridge between *erectus* at Zhoukoudian and modern orientals is provided by the skulls, dating from times after 300,000 BP, from Yunxian, Mapa, Dali and Jinniu Shan in China, all late *erectus*/early *sapiens* in which some of the same traits persist: a similar skull, in a damaged state, was found in India. (But opponents of the multiregional hypothesis draw attention to the occurrence of incisura malaris and face-shortening in the African Broken Hill skull and to the shovelled incisors of an African specimen of *Homo erectus*.) Australasia may be even more supportive of the multiregional idea than China, for there the *erectus* line evidently continued until a late date, and traits that look forward to some of those of the Australian aborigines have been detected in an *erectus* skull from Sangiran on Java at about 700,000 BP, with a further link in the chain of descent at the Javanese site of Ngandong at perhaps as late as 100,000 BP. The skulls from Ngandong, on the Solo River, were once dubbed Neanderthal or at least Neanderthaloid and they do, indeed, resemble contemporary Neanderthal skulls (as some African ones that we have reviewed do too) in their general characteristics as belonging to a broadly similar stage of early *Homo sapiens* evolution, but they lack the really distinctive traits of the true Eurasian Neanderthalers and their cranial capacity is rather closer to *erectus* than *neanderthalensis*. (The Ngandong skulls have, incidentally, been credited with affording evidence – in their smashed skull bases and faces – of head-hunting and trophy-mounting at a date of something over 100,000 BP.)

Some 60,000 years ago Australia, Tasmania and New Guinea were all joined together by the low sea levels of the glacial era in the island continent of Sahul, which could be reached from Java by a run of small islands and a final sea crossing of some 80 km that early people could only negotiate on some sort of raft. (To arrive at Sahul from anywhere else would have required a rather longer crossing.) Fossils dug up in Australia fall into two types, a robustly built group that seems to some anthropologists to take on the Java *erectus* line with big brow-ridges, sloping foreheads, thick skull walls and large teeth, and a more gracile set with much more slenderly made faces. Interestingly, it is the graciles who seem to represent the earlier of the two groups (the best dated being from Lake Mungo at about 30,000 BP, which carries the further distinction of being the world's oldest certain cremation) while the robusts of Kow Swamp appear to date as late as 10,000 BP. Multiregionalists think two waves of population reached Sahul after 60,000 BP, one of them of distinctly Javanese *erectus* lineage and the other perhaps of ultimately Chinese *erectus* stock via the Philippines. On this view, the modern aborigines of Australia are a mixture of both lines, fully *Homo sapiens sapiens* on account of constant gene flow with the wide world of humanity, but retaining certain physical traits long characteristic of their general part of the world. It is indeed a tall order to think that the big prognathous faces and marked brow-ridge development of some Australian aboriginal fossils (and, to an extent, of some living Australians, too) might represent a re-evolution, as it were, of traits formerly seen in the region but later entirely eclipsed by incoming ex-African emigrants who had evolved into fully modern *Homo sapiens sapiens* without these same traits some tens of thousands of years before. As we shall see in the next chapter, a case can be made for the continuity in parts of Europe of Neanderthaler traits in a similar way to that proposed above for local *erectus* traits in Australasia.

The proponents of the 'Out of Africa' hypothesis might concede that the regional continuity of some traits from *erectus* into *sapiens*, and even *sapiens sapiens*, could just possibly point to some limited interbreeding between their conquering heroines and heroes and native people already living in their *Lebensraum*, but they believe that fossils like those from Klasies River Mouth taken together with the mtDNA evidence and in particular the findings of research into patterns of nuclear DNA can only mean that the descendants of a small population of virtually fully modern types spread out from Africa at some time around 100,000 BP, to populate the world with their own kind, to the extinction of the representatives of any other lines of descent that had come down from *Homo erectus* or *Homo heidelbergensis* in the other parts of the world into which the Africans were reaching. The limited genetic variety of *Homo sapiens sapiens* all over the world today (when compared with our close primate relatives) has been interpreted as near proof of this scenario, with the strong implication of a crisis in human affairs through which only a small number of our direct ancestors survived to pass on their genetic make-up to all of us. To complete the picture, it has recently been suggested that worldwide populations of all sorts of humanity were seriously depleted by extremely adverse conditions brought on by an unparalleled volcanic explosion on Sumatra at about 80,000 BP that gave the emigrating moderns their chance to overrun areas previously held by other human types. But evidence for such a decline in human populations is not available in the fossil and archaeological records.

It may seem for the moment a reasonable compromise to admit that modern global humanity's genetic make-up probably carries a preponderance of African inheritance but that this need not all have been exported by pugnacious colonists nor need the genetic contributions of other stocks in other parts of the world have been entirely obliterated on the march to worldwide *Homo sapiens sapiens*.

CHAPTER 12

Neanderthal Nemesis

The first clear epiphany of a modern form of humanity, if we set aside for the moment the people of Klasies River Mouth and their perhaps faintly unreliable African compatriots from Border Cave and so on, is manifest in the caves of northern Israel. We saw in Chapter 3 that pre-war excavations at Mount Carmel turned up a collection of human remains that seemed to cover a range from the very Neanderthal at Tabun to the more or less modern (if rugged) at Skhul; anthropologists wondered for a long time whether they were faced with a single, very variable population on its evolutionary way to modernity, or with a sequence of evolution from older Neanderthalers to later moderns, or with the results of interbreeding between originally separate modern and Neanderthal communities. New evidence, new

Model of the bones of Skhul V as found by excavation.

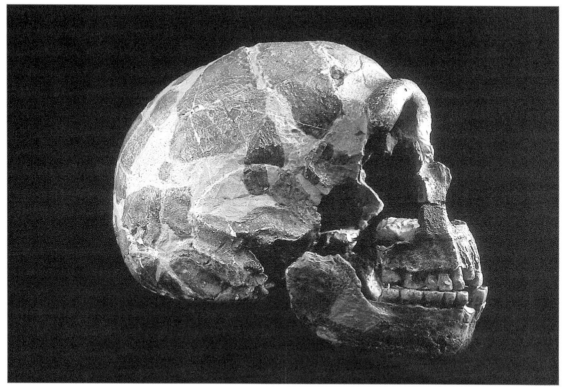

The Tabun Neanderthal woman's skull.

interpretations and in particular new datings from the 1960s on were to create a shifting appreciation of the Mount Carmel evidence that is not entirely cleared up to this day.

The stratigraphy of the Mount Carmel sites is particularly difficult to judge, being nothing like the relatively level and well-separated layering of, say, the French caves, but rather distorted and convoluted by the presence of 'swallow holes' that may have led to mixtures of materials from different periods and certainly makes for uncertainties about precise relationships of human fossil finds in different levels and at different sites with their various associations of tools and animal bones. Consequently, dating interpretations of the finds have had a chequered history. To the original finds from the Mount Carmel caves called et-Tabun and es-Skhul there have been added since the Second World War further finds in northern Israel from Qafzeh, Amud and Kebara, with a clear division between Neanderthal types at Tabun, Amud and Kebara and more or less modern types at Skhul and Qafzeh. All of them, of whichever type, have been found in association with much the same sort of Mousterian tool kit, once thought the technological preserve of the Neanderthalers

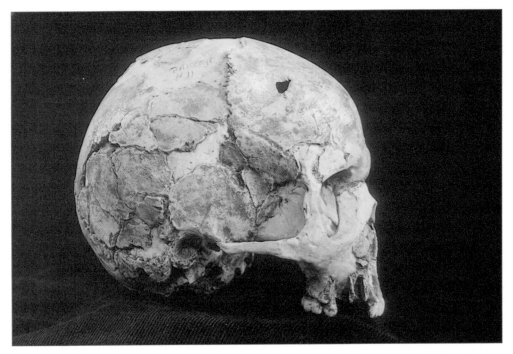

A modern-looking child's skull from Qafzeh.

alone. For a while it was possible to see in the tools a progression from thicker to thinner and flatter flakes that seemed to make (by association) Tabun older than Kebara, and Skhul youngest of all (the sequence of large faunal remains was deemed to back up this picture); a neat advance could be perceived from Neanderthalers with improving tool types to more modern people with most progressed tools. But subsequently it began to look, on the evidence of microfaunal remains (mostly rodent bones), as if the more modern types from Qafzeh predated most of the Neanderthalers in northern Israel. Thermoluminescence dating backed up this interpretation by putting the Kebara Neanderthalers at about 60,000 BP and the Qafzeh moderns at 90,000 BP. Any reservations about the Qafzeh TL dates were largely dispelled by the addition of Electron Spin Resonance dating of tooth enamel (from associated faunal remains) at Qafzeh to 115,000–100,000 BP. The Skhul moderns came out at 100,000–80,000 BP by the same ESR dating method. Taken with the microfaunal evidence, these TL and ESR dates – providing all associations are correctly judged – are powerfully suggestive that uniquely in these sites more or less modern forms of humanity have been found substantially predating the appearance of Neanderthalers at the same sites. The Tabun Neanderthal woman's skull would appear to belong by ESR on seemingly associated animal teeth to about 110,000 BP, roughly the same time as the Skhul and Qafzeh moderns, to complicate the picture further, but it remains a possibility that the Tabun woman's skull, found before the Second World War, represents an intrusion into early levels of the site from a later period, perhaps the same time as the rest of the Neanderthalers of the region.

These Levantine Neanderthal folk are not quite typical of the Neanderthal population as known in Western Europe. The Tabun woman, for example, though brow-ridged in a thoroughly Neanderthal fashion, shows an otherwise rather gracile skull, with the low cranial capacity for a Neanderthaler of about 1250 ml. The Amud Neanderthal male, on the other hand, is the proud possessor of the largest fossil human brain known at some 1700 ml and of the tallest Neanderthal physique at 1.78 m. Additionally, he shows relatively slender brow-ridges, and cheeks less inflated than those of classic Neanderthalers, with something approaching a chin, and a mastoid process closer to the modern size than most of his kind; his skull shape lacks the typical Neanderthal bun at the back but the Neanderthal occipital torus is on display and, seen from the rear, the skull has that rounded rather than loaf-shaped appearance that is invariably seen among the Neanderthalers, while it has Neanderthal length, taken to rather an extreme, when seen from the side. ESR dating on a mammal tooth from the same level suggests some time as late as 50,000–40,000 BP for the adult male Neanderthaler of Amud and, unless with his remains we have stumbled on a very aberrant Neanderthaler, it is tempting to see in them certain indications of evolution towards the more modern form of humanity, either by membership of a population of Neanderthal origin that had taken in a genetic input from moderns (for whom we have not to look far at Skhul and Qafzeh, though some tens of thousands of years earlier on those sites) or by a more general participation in a time of rapid but variable human evolution when a patchwork of traits looking both backwards and forwards could be shared around various populations, manifesting themselves here and there from time to time, while the wider picture tended always to the replacement of the older with the newer characteristics. (The Shanidar Neanderthalers show something of the same non-typical array of features as the late Neanderthal male of Amud.)

The infant Neanderthaler from Amud, with markedly more in the way of Neanderthal character in, for example, the absence of a chin, came from an earlier level of the site and is estimated to date to some

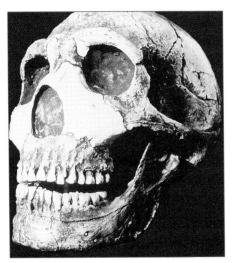

The Neanderthal male of Amud.

60,000–50,000 years ago. The Kebara Neanderthaler, whose hyoid bone and pelvis have proved so useful in settling some questions about Neanderthal speech capacity and birthing, is of about the same age and interestingly, being more or less complete below the neck (or, rather, below the massive, chinless jaw!) shows body proportions of the markedly cold-adapted sort seen in the European Neanderthalers, bolstering the thought that the Neanderthal people of the Levant were not long-term indigenes of the region but had been pushed out of their northerly homelands by the extreme cold of the second phase of the last ice age, which even they could not support. This Kebara male was found, we recall, to have been buried in a deliberately dug grave and the site provided the remains of a hearth fire with carbonized wild peas.

In contrast to the Neanderthalers of Israel, the more or less moderns of the same area present a general physique that looks decidedly warm in adaptation, tall and lanky limbed in a way that fairly suggests genetic antecedence in the south, in Africa. They are not entirely modern-looking in terms of any peoples living in the world today, but even where they show rugged features these are not of a Neanderthal character; for example, the strong brow-ridges of Skhul 5 and Qafzeh 6 are not in the least like Neanderthalers' and their foreheads rise high above them. The whole form of these people is unmistakably modern, particularly in their skulls. Plainly, we are dealing here with *Homo sapiens sapiens*, even if of an early form, and not any sort of *neanderthalensis*. Given the separation in date between the Neanderthalers and moderns of the Levant, with the latter predating the former (except perhaps, for the Tabun woman), we can almost certainly drop the notion of a single variable population and conclude that we are here logging an early appearance of modern humanity – in fact, the best evidenced one – whose ancestry included no specifically Neanderthal forebears, followed by the presence in the same area at a later date of Neanderthalers.

The Levantine moderns were tall on average (like the later Crô-Magnons of Europe), taller than most people today at 1.83 m for males and 1.7 m for females. Shins and forearms were long, unlike those of the Levantine (and other) Neanderthal folk, while pelvis shape was fully modern and un-Neanderthal. Their brains were on average bigger than those of most of us now (a trait they share with the majority of Neanderthalers, though the brains were differently shaped): these brain sizes probably relate to the bigger and more rugged physiques of the time. Seen from the back, the Qafzeh and Skhul skulls are high and parallel-sided just as ours are; cheeks are hollowed like most people's today, and there is none of that distinctive pulled-forward Neanderthal look to the mid-face, though the lower part of the face is often markedly more prognathous (and sometimes rather more chinless) than we generally find among ourselves, with some big teeth in the back of the mouth (but no Neanderthal retromolar gap).

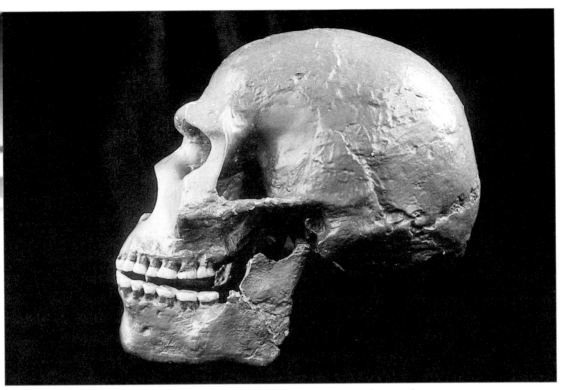

The adult male Skhul V: rugged but non-Neanderthal, despite the heavy brow-ridges.

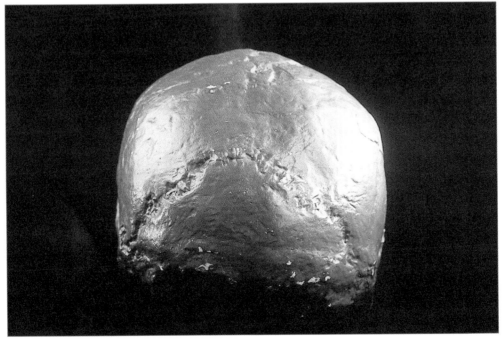

Skhul V from the back, with a modern sort of breadth and height, giving the 'tin loaf' look.

At both the Skhul and Qafzeh sites some ten to twenty individuals were discovered, having been buried (some of them, at least) in deliberately cut graves, with both sexes and adults and children in evidence. The Levantine graves in themselves (like the hearths of the sites) cannot be distinguished in sophistication between the Neanderthalers and the moderns, any more than real differences can be detected in the Mousterian tools found in association with both types. But where the question of grave goods is concerned, there seems no doubt that the moderns were sometimes furnishing their graves with provisions of an ideological intent. We have seen that Neanderthal graves in Europe and in Western Asia cannot unequivocally be said to offer evidence of grave goods in the form of tools or cuts of meat (or garlands of flowers); some of the Mount Carmel graves of modern human types do appear really to have contained animal parts that were intentionally buried with the dead. Skhul 5, for example (a man of between 30 and 40 years of age), lay on his back with the jawbone of a wild boar in his arms. Qafzeh 11 (a child) was buried with the skull and antlers of a deer. (The young female adult Qafzeh 9 was accompanied with the body of a six-year-old child by the feet.) There are associations of ochre and marine shells with the Skhul and Qafzeh graves. These Levantine burials with grave goods, at some 100,000 BP, possibly antedate most if not all of the Neanderthal burials of Europe and Western Asia, though the Teshik Tash Neanderthal boy is probably older – with or without the contentious goat horn arrangement around his skeleton. Certainly the provision of grave goods for some of the Levantine moderns, in a way seen not nearly so clearly at any Neanderthal burial, hints at the development of some differences in the mental sphere between the two groups of people, with the possibility that these early moderns felt a more conscious awareness of death and were truly capable of the symbolic business of making some provision for the dead in an imagined afterlife. (One of the Skhul males, incidentally, evidently died of a severe spear wound to the hip.)

About the only other way in which any distinction can be made between the ways of life of the Levantine moderns and Neanderthalers arises out of some indication, derived from studies of animal teeth on their sites, that the Neanderthalers of Kebara hunted their prey all the year round while the Qafzeh moderns took theirs only in summer; it is as though the Neanderthalers had to work hard all the year round to stay put in their Mount Carmel caves while their modern predecessors came and went more insouciantly, used to travelling around and hunting more confidently. (Later on, Upper Palaeolithic blade industries, with their much greater economy of stone use to produce their more efficient tools, made the peripatetic lifestyle even easier to pursue.) Set against the uniformity of their Mousterian tool kits and their shared lack of bone work, of ornament, and of art, it would perhaps be rather clutching at straws to make very much of the few grave goods of the moderns and their putative hunting superiority to try to draw distinctions between them and the Neanderthalers who came after them in the Levant. But in the end it was the moderns who were to prosper on Earth and the Neanderthalers who were one way or another to disappear; the first hints of the survival advantages enjoyed by the moderns over the Neanderthalers are likely to lie in just such tiny indications of behavioural difference as a piece of meat in a grave or a novel hunting strategy. Meanwhile, it should be noted that the basically Middle Palaeolithic way of life that was shared by the Neanderthalers and these early moderns of Israel went on for tens of thousands of years thereafter with little or no innovation that we can see despite this emergence of *Homo sapiens sapiens* by about 100,000–90,000 BP. It is a good question to ask why it took so long for the moderns to do anything better with those big and thoroughly modern-looking brain-cases of theirs – a question to which we shall return.

A tentative scheme for the comings and goings of evolving humanity in northern Israel from some time back into the Last Interglacial until about 40,000 BP can be constructed as follows. We recall the skull fragment from Zuttiyeh that, back in the 1920s, was the first of the Neanderthal-like remains to be discovered in the region; some anthropologists see in its rather domed forehead and lack of swept-back Neanderthal cheeks, despite the strong and divided brow-ridge configuration, a late and evolved sort of *Homo erectus* or *heidelbergensis*, perhaps on the way to the Neanderthalers or perhaps only representative of the African tendency towards early *Homo sapiens* already seen at Bodo and Kabwe. It is perhaps best to leave the Tabun Neanderthal woman out of the picture as being of slightly dubious provenance in the *c.* 100,000 BP levels to which she has been assigned. The Skhul and Qafzeh remains next appear as early examples, at about 100,000 BP, of almost completely evolved moderns, with strong indications of a heavy dose of African genetic inheritance in their general physiques, as though – plausibly – some good part of their ancestry had come up into the Levant from the East African region during relatively warm times at the end of the Last Interglacial when their African body pattern could emigrate north, along with other warm-loving species of fauna like hippo, ostrich and zebra. Whether these more or less moderns persisted in their occupation of the area after, say 90,000–80,000 BP is unclear. Around 60,000 BP the same region saw perhaps the arrival of cold-adapted Neanderthalers (like those represented by the Kebara remains), coming down into the warmer refuge area of the Levant when the hardships of the consolidating ice age in Europe drove some at least of the Neanderthal folk south, along with brown bear, wolf and woolly rhino. Over the next ten to twenty thousand years the Levantine Neanderthalers seem to have shared to some degree in a local genetic pool that took in some fully *sapiens* tendencies, evolving some traits (seen, for example, in the Amud adult male) that distinguished them from their classic European Neanderthal contemporaries in the direction of the moderns. (The next attested appearance of fully modern humanity in the region occurs at Ksar Akil in the Lebanon, with a juvenile *Homo sapiens sapiens* associated with an Upper Palaeolithic industry at about 37,000 BP, and there are moderns again at Qafzeh at about 35,000 BP.) Whether there was a continual coming and going of both moderns and Neanderthalers in the Levantine area after 60,000 BP is again unclear – we have found too few fossils of either sort to be sure. Perhaps the Levantine moderns largely retreated into Africa at some time after about 80,000 BP with the growing cold, perhaps some stayed on. (A ten-year-old non-Neanderthal child's bones have recently been found in the Nile Valley at about 55,000 BP.) Perhaps, after the arrival of the Neanderthalers in the Levant, the two sorts of humanity coexisted in some way that brought them into little or no direct contact for much of the time, pursuing slightly different hunting strategies, for example, that saw the moderns more prone to travel about and come and go. Their tool kits shared in common make it impossible to settle these questions without more fossils. Perhaps there was some interbreeding to account for the modernish traits of the late Neanderthalers of the area, but equally perhaps the two sorts of humanity largely avoided each other and sexual attraction between them ran at a low ebb. If things had gone so far that any matings between them produced infertile offspring (in other words, they were truly different species) then the modernish traits of Amud, and Shanidar, are difficult to account for (as could be the Neanderthal-like traits of some of the early moderns of Central and Eastern Europe, to be discussed later).

Both the Levantine Neanderthalers and the Levantine moderns who preceded them wielded a Mousterian tool kit, of the sort that is called Middle Palaeolithic in Europe and Middle Stone Age in Africa. The evolution of industrial traditions out of Lower Palaeolithic (African Early Stone Age) through Middle Palaeolithic (African Middle Stone Age) into Upper Palaeolithic (African Late Stone Age) has a history all of its own, largely divorced from the evolution of human physical types by reason of the extreme paucity of these versus the abundance of finds of stone tools. It is consequently possible to trace a technical progression, suggestive of evolving mental enhancement, in the tools found on archaeological sites with no coincidence of human fossil remains to prove absolutely that bigger and more modern brains were behind the improvements in the tool kits. The Levantine finds caution that there is no necessary correlation between Upper Palaeolithic and more or less fully modern *Homo sapiens sapiens*, just as the Chatelperronian finds from France indicate that no such necessary correlation exists, either, between Neanderthalers and Mousterian. Still, it remains broadly useful to conjecture that certain sorts of premature Upper Palaeolithic technological tendencies found in older contexts may hint at the evolution of cleverer, more modern human types to pioneer them. And it is the appearances of blade industries, where many of the struck flakes are much longer and thinner and flatter than those of run-of-the-mill Middle Palaeolithic/Middle Stone Age contexts, that impress as possible harbingers of technological and mental evolution. It was the blade industries of the European Upper Palaeolithic that were found early on in the history of archaeology in clear association with the remains of Crô-Magnon types and their refined bone work, adornments, grave goods, artistic and magical productions. Upper Palaeolithic blades are themselves frequently marvels of lithic sophistication, with many forms adapted to many uses as knives, scrapers, gravers, sometimes finished to a high degree, in marked contrast to the routine and comparatively unimaginative products of Middle Palaeolithic technology. It is easy to see how early dated occurrences of blade manufacture within the time-span of the Middle Stone Age can excite archaeologists on the track of the first footprints of modern humanity.

The Klasies River Mouth site in South Africa, where those early indications of the presence of evolving *Homo sapiens sapiens* were turned up at about 100,000 BP, is also a place where early manifestations of blade manufacture have been identified, though the blades were not found in association with the modernish physical remains (which were accompanied by ordinary enough Middle Stone Age tools, rather as Skhul and Qafzeh were accompanied by Mousterian artefacts). The blades of Klasies River Mouth, of a type found elsewhere and called by the name of the Howieson's Poort tradition, date from about 60,000 or so BP, and are surprisingly sophisticated for their time. They include geometric forms, often tiny like the microlithic products of much later times, in the form of crescents and triangles, and many of them look as

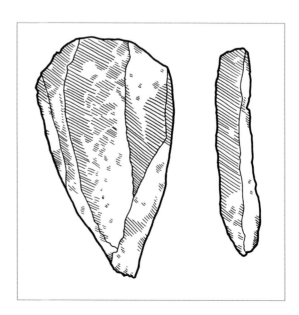

A blade core and blade from Klasies River Mouth.

though they were struck with an intermediary punch made of wood or bone. Some pieces have the appearance of being shaped for hafting as spear points or blades into wooden holders. What is more, stone was fetched from thirty or so kilometres away to make these blade tools, more in the manner of true Upper Palaeolithic than Middle Palaeolithic/Middle Stone Age habits. It is probably fair to say that the Howieson's Poort material (the name site is to the east of Klasies River Mouth) would be called Upper Palaeolithic without a qualm if found in Europe. The Howieson's Poort tradition, with an age range at its various sites between some 75,000 and 40,000 BP, is itself part of a raft of blade manifestations in Africa that appear sporadically from perhaps as early as some 200,000 years ago in Kenya and reach down to true Late Stone Age times (though blades never came to predominate in Africa, nor in the Far East, as they did in Europe). The early appearances of blade technology are rather flash-in-the-pan affairs, coming and going rather quickly without bringing on the establishment of full Late Stone Age (in European terms, Upper Palaeolithic) culture. At Klasies River Mouth the blade episode is succeeded by a return to Middle Stone Age technology. The blades, moreover, are not found in association with other archaeological traits of an Upper Palaeolithic/Late Stone Age character. There is no bone work, for example, so characteristic of the Upper Palaeolithic in Europe, and no sign that the hunting skills of the blade-makers were any better than those of their Middle Stone Age predecessors and successors. It is as though tentative experiments in technological innovation were being haphazardly attempted here and there, without any decisive advantages to show for them among populations that were still not ready to take them further, even if they could hit on them now and then.

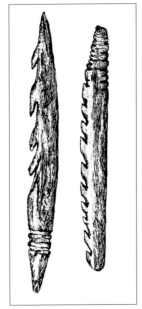

Harpoons from Katanda.

None of the early blade industries of Africa has produced evidence of bone work to go with their advanced-looking stone tools, but there is rather astonishing evidence for sophisticated bone work in itself at a very early date in Zaire. The site of Katanda, on the banks of the Semliki river, has enjoyed a contentious history of attempts to date the archaeological material found there since the late 1980s. It looks now as though the likely date of the levels from which the bone work has come lies somewhere between about 105,000 and 65,000 BP, based on TL and ESR determinations taken together with the geological situation. The stone tools of Katanda are undistinguished flake products of a Middle Stone Age sort, but the bone work includes knife-like pieces and very spectacular barbed harpoons with grooves facilitating mounting on wooden shafts, a feature not encountered in the European Upper Palaeolithic until as late as 15,000 BP. Similar finds have been made at nearby sites (in association with Late Stone Age tools) since the 1950s, with even the reported presence on some bone pieces of linear markings that might represent some sort of numerical recording, but these other finds have been dated by the radiocarbon method to as late as 25,000 or 21,000 BP. At these latter dates, the bone work of all these Zairean sites would not seem wholly out of place, but the very early dating of the Katanda material has been hard to accept without the corroboration of more well-dated sites. Certainly geological and climatological evidence suggests that Katanda is older than the other sites, but so strange and stray at some 80,000 BP are the bone harpoons – which would be an adornment of the European Upper Palaeolithic fifty thousand years or more later – that only the discovery of more such items at other sites with secure dates will satisfy wary archaeologists.

From the number of catfish bones found in the same levels as the archaeological material, we may conclude that the Katanda harpoons were used by their makers to spear fish in the local river. Fishing is not a subsistence strategy much attested at Middle Stone Age/Middle Palaeolithic sites anywhere in the world and so, to the novelty of the sophisticated bone work, is added the unexpectedness of another Upper Palaeolithic trait – of some consequence – at Katanda by perhaps 90,000 or 80,000 BP. It has even been suggested that the finding of two separate clusters of debris at Katanda might indicate the ancient presence of two neighbouring nuclear families of prematurely Upper Palaeolithic people.

It is another rather tallish order to think that a tradition of such sophisticated bone work, evidenced nowhere else in the world at such an early date, nor for tens of thousands of years subsequently, should have apparently gone on in the same area for so long (down to 20,000 BP) without communicating itself to any other early populations of humanity that we know of. Katanda hints at the long persistence in one, perhaps rather isolated, area of an innovatory technology and perhaps a whole way of life pioneered tens of thousands of years before they appeared elsewhere in the wider world. Perhaps there are more sites like Katanda to be discovered in Africa, where we may hope that human remains might be found to throw light on the evolution of the sort of humanity that could produce the Katanda harpoons and fish with them. Certainly, until further finds are made and dated to everyone's satisfaction, the Katanda harpoons cannot clinch the argument that fully modern humanity and the modern mode of life originated in Africa at some time around 100,000 BP and spread out from there to the rest of the world. But it has to be said that it must have been in such small and isolated ways that the very first steps were taken somewhere towards the way of life that was to spread far and wide with *Homo sapiens sapiens* and the Upper Palaeolithic. A patchwork of initially intermittent or isolated manifestations of the components that eventually came together as the Upper Palaeolithic is quite plausible.

It is tantalizing that no single line of evidence – whether to do with genetics or fossils or archaeological finds – amounts to proof of an African antecedence for *Homo sapiens sapiens*, or at least for the best part of his genetic make-up and technological equipment; taken as a whole, the body of evidence of different lines of enquiry is powerfully suggestive to many anthropologists of the African origins of modern humanity, but with no conclusive proof of the case in any specific department.

No more bone work of the sort seen at Katanda (or really of any sort at all) is known from the archaeological record elsewhere over all the years that separate the Zairean finds at some 90,000 or 80,000 BP (if the dates stand up) from those of the European Upper Palaeolithic after about 40,000 BP. But blade industries do continue to manifest themselves here and there between the time of the early South and East African appearances and the emergence of the true blade-based Upper Palaeolithic cultures. These blade manifestations necessarily occur against a background of generally Middle Palaeolithic/Middle Stone Age traditions (sometimes even of Lower Palaeolithic/Old Stone Age ones, where these lingered on); it is common to find the blade industries underlain and/or overlain by Middle Palaeolithic/Middle Stone Age material, as is the case at Klasies River Mouth. The same sort of situation obtains at Haua Fteah in Libya, at Abri Zumoffen in Lebanon and at Mount Carmel in Israel, though none of the human remains of the latter area was found in association with the blade material, which archaeologists know by the name 'Amudian' after the same site in which – at different levels – the Neanderthal remains were found. In both Libya and the Levant the blade episodes (at about 70,000 BP) are succeeded by a return to Mousterian material, well before the establishment of true Upper Palaeolithic industries in both areas after about 45,000 BP. Whoever was making these flash-in-the-pan blade industries of North Africa and the Levant, and whatever the potential advantages of their innovatory tool kits, in the aftermath it was always back to the Mousterian for the time being. The more or less moderns of Skhul and Qafzeh wielded Mousterian tools, with no blade element, so if we are tempted (reasonably) to identify the blade manifestations with evolving modern *Homo sapiens sapiens*, we have to conclude that blade-making was not an idea that recommended itself to all the populations of moderns all the time, but was rather something tried now and then by some groups (maybe for particular reasons at the time) and then dropped for a while, perhaps to be taken up again later, or not. It is as though the intermittent blade-makers were clever enough to hit on the idea of blades but not yet able to integrate this promising technology into their entire imaginations and think it through to get the best out of it. Indeed, we may speculate that they yet lacked any integrated and entire imagination into which all the experiences of their lives could be pooled, to make fruitful connections between every aspect of their existence. Modern looking as the brain-cases of the early moderns are (at Skhul and Qafzeh, for example), we may well conclude that consciousness as we know it was absent within them – whether because some further brain evolution, invisible in the fossil record, was still to be accomplished or because a necessary groundwork of cultural evolution, in terms of acquired habits of mind (perhaps involving language developments), was not yet in place. Perhaps too many parts of the mind were still on separate automatic pilots, with no all-embracing and directing consciousness. All this remains for the moment highly speculative, of course, but it is to these areas of enquiry that we must look to try to explain the emergence of modern humanity with the Upper Palaeolithic of some 45,000 years ago. Meanwhile, it may be salutary to note that the very development of blade technology, which we so firmly associate in Europe with the self-evident glories of Upper Palaeolithic modernity in the shape of art and burial rites, social and cultural elaboration, was never in any case the be-all and end-all of sub-Saharan or Far Eastern Late Stone Age tool traditions – blades were not an important part of the tool kits of the people of these regions.

The final triumph of the blade-making tendency seems to have been achieved in the Levantine region at some time soon after about 50,000 BP. Sites like Boker Tachtit in the Negev and El Wad at Mount Carmel may be witness to the emergence of the Upper Palaeolithic with blades out of the local Mousterian with flakes. Thereafter the Upper Palaeolithic spread quickly in the area and was soon making its way into Europe, its progress probably facilitated by a relatively warmer phase of the Last Ice Age which encouraged its makers, of presumably warm-loving build, to venture into the erstwhile colder regions. Once again we are faced with the dual lines of evidence afforded on the one hand by a few fossils of human types and on the other by rather more in the way of archaeological artefacts.

In Europe, in the domain to date of the Neanderthalers with their Mousterian version of Middle Palaeolithic/Middle Stone Age toolmaking, it is possible to track the progress of the blade-based Upper Palaeolithic out of the Levantine region. At Ksar Akil in Lebanon, a properly Upper Palaeolithic blade industry dates to about 44,000 BP, while the oldest Upper Palaeolithic of Europe that has been discovered so far appears to be the Aurignacian material from Bacho Kiro in Bulgaria, from before 43,000 BP. The gap between these sites and a proto Upper Palaeolithic site like Boker Tachtit, at 47,000 BP, is small enough; the gap between Ksar Akil and Bacho Kiro is vanishingly small. At Boker Tachtit the emergence of the Upper from the Middle Palaeolithic is evidenced by the occurrences of cores from which first large Levallois flakes and then smaller true blades were struck; at Bacho Kiro the Aurignacian toolmaking tradition, the first of the European Upper Palaeolithic cultures (and the most uniformly widespread), is in place. It took perhaps some 3,000

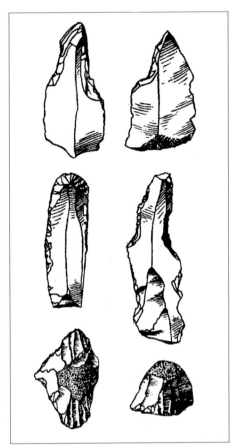

Aurignacian blades and scrapers (the longest about 5 cm).

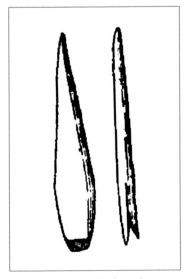

An Aurignacian split-base bone point, about 10 cm long.

to 5,000 years more for the Aurignacian to reach right across Europe to Spain, by about 39,000 BP.

The appearance of the Aurignacian in Europe seems to coincide with relatively warmer times that facilitated its spread out of the Levantine region first into south-east Europe and then westwards across the continent. The strong presumption must be that the Aurignacian was carried into Europe by a population movement of modern types of humanity into the Mousterian territory of the Neanderthalers; wherever human remains have been found in association with the Aurignacian tool kit, those remains have always been of modern and never of Neanderthal type. It was not, of course, some purposeful invasive trek of moderns bent on reaching the Atlantic in short order but rather a slow spread like that, more than 30,000 years later, of the first farmers of Europe out of much the same Middle Eastern homelands.

The Aurignacian is a very distinctive toolmaking tradition, markedly different in so many ways from the Mousterian. The emphasis is on narrow blades from carefully prepared cores rather than broad flakes, with characteristic end-worked and steeply retouched scrapers rather than Mousterian side-scrapers, and with bone and ivory points that are signally missing from Mousterian assemblages (as are items of personal decoration like beads which feature in the Levantine and European Aurignacian from the first). With very few exceptions, most of which can probably be explained by accidental mixing of material from different levels before or during excavation, there are no European instances of anything like the Negev and Mount Carmel sites where Upper Palaeolithic blade techniques emerge from within Middle Palaeolithic industries: the Aurignacian did not evolve out of a European Mousterian background. The exceptions, however, do look like cases of acculturation, where local Mousterian traditions took on board some Upper Palaeolithic traits and turned themselves into short-lived and geographically restricted pseudo Upper Palaeolithic cultures within the Aurignacian range. Two such acculturated Mousterian pockets may be represented by the Szeletian of Hungary and the Uluzzian of Italy, where a basically Middle Palaeolithic tradition with side-scrapers and denticulates is distinctively supplemented by Upper Palaeolithic elements like end-scrapers and burins (together with novel leaf-shaped points for the Szeletian that are really no more Upper than Middle Palaeolithic). Even these two cases (and something similar in southern Russia) of apparent acculturation may owe their character to mixing from Mousterian and true Upper Palaeolithic levels.

All the same some acculturation between the incoming Aurignacian and the indigenous Mousterian (in a one-way direction from the former to the latter) seems quite likely to have occurred as the Upper Palaeolithic and its makers spread into Eastern and Central Europe – for it almost certainly happened later on in Western Europe as we shall shortly see. In the west it happened without any sign of physical interbreeding between Neanderthalers and moderns, but there is some reason to think that in the east a certain amount of interbreeding may have occurred. Staunch supporters of the 'Out of Africa' school of anthropology point to the mtDNA evidence, particularly in the light of the distance in terms of mtDNA of the original Neanderthal Man from any modern populations, as a strong argument against the Neanderthalers' having had any part to play in the descent of modern Europeans through contact with the Aurignacian people. But it remains a possibility that Neanderthal nuclear DNA, which after all is the genetic material that actually controls our development, was imported for a time into the early *Homo sapiens sapiens* gene pool. Put bluntly, it is possible that Neanderthal males did on occasion impregnate early modern females, to produce offspring with some Neanderthal-derived traits that may even survive to the present in, mostly, European populations. The mtDNA evidence, aided perhaps by shrewd conjecture, does appear to rule out (so far as the published results from only the one Neanderthal specimen go) any likelihood that Aurignacian males regularly favoured Neanderthal females as partners. The anatomical evidence to support the idea of some Neanderthal input into the modern gene pool is not overwhelming by any means, but suggestive. There are specific details of nose and brow forms, of the shape of the back of the skull, of teeth and of the femur that persuade some anthropologists that something of the Neanderthalers came through into the earliest populations of *Homo sapiens sapiens* in Europe. Even among modern Europeans, thirty to forty thousand years further on, there is a higher incidence of something like the occipital bun, that was such a distinctive feature of the Neanderthal skull, than occurs among other peoples of the world today. Many of the fossils of early moderns in Europe also show a bony ridge over a nerve opening in the lower jaw that was common in the Neanderthalers; it is rarely seen in non-European fossil moderns and never among early *Homo sapiens sapiens* fossils from Africa. Front teeth of both Neanderthalers and some early moderns show a similar shovel shape. Committed supporters of the 'Out of Africa' hypothesis dismiss these details as unmeaningful coincidences, while die-hard multiregionalists lean on them to try to maintain, even with the European Neanderthalers, the notion that all the human populations of the world have come up together through more or less the same evolutionary stages at more or less the same speed, retaining local characteristics as they come. In the light of the archaeological evidence of the spread of the Aurignacian as a new and uniform tradition without Mousterian antecedence in Europe and of the complete dearth of European Neanderthalers with any signs of evolving fully *sapiens* physical traits, it has to be concluded that the multiregional hypothesis – whatever its merits in regard to the Far Eastern and Australasian evidence – breaks down where the Neanderthalers are concerned. The most that can be proposed is that some Neanderthal inheritance was mixed in Europe (and probably in the Levant, too) into the modern gene pool.

The first moderns of Europe tend to be a ruggedly built crew, though without the cold-adapted body proportions and limb shapes of the Neanderthalers. Indeed, the warm-adapted, and so 'African', look of the long forearms and shins of many of the early moderns of Europe are features that argue against much in the way of interbreeding with the squat Neanderthalers. Though their relatively long legs may have gone back to experience in warmer climes, it is likely that they were still of advantage to the early moderns of Europe, in keeping with their active and roaming style of life which saw them hunt further from 'home' and fetch their raw materials from further away than the Neanderthal folk did. Compared with the Neanderthalers, even the tallish and rugged early moderns of Europe were somewhat lightly built; this too may have been an advantage to them in northern climes, needing a little less food to fuel their bodies, for their lack of Neanderthal-style cold-adapted body proportions could be offset by their technological superiority and greater hunting powers.

The skull shapes of the European early moderns may vary to a degree (and even display some traits that may relate them to the Neanderthalers as we have seen) but essentially they display high-rising foreheads over unpronounced brows (though males show more than females) that seldom if ever meet in bars over the eyes; high brain-cases that are short when seen from the side and parallel-sided when seen from the back (though they can sometimes be longer and lower than is usual today); short

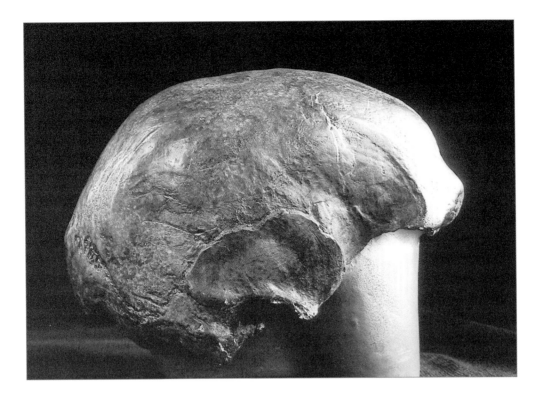

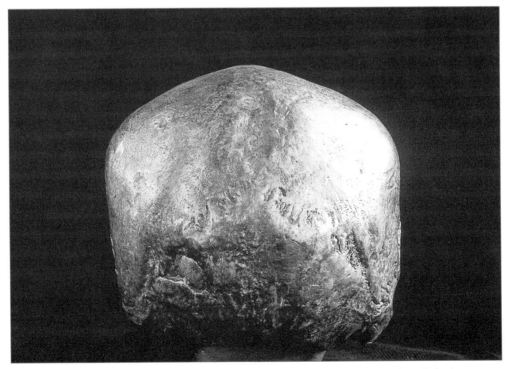

A skull from Mladeč, with something of a bun at the rear, but high and straight-sided when seen from the back.

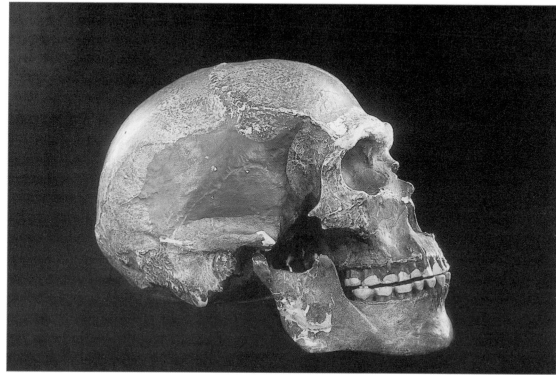

An adult male from Předmosti.

and tucked-in faces without inflated cheeks and that Neanderthal pulled-out look; and, usually, rather delicate jaws with smallish teeth and marked chin development to act as a strengthener when overall jaw robusticity was reduced. Improvements in the range and usefulness of Upper Palaeolithic tools, and perhaps of cooking techniques too, helped to facilitate jaw and teeth reduction when great strength in the mouth was no longer so badly needed. The tucking-in of the jaw under a shorter, higher skull has been judged, also, to coincide with an increased flexing of the skull base and repositioning of the pharynx needed for full articulation of speech.

Among the first appearances of modern types (all with Aurignacian tool kits) in the European territory hitherto populated by the Neanderthalers (with their various sorts of Mousterian) we may note finds at Bacho Kiro in Bulgaria at 43,000 or more years ago (jaw and tooth fragments), at Velika Pečina in Croatia at more than 34,000 BP (skull pieces with high forehead and slight brows), at Mladeč in Moravia at some 35,000 BP (several strong-browed males and unbrowed females with, in some cases, those Neanderthal-like buns but flat and reduced faces), at Vogelherd in Germany at about the same age as Mladeč (and of about the same character), at Předmosti in Moravia at before 30,000 BP (a mass grave of mammoth hunters

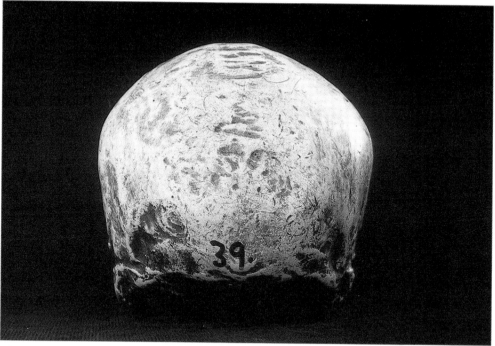

The old man's skull from Crŏ-Magnon, back view.

includes some skulls with rather prominent brows, prognathous faces and suggestions of a bun that are otherwise fully modern in type), and – best known of all – at the Crô-Magnon shelter at les Eyzies in France. This site has given its name to the entire type of early European moderns and it is still convenient to use the name, with reservations.

The Crô-Magnon 'mausoleum', with three adult males, one adult female and a child, was discovered as long ago as 1868 by workmen labouring on the laying of the railway track that still runs just across the road from the subsequently built Crô-Magnon hotel. Obviously, the Crô-Magnon shelter was not investigated with any modern archaeological finesse but it seems clear that the skeletons were laid to rest in a context with Aurignacian tools and faunal remains of reindeer, bison and mammoth – pierced animal teeth and shells appear to have constituted the grave goods of the departed. To go by the Aurignacian tools in a French context, we may estimate the date of the human remains to be some 34,000–30,000 BP. The skulls are of such fully modern type and the limb bones show the long shins and forearms of the moderns to such a degree that doubts have occasionally been raised as to the early date of the remains, which were lying on the surface of the rock shelter floor – but then, so were the animal bones and tools, and the Crô-Magnon skeletons are no more outlandishly modern than the bones from Mladeč and Předmosti. At Crô-Magnon, too, there is variation between the skulls in extent of brow-ridge development and in the shape at the back. The 'old man' of Crô-Magnon (who has distinctively rectangular eye sockets) presents a face pitted by fungal infection (see p. 20), while the woman survived a fractured skull and there is evidence of fusing of neck vertebrae: all features that point to a hard life where the status of old man meant being barely middle-aged in our terms. By the time the moderns were reaching south-west Europe, life was indeed hard with the beginning of a return to glacial conditions after the interstadial improvement that helped to usher them out of the Levant and into south-east Europe a few thousands of years before.

The bones of the early Upper Palaeolithic people, from all over Europe, go to make up a picture of a varied population of *Homo sapiens sapiens*, with quite a range of types that sometimes resemble not only modern Europeans but also people living in other parts of the world today. Not too much should be made of this as it is mostly a matter of skull details in a small sample that has come down to us from a small population in the first place. We do not know what skin colour they had, nor the colour and character of their hair. (Though the Upper Palaeolithic people often painted animals on cave walls with considerable naturalism, their few pictures of themselves are very stylized and useless for getting any idea of what they really looked like.) In the past the matter of their body build and stature has been overdone by writers intent on making comparisons that were unfavourable to the Neanderthalers: the Crô-Magnon folk were on average about 1.73 m tall for males and 1.55 m for females, with male brains averaging just under 1600 ml and female ones just under 1400 ml. Though slender, their limb bones were not always all that long even by comparison with average Neanderthalers. Whatever population growths and movements have happened since their day, it is certain that modern European populations still carry many of their genes.

Chatelperronian knives.

Crô-Magnon type bones have been found in association with Aurignacian tools at another French site called les Rois; the people and the toolmaking tradition appear to have arrived together in Western Europe by some time after 40,000 BP. (They may have reached Spain earlier than south-west France, along the Mediterranean coast.) For the ensconced Neanderthalers of the region, this was the time of their first encounter with very different people equipped with a different and better tool kit and, it seems certain, a better strategy to survive and prosper even in the harsh climate to which the Neanderthalers had made such a complete adaptation. The Neanderthalers were not to long outlive the encounter. At some sites in northern Spain and France there seems to be a change without hiatus from underlying Mousterian to immediately overlying Aurignacian; at others there is a sterile interval between the two occupations, as though the Neanderthalers who made the Mousterian had gone away never to return before the fully moderns arrived with their Aurignacian. In no case does a Mousterian assemblage overlie an Aurignacian one. But at three sites, two of them in France, and one in Spain, a tool tradition called Chatelperronian, that contains many Mousterian elements alongside Upper Palaeolithic ones, has been found interstratified with Aurignacian. This interstratification of the two cultures, showing that their makers came and went and returned to the same sites in these three instances, demonstrates a period of coexistence between them, with the possibility at least of some interaction. There is no doubt that the Chatelperronian is rooted in the late Mousterian variant called MAT-B (Mousterian of Acheulian Tradition, later version, where the small hand-axes of the variant are not abundant but backed flakes – blunted along one edge – are). The Chatelperronian shows such MAT-B elements as backed flakes, side-scrapers, denticulate pieces and even some small bifacial axes; its geographical distribution is the same as the MAT-B's. But at the same time there are in the Chatelperronian true blades, end-scrapers, burins, some bone and antler tools and ornamental pieces like perforated animal teeth: items very rare (to say the least) as individual pieces in Mousterian assemblages and never seen together in force. At one time it was thought that this Chatelperronian might be an independent local innovation out of the MAT-B at the very beginning of the Upper Palaeolithic, predating the Aurignacian, and even that the makers of the MAT-B might already have evolved from Neanderthal ancestors into modern types well before developing the Chatelperronian. But dates for the Aurignacian and the Chatelperronian soon showed that the European-wide Aurignacian had arrived in France and Cantabria by the time of the Chatelperronian, and the subsequent discoveries of interstratification proved them contemporaneous, without any priority for the Chatelperronian. Human teeth found with the Chatelperronian at the Grotte du Renne at Arcy-sur-Cure in the Paris Basin hinted strongly that this culture was the work of Neanderthalers and then the discovery, in 1979, of a human skeleton in association with the Chatelperronian at Saint-Césaire in the Charente-Maritime clinched the matter – for the skeleton was that of a classic Neanderthaler. It was now to all intents and purposes certain that the Chatelperronian, with its mixture of Mousterian and Upper Palaeolithic traits, was the work of pure Neanderthalers.

Acculturation seems to be the only explanation for the Chatelperronian. Its Neanderthal makers, with their long Mousterian inheritance, must have been influenced by the incoming Aurignacian to introduce various Upper Palaeolithic elements into their toolmaking tradition, and indeed into other aspects of their lives (like the wearing of personal adornments). Even so, Chatelperronian tools were still made by different techniques and from differently sourced raw material *vis-à-vis* the Aurignacian products. Where they overlapped in their use of the same sites at different times, the makers of the Aurignacian seem to have favoured the hunting of reindeer as their speciality while the Chatelperronians hunted (and perhaps scavenged) less discriminately, taking horse, bovids and red deer in addition to reindeer. Perhaps, in the early days, while Aurignacian population numbers were still small, it was the differences in lifestyles between the two peoples that allowed a measure of coexistence. Perhaps the Neanderthalers had been weakened by the decline, during the milder interstadial that saw the entry of the Crô-Magnon types into Europe, of their familiar world of ice age conditions to which they had become so attuned. It is fascinating to wonder just how the coexistence of the two sorts of people went on in practice and how the acculturation of the Neanderthalers into Upper Palaeolithic ways was achieved.

The physical remains of the Saint-Césaire Neanderthaler come from the higher (later) of two Chatelperronian layers of the site, dated by TL to around 36,000 BP. The body of this male Neanderthaler was flexed and buried in a small oval grave, in which were preserved the right half of the skull, a shoulder blade, robust arm bones, some ribs and fragments of shin and kneecap. The skull is classically Neanderthal in character, except perhaps for some reduction in the typical mid-face prognathism of the breed which does not look sufficient to set us guessing at any interbreeding with Crô-Magnon types or at any rapid evolution towards modern *Homo sapiens sapiens*. (With modern types already in full swing at places like Vogelherd by about 35,000 BP, there seems insufficient time, in even the most optimistic multiregional terms, for the European Neanderthalers to have evolved into European moderns in situ, now that we find classic Neanderthal types still around at 36,000 BP and later, as we shall also see.)

At Arcy the Chatelperronian levels incorporate evidence of hut building in the form of a rough circle of eleven post holes enclosing a 4 m wide area (with two hearths) partially paved with limestone slabs – the holes probably for mammoth tusks and bones as structural elements in view of the abundance of such bones on the site and the dearth of tree pollen to indicate the availability of timber. The huts, the Upper Palaeolithic tools and the bone points are impressive enough innovations for Neanderthalers of Mousterian background; they demonstrate the ability of these people to pick up on new ideas if not to pioneer them. But perhaps we should set most store by the Chatelperronian adoption of items of personal decoration (the pierced animal teeth) when we come to give them their due. Apart from the possibility of body painting (or decoration of clothing) which is unlikely ever to be

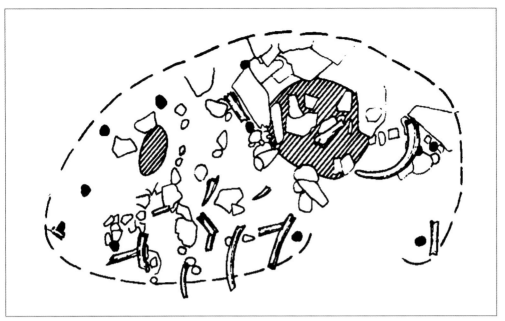

Hut emplacement at Arcy with stones, mammoth bones, post holes (black) and hearths (hatched areas).

established, the Neanderthalers show no signs of personal adornment until the Chatelperronian episode. To have seen the point of body decoration with beads of pierced teeth and to have taken it up as a habit perhaps says more about Neanderthal mentality than anything else; personal adornment is a very social thing, with potential implications about status in terms of sex and hierarchy as well as about aesthetic sensibility. Nothing about the archaeology of the Neanderthalers, except to an extent for their graves and their bear 'cult', has had much light to shed on this side of their natures until the Chatelperronian beads at more or less the end of the Neanderthalers' career on earth. Even so, the personal adornment of the Chatelperronian is a poor thing by comparison with what was soon to go on among the Upper Palaeolithic people, and the Chatelperronians produced absolutely no art that we know of. They seem to have been capable of seeing some point to personal decoration, but not to have been able to innovate it for themselves, except by imitation.

The Chatelperronian was a short-lived late flowering of Neanderthal potential, probably only a few thousand years in duration. A Neanderthal temporal bone from Arcy is dated to about 34,000 BP with Chatelperronian associations. And despite the emergence of the Chatelperronian from a MAT-B background, it did not supersede all forms of Mousterian either in France or Spain. The latest French Mousterians, at les

Cottés and la Balme, are dated by C14 to about 30,000 BP but should probably be corrected to a slightly earlier date as a result of refinements of carbon dating. In Spain a Neanderthal lower jaw found at Zaffaraya dates to some 33,000 BP (perhaps even a little later) and was discovered in association with a Mousterian industry; bones in a hearth at the site suggest the cooking of goat meat and the melancholy thought may cross our minds of Neanderthal Man's eating a hearty breakfast for his last meal in his final refuge, with the Crô-Magnonards beating at the door.

But perhaps after all, the Iberian Neanderthalers at least did not perish altogether without issue. A newly reported find from Leiria, north of Lisbon, offers possible evidence for the survival of Neanderthal physical traits into Crô-Magnon times. The skeleton of a little girl, buried with a seashell necklace and coloured with red ochre, is said to show at about 24,500 BP a Neanderthal stockiness of trunk and leg bones alongside more Crô-Magnon features of chin development, teeth and arm bones (though the top of the skull, where the brows might have told us more, was broken by a farm tractor before discovery). Claims for a period of interbreeding between Crô-Magnon and Neanderthal types have again been advanced on the basis of this new find.

In all probability the Neanderthal folk who survived unchanged into Aurignacian times were simply outcompeted and marginalized to extinction rather than hunted down and exterminated. Though they were evidently able to coexist for a time with the moderns and to acculturate from them in some circumstances, even to interbreed with them to some extent, it seems likely that differences persisted in habits, in technological aptitude, in hunting prowess, in language (and language skills), in appearance, in mating predelictions and in social arrangements, and that all these differences and others we cannot now discern might have kept the two sorts of humanity largely apart. The moderns, from everything we know of their technological and ideological achievements, were cleverer and more flexible than the Neanderthalers; as climate deteriorated again at around 30,000 BP, it might only have taken one or two thousands of years of slightly inferior hunting performance, slightly shorter life expectancy, slightly lower birth rate and slightly higher infant mortality for the Neanderthalers to disappear in the face of the moderns' better record in all these areas. It is rather like the decline of Britain's native red squirrels in the face of the imported grey species; interestingly, the reds were already in slight decline before the arrival of the robust greys, who are more successful hunters and produce more offspring, but do not physically attack the reds. A natural sympathy for the underdog and the disadvantaged lends a sad poignancy to the fate of the Neanderthal folk, however it came about.

CHAPTER 13

Epilogue

As the evidence currently stands, it looks extremely unlikely that the classic Neanderthalers of Europe can have evolved directly into the Upper Palaeolithic people. There is not a big enough time gap between the last of the Neanderthalers at places like Saint-Césaire and the first of the moderns who brought in the Aurignacian – indeed there is no gap at all, and we have seen the evidence for moderns in Africa and the Levant at much earlier dates. In Western Europe there is, moreover, no body of evidence of any admixture at all of Neanderthal physical traits into the early modern inhabitants of the Aurignacian and succeeding periods, even though the case of the Chatelperronian indicates that cultural, if not genetic, traits could cross between the two peoples (though seemingly only by the one-way street from moderns to Neanderthalers). In Central and Eastern Europe there is perhaps slightly stronger indication that some interbreeding between Neanderthalers and moderns may have gone on, though here too the evidence never approaches the implication that any wholesale evolution from Neanderthal to modern types can have taken place, even with genetic input from outside. The evidence of physical anthropology (with remains like those of the Levantine moderns at 90,000 BP), the evidence of genetics (with the great distance of the Neanderthal mtDNA from that of any people in the world today) and the evidence of archaeology (with the spread of the Aurignacian, never associated with anything but moderns' bones, out of the Levant after about 45,000 BP) all point to the sidelining of the Neanderthalers of Europe in the face of the arrival of the moderns. The moderns carried the day and the question forces itself upon us as to the secret of their success. And even if the views of the most extreme multiregionalists were one day to be vindicated by new evidence to bolster the idea of rapid Neanderthal evolution into *Homo sapiens sapiens* in Europe, we should still have to ask why the modern sort of humanity took hold so quickly and completely (and not just in Europe, but all over the world). What was it about the moderns that ultimately let them thrive so readily, to the eclipse of other sorts of humanity like the Neanderthalers and their cultural traditions?

We have seen that modern physical types, as far as we can tell from their bones, were on the scene in Africa and the Levant by about 90,000 BP. Unless some breakthrough in the interpretation of interior skull formation allows us to come to firm conclusions about differing levels of brain performance among different fossil remains in comparison with ourselves, we shall not get any further with an answer to the question about the origins of modern human behaviour from the physical remains themselves. It seems unlikely any such breakthrough will be made, so we have only the archaeological evidence of what human beings were doing to go on when we try to characterize and account for the beginnings of the modern human career. In fact, the archaeology of the Upper Palaeolithic, though it can only represent a few surviving traces of past activity in the shape of flints and bone work, graves and artistic productions, is really very rich and suggestive. The Aurignacian culture, the first of the Upper Palaeolithic succession, comes in with a surprising uniformity across Europe from the Middle East. (This situation in itself argues against any evolution out of the preceding Mousterian for the Aurignacian, since the various versions of Mousterian across the range to be colonized by the Aurignacian were themselves not so very uniform, with distinct regional differences, though at the same time less rich in detail than the Aurignacian.) But after a few thousand years of the Aurignacian, real cultural diversity set in for the rest of the Upper Palaeolithic sequence with relatively short-lived and regionally diverse toolmaking traditions that show great inventiveness and sheer style in a way that the Mousterian never did. These traits must bear witness to a very different state of mind on the part of the makers of the upper Palaeolithic traditions from that of any previous peoples, including those very early moderns of Africa and the Levant who contented themselves with Middle Palaeolithic/Middle Stone Age tools just like their Neanderthal contemporaries.

People have speculated as to whether some brand-new neurological evolution took place in the brains of the early moderns, between the time of the Klasies River Mouth and Mount Carmel specimens and the time of the first makers of the Aurignacian in the Middle East and Europe: some neurological evolution deep inside the neocortex of their brains that is quite invisible to us when we examine the brain casts on the inside of their skulls. This speculation remains valid, but it also remains possible that the brains of the first moderns of a hundred thousand years ago were already every bit as versatile from the first as yours and mine but not yet put, for cultural reasons, to the sort of uses that have characterized humanity since the establishment of the Upper Palaeolithic – not until culture, in the broadest sense, had elaborated itself into complex social relations, complex linguistic expression and complex symbolism could the brains of the moderns fully flower. But, of course, those brains would never have evolved in the first place unless nature set some store by them in a way that gave their owners selective advantage over rivals – mostly other forms of humanity – for the ecological niche they exploited. Without making better tools than their Neanderthal (and, in some parts of the world, late *erectus*) contemporaries, the first of the moderns may well have already been doing something better with their evolved brain-cases; those slightly superior hunting strategies in Palestine mentioned in the previous chapter may be among the things they were doing better, and perhaps their grave-goods point to some greater social cohesion, some better network of supportive relations that could be manifested even in death. Both of these traits would be examples of better functioning of more fully integrated minds: in one case, of reading the signs of the natural world better, to hunt more flexibly and economically in terms of effort by season; in the other case, of more vividly recognizing family and kinship relations to the point where not just the old and infirm but even the dead could be imaginatively brought into the fold of human mutuality.

As far back as the early moderns of Israel at some 90,000 BP, the evidence for distinctively modern human behaviour (and, it has to be said, the interpretation of that evidence) is thin: the seasonal hunting and perhaps more certain grave-goods of the Levantine early moderns vs. the Neanderthalers do not amount to so very much. When we come to the European Upper Palaeolithic, the difference between Neanderthal behaviour (indeed, all former human behaviour) and Crô-Magnon behaviour is striking indeed. Where the tools are concerned, there is variety and sophistication on a scale not evidenced before: many more blades than were ever seen among the stray blade manifestations of earlier times, made with soft hammers and punches (of wood and bone) to judge by the percussion patterns on them; new blade-based forms like keeled and nosed scrapers, complex burins (the bone carving and engraving tools), edge-retouched blades and microlithic bladelets; much use of bone and antler to make spear points (some split-based for hafting), rods and tubes unknown in the Middle Palaeolithic (though we recall the enigmatic harpoons of Katanda). By about 25,000 BP needles were being made of bone in Central Europe, a little later on in France: sewn clothes, of animal hides, must have been much more tailored than ever before. At Sungir in Russia elaborate clothing is indicated by patterns of beads that were attached to the clothes, while the sites of Barma Grande and Arene Candide in Italy suggest that different dress codes could be applied to men and women. Entirely new in the Upper Palaeolithic is the marked adoption of articles of personal adornment like perforated animal teeth and shells and beads made of ivory and attractive stones like steatite and serpentine. The widespread production and wearing of such ornaments must bear witness to a great change in human social relations and psychology: visual differentiation among individuals points to complexity of social relations across a network of people who know and recognize one another and have their places in the social scheme. Personal adornment similarly hints at a developed sense of self *vis-à-vis* one's fellows – it may be that the arrival of the self as a fully conscious entity is memorialized by the appearance of beads in the archaeological record. It is interesting to note, too, that population sizes increased with the Upper Palaeolithic, with many more archaeological sites and evidence for the transport of materials (like favoured flint supplies and decorative materials) over much greater distances than had occurred in Mousterian times. There were more people, more societies and more interchanges between societies in networks over greater distances.

Among these Upper Palaeolithic societies cultural diversity soon manifested itself, in contrast with the painfully slow evolution of Mousterian (and all previous) culture. By about 28,000 BP the Gravettian tradition replaced the Aurignacian, with small and parallel-sided blades, often pointed and very steeply retouched ('backed') along one edge, and bone awls and punches but no Aurignacian bone points. For a few thousand years around 20,000 BP the distinctive Solutrean culture flourished in France, producing a range of leaf-shaped flints of such exceptional (and otiose) workmanship that we are tempted to see the Solutrean as a fashionable *jeu d'esprit* like art deco, though lasting about three hundred times as long (still short, of course, by previous standards of cultural change). After about 18,000 BP the Magdalenian

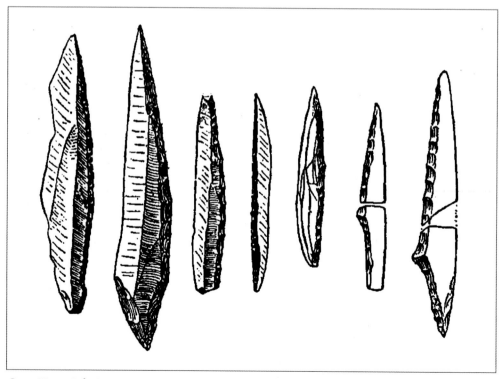

Gravettian artefacts.

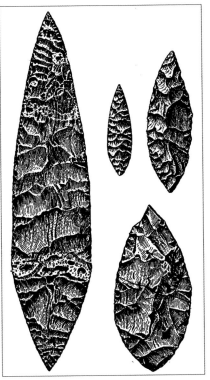

Solutrean artefacts.

Magdalenian harpoons.

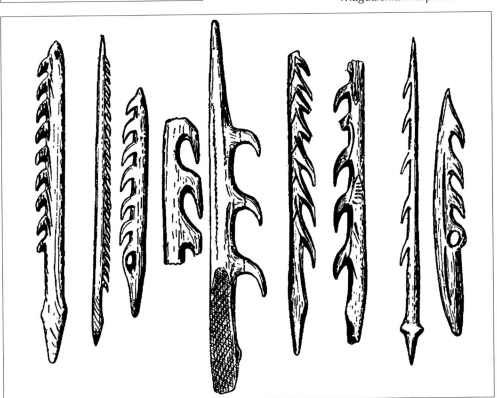

tradition began, itself to pass through many phases, with great abundance and variety of bone and antler work, some of it highly decorative in character, and a range of often microlithic products that were clearly employed in composite tools with bone and wooden handles. The Magdalenian and its derivatives reached to the end of the last ice age in Western Europe.

The Upper Palaeolithic people were making better tools out of their better-exploited raw materials, they were hunting better and enjoying more complex social relations (and they were also, as their bones show us, living longer and suffering a bit less physical trauma in the course of their lives). The houses built by Gravettian people in Eastern Europe, where there were no caves in which to take up residence, not only attest to the superior technical skills of their builders but also point to increasing social differentiation. Huts built of mammoth bones at the site of Kostienki on the Don river show a progression from communal arrangements with shared storage pits to concentration of storage in one hut bigger than all the rest, as though chiefs and/or medicine men were rising to power in a more hierarchically organized society. (It was probably the salmon runs of the local rivers that supported the wealth of such societies – fishing was never much of a Middle Palaeolithic accomplishment.) The hearth arrangements of the Upper Palaeolithic people, whether in the huts of the east or caves of the west, show a clear advance over Mousterian efforts, with more built structures including ventilating flues.

With the graves of all these Upper Palaeolithic peoples we sometimes find ourselves faced with obvious grave-goods of incontestable ideological intent. Some individuals at least were being buried in communal interments, like the one at the Crô-Magnon site, and in all their finery, with personal adornments that they wore in life or were treated to in death. At Dolni-Věstonice in Moravia, and dating to about 27,000 BP, a triple burial of two men and a crippled girl is disposed in a manner irresistibly suggestive of sex and murder: one of the males was buried arms linked with the spinally deformed girl, while the other – who had been pierced through the hip with a wooden spear (and may have been wearing a sort of painted wooden mask) – was laid out with his hands at the pubic area of the girl where red ochre was liberally splashed around. Well, there was nothing like this in the Middle Palaeolithic. . . . We can think up any number of stories to account for such a burial (including respectable ones like death in childbirth followed by distraught husband's revenge on the attendant medicine man and own suicide) without any hope of knowing what really happened and what it all means; what we do know is that with scenes like this we are certainly faced with the all-too-human in some form or another, in a way absolutely not seen in earlier times. These were people like ourselves, engaged in complex and problematic behaviour with a heavy dose of imagination and symbolism.

It is the art of the Upper Palaeolithic people that so decisively separates them from all that had gone before. Before 30,000 BP at the Chauvet cave in France Aurignacian artists created cave paintings as good as any to come over the next fifteen thousand years or so at famous places like Altamira in Spain or Lascaux near les Eyzies; one of the Chauvet paintings features a half-man and half-bison figure; from the Höhlenstein-Stadel cave in southern Germany comes, with equal antiquity, the astonishing figure of a lion-headed human being in mammoth ivory. Sites like these stand at the start of a long line of archaeological finds of ice age art in Europe that mark a total break with Lower and Middle Palaeolithic products. (Important claims of equally old or perhaps even slightly older artistic efforts have been made for Africa and Australia, but the west European Upper Palaeolithic art – evidently created in a rich world of relatively easy living, ice age notwith-standing – remains the most varied and vivid of the palaeolithic productions.) There really is no Middle Palaeolithic art:

The venus of Willendorf, Austria.

only scratched lines here and there and lumps of ochre. Upper Palaeolithic art is abundant and sophisticated, from detailed engravings on cave walls or pieces of bone to polychrome paintings of amazingly well-observed naturalism, with sex symbols and apparently abstract motifs, and a positive cult, widespread across Europe, of small female statuary in stone, bone, ivory and even fired clay, at whose potential meanings we can only guess. (Everything to do with sex would, of course, have been vastly altered by the inauguration of the modern mind – the sexual, previously conducted like so much else on automatic pilot, would have become the erotic with the conscious application of imagination, to make the most colossal impact on all aspects of behaviour.) Even the most representational of art is, of course, already a symbolic enterprise, but there is in the Upper Palaeolithic art – though we cannot always discern the intent of much of it – an unmistakable extra component of symbolism and magic, with evident reference to themes like sexuality, fertility, hunting prowess and shamanism. And there is a strong possibility that music was a feature of Upper Palaeolithic life: a very debatable bone 'flute' is reported from a Mousterian context in Slovenia whose holes are most likely only the effects of animal teeth, but a very flute-like object comes from an Aurignacian site in south-west France, 10 cm long with four holes on one side and two on the other, staggered as though for fingers and thumb, that can certainly be played as a flute to this day. Later on in the Upper Palaeolithic there are several bone recorders and even a picture showing a figure playing a bowed instrument. The people who created all these things, from statuettes to wall paintings to musical instruments, plainly had minds like our own, capable of imaginative insight and symbolic representation – and, by the same token, former people like the Neanderthalers who achieved none of these things cannot possibly have had minds anything like ours, even when they were housed in brains bigger than our own.

Invisible in the archaeological record, except in indirect ways, is any evidence for the language capacity of the moderns of the Upper Palaeolithic. Some bone scraps carry markings that have, probably very plausibly, been interpreted as numerical notation, perhaps hunting tallies or even moon-phase records, but there was to be no writing of any sort until long after the ice age world had passed away – not until, in fact, the agricultural revolution had progressed to wealthy and settled living with developed social and economic stratification some five-and-a-half thousand years ago. Indirectly, the graves, houses, sophisticated tools and above all the art do tell us that elaborate language with high symbolic content must have been employed by the moderns who made the Upper Palaeolithic – and, certainly, their skull and jaw anatomy confirms their capacity to form fully all the sounds that languages use today. At what point grammatically sophisticated language came into use is hard to say; the Klasies River Mouth moderns, certainly the Skhul and Qafzeh people, are quite likely to have been capable of it (unless some later rewiring of the brain brought about full language capacity along with an all-round mental enhancement at some time after 90,000 BP). But it is tempting to relate the development of the modern sort of language use to about the same time as the development of the complex panoply of Aurignacian tools, on the assumption that a parallel process of thought between the logical and conceptual steps of toolmaking and of sentence building was always in place from the earliest days of toolmaking. In a rough and ready way, we might expect Oldowan tools to go with something little better than a sort of vocalized chimpanzee signing, Acheulian axes to accompany the use of rudimentary and limited expressions, Middle Palaeolithic tools to indicate a little greater complexity and flexibility and the innovations and variety of Upper Palaeolithic products to be matched by the habitual use of grammatically complicated and imaginative speech.

(But it is salutary to note that the moderns of Australia, to whom belong the world's oldest known cremation burials at about 25,000 BP and some of its earliest art, perhaps before 30,000, achieved their modernity of behaviour to the accompaniment of a not even Middle Palaeolithic stone toolmaking tradition.)

By modern language, we mean to emphasize the availability of complicated tense arrangements like the pluperfect or moods like the subjunctive, and imaginative rehearsals in the mind's eye like metaphor and analogy. All these things come naturally to human children, who only need exposure to language use around them and at them to pick them up quite effortlessly, as though their brains come ready wired for language use. It is possible that the development of complex language and brain improvement went hand in hand under the pressure of natural selection to promote a phase of very rapid evolution among the early moderns of Africa and the Levant; those with better capacity for complex speech (and therefore with better thinking minds) enjoyed such clear survival benefits over their duller fellows, in their own tribes or outside, that they prospered and bred, spread their genes abroad and extended their domain. It may be that the long period of coexistence between Neanderthalers and early moderns in the Middle East only came to an end when the early moderns alone evolved the fully modern mental capacity that facilitates complex thought and speech. Once that capacity was in place, there was no stopping the moderns, who took the opportunity of the climatic amelioration of about 40,000 BP to penetrate into Europe. (They appear to have started their spread towards the Far East at an even earlier time, perhaps from the Horn of Africa rather than the Levantine region, reaching Australasia by possibly as early as 60,000 BP. It is hard to believe that these feats too were not accompanied by fully modern language use.)

It is tempting to think that language use all by itself might have forced the evolution of greater mental powers along the lines sketched above, when natural selection favoured the complex speakers (and thinkers) over the rest. But there are a number of reasons to doubt that conclusion. Although complex thought is apt to seem impossible to us without complex language to give shape to it, as though the words themselves foster the ideas, it remains a fact that not only not-yet-educated children but also some natural-born idiots (otherwise terribly limited in their mental possibilities) display a well-developed capacity to wield complex grammatical construction, if only for the most part in the interests of uttering fluent nonsense. Conversely, some stroke victims apparently remain fully capable of thought formulation while losing all ability to express thought in words, which just will not come. It looks as though language use, even with complex grammar, is at base a rather limited and technical capacity of the brain, inherent in almost every one of us however disadvantaged in terms of physiology or education: a capacity, moreover, with a long development in the course of human evolution since faint beginnings in the times of *Homo habilis*. It must have been some other change in the minds of the first moderns that enabled them to use language much more symbolically, alongside the rest of their startling ideological advances that are made manifest in their graves, their houses, their adornments, their art and their magic. With the flowering of imagination and symbolic thought that made ideology a reality for the first time in the history of humankind, the phenomenon of cultural evolution was initiated. Culture has been well described as a second system of inheritance, to go alongside genetic descent from one generation to the next, with its own unique method of transmission by language, symbol and example, so that culture can spread quickly between genetically unrelated individuals and even whole peoples, sometimes at astonishing rates and intensities. We owe to culture all the real glories of humanity – music, art and literature – and also its worst excesses – racial, political and religious fantasies.

We have seen that a big part of mental enhancement began with the primates (as with other social animals) as an aid to self-promotion in the context of group living. The brightest and best of primate intelligence is of a social character, concerned with the favourable negotiation of social encounters in the group. The second-guessing of other individuals' moods and intentions in the light of one's own (as a basis for action to one's advantage) is among the most humanlike of the behaviour traits we spot in the chimpanzees; to the sort of vegetative general intelligence that all living creatures show to some degree in adaptation to their environments, the top primates have added an unusual degree of social intelligence. It is their hallmark, and much of the archaeological record of that exceptional primate, the human being, can be read as witness to the growth of social intelligence over several millions of years of brain expansion, with enlarging group sizes, standardization of tool types, communal life around cave hearths, survival in harsh environments, support for the aged and infirm, burial of the dead, extended ranges of raw material transport and long-distance exchange. Developing social intelligence was no doubt accompanied by the development of language use, but it was very likely language of an almost exclusively social application, to groom and persuade and deceive. It is not at all impossible that such social language became, well before the emergence of the moderns, quite grammatically sophisticated with the power to handle past and future and 'what if?'. But it would not have embraced much in the way of non-interpersonal activity, not even the socially conducted businesses of hunting and toolmaking which remained separate mental domains of natural history lore and technical procedure, not subject to the fruitful scrutiny of social intelligence but rather going along in an unconscious, automatic pilot mode. The painfully slow progress of food gathering strategies and tool technologies and the virtual absence of evidence for symbolic behaviour until the end of Middle Palaeolithic times are all pointers to the compartmentalizing of the mind – until the Upper Palaeolithic era. A form of consciousness, to us bafflingly limited to the social scene, was very likely evolved from *habilis*, perhaps even Australopithecine, times onwards; toolmaking, plant gathering and hunting were carried on rather like sleepwalking, or like the way we drive to work without much consciousness of the journey at the time and even less memory of it afterwards. But whereas we can will ourselves into vivid consciousness of everything we do and retain memory of it all afterwards (if we really want to, if it means something to us, if we're under fifty), it seems certain that our pre-modern ancestors can only have been much less conscious at the time of all their doings outside the social sphere and altogether more oblivious afterwards.

The trick of the moderns was to acquire integrated minds, where the subtle intelligence evolved for social interactions could be brought to bear on so many more aspects of their lives. Social intelligence became general intelligence again, vastly superior – thanks to millions of years of refinement as social intelligence – to what we have called the vegetative general intelligence of lower forms of life. Social language became general language, able to be extended to the whole world of the senses and of human action. Procedures that had formerly been undertaken on automatic pilot were now open to conscious reflection. Not surprisingly, everything brought into a consciousness previously devoted to social conduct was invested with a heavy dose of anthropomorphizing: the natural thing to do was to imagine everything in terms of human feelings and human instincts to action. Animals, especially perhaps animals of the hunt, were credited with human reactions and intentions and a kinship was felt with them that has been expressed, among recent hunter-gatherer peoples, as totemism: we recall the man-bison and man-lion from the earliest phase of Upper Palaeolithic art. This anthropomorphizing was extended almost certainly to all sorts of living and inanimate things, as has also been the way with recent foragers. (The putative Neanderthal cult of the bear is worth recalling at this point, as it does look very much like a tentative manifestation of the anthropomorphizing tendency in a pre-modern human species, possibly to be explained by the rather blatantly humanoid appearance of bears that even the Neanderthalers could not miss.)

In the moderns the anthropomorphizing tendency ran riot, as it does with us to this day: the firm habit of reading all the world outside ourselves, and not just the other people in it, as somehow like ourselves, to be cajoled, threatened, deceived, manipulated, placated to our best advantage. The human mind has been rightly credited with 'a passion for analogy', for seeing similarities and relationships in different parts and aspects of the world at large and basing actions upon these perceived analogies, often with fruitful and useful outcome. This passion for analogy is an extension of the anthropomorphizing tendency where we see everything in the world in human terms and therefore potentially akin. The uses of the passion for analogy range from, say, practicalities like the avoidance of poisonous plants, on the plausible grounds of one such plant's similarity to another, to exalted achievements like mathematics and science, though the awkward philosophical fact remains that no two or more pieces of space-time can ever really be said to be 'the same' and, indeed, space-time as a whole really has no discrete pieces to be compared. For all that, practically speaking, we can all see that our capacity for imaginative analogizing has been immensely useful to the human race in so many ways, with its ready appreciation of relationships among the phenomena we face in our lives and its speedy devising of ways to exploit every sort of situation; we have also to acknowledge that it can equally be appallingly misleading as every sort of political and religious irrationality rests on passionately misapprehended 'analogies'. The mental ability to analogize and in general to bring many facets of experience into consciousness must depend on workings of the neocortical part of the brain in which data and memories can be brought together without much reference back into the older and more primitively operating regions of the brain – so it looks likely that it must have been some crucial reorganization of the neocortex and its internal pathways that made possible the emergence of the moderns' minds and patterns of behaviour. As to what the seemingly presidential consciousness of the modern human mind really is, which feels as though it spends its waking hours knowing and deciding everything we do (being our very self, we might say), nobody has ever come up with anything very enlightening to say about it beyond noting the usefulness in Darwinian terms of such an executive self as coordinator and arbiter of all the neural circuitry that busies itself with every aspect of our interaction with the world. Even so, it is hard to see why 'we' have to know consciously that the coordination and arbitration is going on, but each of us does know it, and what 'we' are, in reality, is that knowing. Beyond that, the problem of consciousness (if such it be) is a philosophical hall of mirrors and some thinkers have concluded that in the nature of things, consciousness can get no further with thinking about itself. We leave the topic with a reminder that our consciousness is in any case a constantly changing thing (which, moreover, shuts down for hours every day) and that our conviction of our own existences as fixed selves can easily be suspected of an illusory nature.

At all events we can say that the art, in particular, of the Upper Palaeolithic peoples and their relatives around the world constitutes proof that the modern mind had evolved by at least thirty thousand years or more before the present. Once evolved, the modern mind – with all its advantages of perception and invention – was indispensable and there was no going back on it. Close competitors without it were ultimately doomed. The modern sort of humanity spread all over the world, into areas previously peopled by older forms of human being like the Neanderthalers of Europe or late *Homo erectus* descendants in the Far East. It is possible that populations of these older sorts of humanity, never large in numbers, were recently depleted at the time of the spread of the moderns by adverse conditions associated with heavy volcanic activity and climatic deterioration. In some parts of the world, like inhospitable Siberia, the moderns were the first people ever to take up residence – even the hardy, long-suffering, cold-adapted Neanderthalers had never done it. From Siberia the Americas were colonized, perhaps in a small way from about 20,000 BP and then more intensively after about 12,000 BP.

The spectacular triumph of the modern human species, *Homo sapiens sapiens*, is owed to the unprecedented cleverness of the human brain, a Darwinian adaptation that has proved so successful over the past forty thousand years or so. There are times today when the cleverness of the brain of *Homo sapiens sapiens* is apt to look about to become terminally non-adaptive. Only a creature as clever as *Homo sapiens sapiens* could have devised runaway population explosion, pollution, the hydrogen bomb. *Homo sapiens neanderthalensis* had no such problems, only a very hard life and a – perhaps mercifully – limited awareness of it. Left to themselves, the signs are that the Neanderthalers would never even have achieved the Chatelperronian. So like us in general physique and even brain size, so unlike us in behaviour, the Neanderthal folk stand as the last and most vivid representatives of all the former sorts of evolving humanity, inviting us to go on reflecting on the real nature of our own very evidently different mental processes, unique in the long history of life on earth. Every dog will have his day and the Neanderthalers' day was a respectably long one – our own, in our fully modern form, has so far lasted for only a quarter of their span. If we think of what might come after us in terms of further biological evolution or, more likely, hybrid biological and artificial intelligence then we may be sure that our successors' minds will be as unknowable to us as ours must have been to the Neanderthalers.

Further Reading

Bahn, Paul G. *Journey through the Ice Age*, London, Weidenfeld & Nicolson, 1997

Bradshaw, John L. *Human Evolution, A Neuropsychological Perspective*, Hove, Psychology Press, 1997

Cavalli-Sforza, Luca and Francesco. *The Great Human Diasporas*, Reading Massachusetts, Addison Wesley, 1995

Conroy, Glenn C. *Reconstructing Human Origins*, New York and London, W.W. Norton & Co., 1997

Deacon, Terence. *The Symbolic Species*, London, Allen Lane The Penguin Press, 1997

Dennett, Daniel. *Consciousness Explained*, London, Penguin Books, 1993

Foley, Robert. *Humans before Humanity*, Oxford, Blackwell, 1997

Gamble, Clive. *Timewalkers: The Prehistory of Global Colonization*, Cambridge Massachusetts, Harvard University Press, 1994

Gowlett, John A.J. *Ascent to Civilization*, New York and London, McGraw-Hill, 1993

Johanson, Donald and Edgar, Blake. *From Lucy to Language*, New York, Simon & Schuster, 1996

Jones, S., Martin, R., Pilbeam, D. (Eds) *Cambridge Encyclopaedia of Human Evolution*, Cambridge University Press, 1992

Kingdon, Jonathan. *Self-made Man and His Undoing*, New York, Simon & Schuster, 1993

Klein, Richard G. *The Human Career*, Chicago University Press, 1989

Lewin, Roger. *Principles of Human Evolution*, Oxford, Blackwell, 1998

——. *Human Evolution, An Illustrated Introduction*, Oxford, Blackwell, 1999

Mellars, Paul. *The Neanderthal Legacy*, Princeton University Press, 1996

Mithen, Steven. *The Prehistory of the Mind*, London, Thames & Hudson, 1996

Moser, Stephanie. *Ancestral Images*, Stroud, Sutton Publishing Ltd, 1998

Pinker, Steven. *How the Mind Works*, New York, W.W. Norton, 1997, and London, Allen Lane The Penguin Press, 1998

Renfrew, Colin, and Zubrow, Ezra (Eds) *The Ancient Mind*, Cambridge University Press, 1994

Shreeve, James. *The Neanderthal Enigma: Solving the Mystery of Modern Human Origins*, London, Penguin Books, 1997

Stringer, Christopher and Gamble, Clive. *In Search of the Neanderthals*, London, Thames & Hudson, 1993

Stringer, Christopher and McKie, Robin. *African Exodus*, London, Jonathan Cape, 1996

Tattersall, Ian. *The Fossil Trail*, Oxford University Press, 1995

Trinkaus, Erik and Shipman, Pat. *The Neanderthals: Changing the Image of Mankind*, London, Jonathan Cape, 1993

Walker, Alan and Shipman, Pat. *The Wisdom of Bones*, New York, Alfred A. Knopf, 1996, and London, Weidenfeld & Nicholson, 1996

Wolpoff, Milford H. *Paleoanthropology* (2nd edn) USA, McGraw-Hill Inc., 1999

Wymer, John. *The Palaeolithic Age*, London, Croom Helm Ltd, 1982

Index